THE CAMBRIDGE
COMPANION TO
THOMAS HARDY

Thomas Hardy's fiction has had a remarkably strong appeal for general readers for decades, and his poetry has been acclaimed as among the most influential of the twentieth century. His work still creates passionate advocacy and opposition. The Cambridge Companion to Thomas Hardy is an essential introduction to this most important and enigmatic of writers. These newly commissioned essays from an international team of contributors comprise a general overview of all Hardy's work and specific demonstrations of Hardy's ideas and literary skills. Individual essays explore Hardy's biography, aesthetics, his famous attachment to Wessex, and the impact on his work of developments in science, religion, and philosophy in the late nineteenth century. Hardy's writing is also analyzed against developments in contemporary critical theory and issues such as sexuality and gender. The volume also contains a detailed chronology of Hardy's life and publications, and a guide to further reading.

Dale Kramer is Emeritus Professor of English at the University of Illinois, Urbana. He is the author of *Thomas Hardy: The Forms of Tragedy*, and has edited *Critical Approaches to Thomas Hardy* and *Critical Essays on Thomas Hardy*.

CAMBRIDGE COMPANIONS TO LITERATURE

THE CAMBRIDGE
COMPANION TO
THOMAS
HARDY

EDITED BY

DALE KRAMER

CAMBRIDGE
UNIVERSITY PRESS

PUBLISHED BY THE PRESS SYNDICATE OF THE UNIVERSITY OF CAMBRIDGE
The Pitt Building, Trumpington Street, Cambridge CB2 1RP, United Kingdom

CAMBRIDGE UNIVERSITY PRESS
The Edinburgh Building, Cambridge CB2 2RU, United Kingdom
http://www.cup.cam.ac.uk
40 West 20th Street, New York, NY 10011–4211, USA
http://www.cup.org
10 Stamford Road, Oakleigh, Melbourne 3166, Australia

© Cambridge University Press 1999

First published 1999

Printed in the United Kingdom at the University Press, Cambridge

Typeset in Sabon 10/13 pt. [CE]

A catalogue record for this book is available from the British Library

Library of Congress cataloguing in publication data
The Cambridge companion to Thomas Hardy / edited by Dale Kramer.
p. cm.
Includes bibliographical references and index.
ISBN 0 521 56202 3 – ISBN 0 521 56692 4 (paperback)
1. Hardy, Thomas, 1840–1928 – Criticism and interpretation.
I. Kramer, Dale, 1936– .
PR4754.C23 1999
823'.8–dc21 98–38088 CIP

ISBN 0 521 56202 3 hardback
ISBN 0 521 56692 4 paperback

Dedicated to the memory of
Kristin Brady (1949–1998)

CONTENTS

CONTENTS

PENNY BOUMELHA has held the Jury Chair of English Language and Literature at the University of Adelaide since 1990, having previously taught at the University of Western Australia. Her publications include *Thomas Hardy and Women* (1982) and *Charlotte Brontë* (1990). She is the editor of the volume on *Jude the Obscure* in the New Casebooks Series. She is currently working on gender and nationality in late-nineteenth-century writing in and about Ireland.

KRISTIN BRADY, Professor of English at the University of Western Ontario, was the author of *The Short Stories of Thomas Hardy: Tales of Past and Present* (1982) and *George Eliot* (Macmillan Women Writers Series, 1992), as well as of articles and reviews on nineteenth-century fiction and on feminist theory. At the time of her death in 1998 in an automobile accident in France, she was editing a two-volume edition of Hardy's short stories for Penguin and writing a book on the representation of the Gypsy from William Wordsworth to Virginia Woolf.

SIMON GATRELL is Professor of English at the University of Georgia. He has published critical editions of three of Hardy's novels, one (*Tess of the d'Urbervilles* [Clarendon Press, revised edition 1986]) with full critical apparatus, the others (*Under the Greenwood Tree* [1985] and *The Return of the Native* [1990]) in the Hardy volumes, for which he was also general editor, in the Oxford World's Classics Series. He has edited the manuscripts of *Tess of the d'Urbervilles* and *The Return of the Native* (Garland, 1986), and from his work with all of Hardy's fictional texts springs his *Hardy the Creator: A Textual Biography* (1988). He has also published *Thomas Hardy and the Proper Study of Mankind* (1993). He is currently completing a biography of William Allingham, and preparing a book-length expansion of his essay in this volume.

DALE KRAMER, Professor of English Emeritus at the University of Illinois at Urbana-Champaign, is the author of *Thomas Hardy: The Forms of Tragedy* (1975) and a study of *Tess of the d'Urbervilles* in the Landmarks of World Literature Series (Cambridge University Press, 1991), and the editor of critical editions of *The Woodlanders* (Clarendon Press, 1981) and *The Mayor of*

Casterbridge (Oxford University Press, 1987) and of two previous collections of essays on Hardy.

JAKOB LOTHE is Professor of English at the University of Oslo. His books include *Conrad's Narrative Method* (1989) and *Narrative in Fiction and Film* (forthcoming). He has written a number of articles on modern literature and is the editor of *Conrad in Scandinavia* (1995).

MICHAEL MILLGATE, University Professor of English Emeritus of the University of Toronto, has written *Thomas Hardy: His Career as a Novelist* (1971, 1994) and *Thomas Hardy: A Biography* (1982), coedited *The Collected Letters of Thomas Hardy* (7 volumes, 1978–88) and *Thomas Hardy's "Studies, Specimens &c." Notebook* (1994), and edited *Life and Work of Thomas Hardy by Thomas Hardy* (1984), *Letters of Emma and Florence Hardy* (1996), and the forthcoming *Thomas Hardy: The Public Voice*.

NORMAN PAGE is Emeritus Professor of the University of Nottingham and the University of Alberta. He has written widely and lectured in many parts of the world on Hardy and other nineteenth- and twentieth-century authors, his publications including *Thomas Hardy* (1977), the edited volume *Thomas Hardy: The Writer and his Background* (1980), and editions of *Jude the Obscure* (Norton, 1978), *The Woodlanders* (Everyman, 1994), *The Well-Beloved* (Everyman, 1997), and *The Mayor of Casterbridge* (Broadview Press, 1997). He has been editor of the *Thomas Hardy Annual* and the *Thomas Hardy Journal* and is currently editing The Oxford Reader's Companion to Thomas Hardy. He is a Vice-President of the Thomas Hardy Society.

JOHN PAUL RIQUELME is Professor of English at Boston University. He has published books and essays on Joyce, Yeats, Eliot, Wilde, and Hardy. His case studies edition of *Tess of the d'Urbervilles* was published by Bedford Books in 1998. Riquelme's future projects include a study of the origins of literary modernism in 1890s Britain, essays on Samuel Beckett, and a commentary on Mona Lisa as a cultural icon.

ROBERT SCHWEIK is Distinguished Teaching Professor, Emeritus, of the State University of New York, editor of the Norton Critical Edition of *Far from the Madding Crowd* (1986), and author of eleven other books or parts of books, as well as numerous articles on Hardy, Tennyson, Browning, J. S. Mill, analytic bibliography, rhetoric, and cultural history in the nineteenth and early twentieth centuries.

LINDA M. SHIRES, Professor of English at Syracuse University, is the author of books on British war poetry and on narrative theory and of many articles on Victorian subjects. She is the editor of Hardy's *The Trumpet-Major* for Penguin Books (1997) and of *Re-Writing the Victorians* (1992). Her current book project is tentatively entitled "Victorian Fame: The Transformation of Authorship in the Nineteenth Century."

DENNIS TAYLOR is a professor at Boston College, and editor of the journal *Religion and the Arts*. His books include *Hardy's Poetry 1860–1928* (revised edition, 1989), co-winner of the 1990 Macmillan/Hardy Society Prize; *Hardy's Metres and Victorian Prosody* (1988); and *Hardy's Literary Language and Victorian Philology* (1993). He is editor of the new Penguin edition of *Jude the Obscure* (1998). He has also published articles on Drayton, Wallace Stevens, the *OED*, Wordsworth, Kierkegaard, and religious autobiography. He is known at Boston College for his course, "The Literature of Spiritual Quest."

PETER WIDDOWSON is Professor of Literature at Cheltenham and Gloucester College of Higher Education. He has published extensively on nineteenth- and twentieth-century fiction and on critical theory, but it has been his work on Thomas Hardy which has brought these interests together. A collection of his essays, *On Thomas Hardy: Late Essays and Earlier*, was published in 1998, and he is currently writing the volume on *Literature* for Routledge's New Critical Idiom Series.

PREFACE

Thomas Hardy's fiction has had a remarkably strong appeal for general readers for decades, and draws increasingly provocative attention from academic readers. His poetry more recently has come to acclaim as among the most influential of the twentieth century. Hardy presents the extraordinary case of a master in two genres whose career spanned major parts of two literary eras – one genre per era. (He published nearly all of his fiction during the reign of Victoria, nearly all of his poetry during the twentieth century.) His work in each genre reflects upon the other, and he exceeds narrow literary or historical definitions of the eras he lived through. Hardy's standing as a novelist has grown to eclipse everyone in the nineteenth century but Dickens, just as his large role in shaping the poetic output of the twentieth century is gaining acceptance as a near-cliché.

Hardy is at once an easy and a difficult "read," as this volume demonstrates in several places. He is lucid and direct in both verse and prose. His subject matter while to some degree necessarily is "local" and temporally fixed, in most respects is concerned with matters of permanent concern: neither his politics nor his philosophy requires subtle explication. However, a *Companion* can reveal to both first-time and more advanced readers the benefits to be gained from readings founded on a canvass of previous commentary and ambitious to stimulate curiosity and to expand current knowledge. Hardy's work still raises hackles and creates passionate advocacy and opposition; the essays in the *Companion* intend to provide, on the one hand, a dispassionate survey of general characteristics and specific demonstrations of Hardy's ideas and skills. From this base, users of this volume can set out to clarify their own concepts. Nonspecialist readers can perhaps ascertain some of the reasons for their own admiration or interest; readers of all degrees of sophistication might also find some reasons to critique the author they love. What this collection has no intention of providing is an array of "answers" to the many still lively disputes in the long history of efforts to comprehend all that Hardy offers.

A significant inducement to read and study Hardy at the present time arises from his paradoxical relationship with literary criticism. Unlike such a writer as Dickens, whose work is always among the earliest to be examined in terms of each new theoretical fashion, Hardy's fiction and poetry are peculiarly resistant to Procrustean beds and critics with agendas. His works tend to test the validity of matured theories more than they offer early opportunities for theoretical display. Although this preface refers to critical and theoretical approaches, the essays in the volume do not comprise a critical sampler. It is an elementary truth that theoretical approach is inextricable from writing about literature, whether or not the contributor considers him- or herself inclined toward a special theory. The simple fact is, you cannot comment on a subject unless you have a perspective. Each of the contributors is aware of theory and its due place in literary analysis, but there is no felt need either to downplay or to elevate theory in a conspicuous or explicit manner in order to address more clearly the issues being dealt with.

Like every classic writer Hardy is always undergoing reassessment, and the numerous excellent analyses over the past forty years and more have created a core of knowledge and developed areas of controversies that of course affect these essays. Controversies in Hardy's biography, for example, have brought anguish to some readers and fury to others, but readings of the fiction and poetry have continued to make aesthetic discriminations even while suspicions that the man who wrote so sympathetically about Tess might not have been a superb companion for her in life have been frequently voiced.

While the essays necessarily concentrate on the more widely read novels, the two essays on the poetry are among the more substantial available anywhere, and there are numerous forays into the minor novels and the short fiction. The essays are not arranged in order to foster a particular interpretation. The first essays develop general topics, and the later ones concentrate on a selected few of Hardy's works; but all of the essays aim to correlate broad concepts with fresh readings of specific works.

Inevitably there is overlap in the coverage of some of these essays, such as Hardy's sexuality in his life, characters' sexuality in the novels, and revisions involving sexuality. Several contributors address the same issues, and evaluate the same critics, with assorted results. Contributors judge novels and characters on distinctive criteria, find disparate themes in the novels, and interpret ethical slants diversely. That essayists often comment on the same passages in Hardy's autobiography – for example, his reflection on the consequence of the principle that art distorts reality – may reflect the widespread concern of the 1990s for artists' consciousness of the manipulations they perform, but it is not part of a volume-long scheme. Likewise, there are distinct views on, and discrete ways of viewing, Wessex; and several contributors discuss the same poems while making dissimilar points about them and about their author. Such internal inconsistencies in this volume point up primary characteristics of Hardy studies – the liveliness and frequent disagreements, usually friendly, amongst the participants – and of literary studies – that a variety of viewpoints more often are complementary than conflictual.

I wish to thank John Paul Riquelme and Dennis Taylor for advice toward choosing a citation text for poetry, and John Paul Riquelme for help in writing the "Notes and Abbreviations" section on the poetry. I also extend gratitude to Kevin Taylor, Sarah Stanton, and Ray Ryan of the Cambridge University Press staff for their encouragement and congenial advice. Each and every one of the contributors met his or her obligations in good spirit and, with only occasional and understandable exceptions, timeliness. Thomas Hardy seems to bring out the best in those who admire and think about his writing.

1840   Thomas Hardy born 2 June, Higher Bockhampton, Dorset, first child of Thomas (a master-mason) and Jemima Hardy (born Hand) (before marriage a cook for a local clergyman). Nearly placed aside as stillborn, and a frail child in his early years.

1848–56   Attends various schools, including the National School (Church of England) in Lower Bockhampton; the British School in Greyhound Yard, Dorchester, run by Isaac Glandfield Last; and an independent school for older students, also run by Last. Is encouraged, and counseled in reading, by Horace Moule, son of the vicar of St. George's Fordington, and by Horace's brothers.

1856–62   Articled to John Hicks, a Dorchester architect, for four years, then employed by Hicks as architect's clerk.

1862   Begins work in London for Arthur Blomfield, who designed and restored churches.

1863   Awarded prize for architecture, but denied a cash prize. Millgate believes Hardy became engaged to Eliza Bright Nicholls, a lady's maid in London.

1865   Publishes a prose sketch in *Chambers's Journal*, "How I Built Myself a House," winning his first money as a writer. Increases the writing of poetry and the study of writing.

1866   Abandons ambition to attend university and enter the Church.

1867   Suffering from ill health, Hardy returns to Bockhampton and employment with Hicks. Breaks his engagement with Eliza Nicholls.

1868   Sends manuscript of first novel, "The Poor Man and the Lady," to the publisher Alexander Macmillan, who rejects the novel but offers encouraging advice, as does his reader, George Meredith. Although no copy of this novel remains, ideas and sections from it appear in later novels.

1869   John Hicks dies. Hardy moves to Weymouth to work; also begins writing *Desperate Remedies*.

1870   Macmillan rejects *Desperate Remedies*; William Tinsley agrees to publish it on receipt of £75 from Hardy. Hardy meets and becomes engaged to Emma Lavinia Gifford while planning the restoration of a church in St. Juliot, Cornwall.

1871   *Desperate Remedies* published, to mixed reviews. Offers manuscript of *Under the Greenwood Tree* to Macmillan, who suggests Hardy resubmit it early in the next year. Hardy instead sells it to Tinsley.

1872   Publishes *Under the Greenwood Tree*, which is reviewed enthusiastically.

1873   *A Pair of Blue Eyes*, Hardy's first novel to be published under his name, receives positive reviews. Hardy's friend Horace Moule commits suicide in his Cambridge rooms.

1874   *Far from the Madding Crowd* serialized in *Cornhill Magazine* and published as a book. Marries Emma Gifford on 17 September; they honeymoon in France, the first of many trips to the Continent during their marriage.

1875   First published poem, "The Fire at Tranter Sweatley's" (later named "The Bride-Night Fire"), in *Gentleman's Magazine*.

1876   *The Hand of Ethelberta* published. The Hardys move to Sturminster Newton, north Dorset. Hardy intensifies his reading program, especially in philosophy, the classics, and history (including local Dorset history).

1878   *The Return of the Native* published. Emma's social aspirations bring the Hardys back to London, to the suburb of Tooting.

1879   *New Quarterly Magazine* publishes two short stories, "The Distracted Young Preacher" and "Fellow-Townsmen."

1880   *The Trumpet-Major* published. Hardy falls ill during the writing of *A Laodicean*. While bedridden, he dictates the rest of *A Laodicean* to Emma. Without Emma's consent, Thomas decides to build a home in Dorchester.

1881   The Hardys move to Wimbourne for Thomas's health. *A Laodicean* published.

1882   *Two on a Tower* published, and criticized for its immorality.

1883   Publishes "The Three Strangers," "The Romantic Adventures of a Milk-Maid," and "The Dorsetshire Labourer." The Hardys move to Shire-Hall Place in Dorchester, after leasing land (from the Duchy of Cornwall) on which his father and brother construct Max Gate under his supervision.

1884   Appointed a Justice of the Peace for the Borough of Dorchester. Joins local antiquarian societies and becomes friendly with local gentry. Reads extensively in local records and newspapers in the Dorset County Museum.

1885   Thomas and Emma move into Max Gate in June.

1886   *The Mayor of Casterbridge* published.

1887   *The Woodlanders* published; the Hardys travel in France and Italy.

1888   *Wessex Tales* published, as is the essay "The Profitable Reading of Fiction."

1889   Hardy meets Agatha (Mrs. Hamo) Thornycroft, who may have been the physical model for Tess Durbeyfield, though Hardy may have begun working on *Tess* in 1888. As had occurred with earlier novels (*The Return of the Native*; *The Woodlanders*) and with later (*Jude the Obscure*), Hardy's original ideas were resisted by his periodical publishers. Tillotson's newspaper syndicate refuses to publish *Tess* after Hardy declines to make requested changes.

1890   "Candour in English Fiction" published as part of a symposium in the *New Review*.

1891   "The Science of Fiction" published in the *New Review*. *A Group of Noble Dames* (short stories) published. *Tess* published by Osgood, McIlvaine; reviews are split in assessment, but more in favor than against.

1892   Hardy's father dies on 20 July. *The Pursuit of the Well-Beloved* published as serial; the thinly veiled exploration of Hardy's dissatisfaction with his marriage causes further deterioration of his relationship with Emma.

1893   Whilst on a trip to Ireland with Emma, meets and is immediately attracted to Florence Henniker, author of three novels and wife of Arthur Henry Henniker-Major.

1894   Begins extensive revisions of his novels for the Wessex Novels Edition (Osgood, McIlvaine), published 1895–96.

1895   Diluted version of *Jude* published serially. The book edition arouses much hostility, as well as strong praise. The first maps of Hardy's fictional Wessex printed. The Hardys' marriage continues to deteriorate. Emma becomes more involved in various humanitarian and feminist causes; her attempts to publish her own literary works are unsuccessful.

1896   The Hardys travel in England and Belgium, revisiting their honeymoon hotel without reviving original feelings.

1897   *The Well-Beloved* published in book form. Critics not happy with its sexual theme despite thorough-going revisions. Determined to write no more novels, Hardy begins to gather poems for a book. After a year of negotiation and some revision, Hardy's dramatic version of *Tess* is performed, in New York (a copyright performance also is given in London).

1898   *Wessex Poems and Other Verses* published, to the amazement of readers and critics. Reviews are mixed; Hardy resents being labeled a pessimist. Emma responds negatively, probably because of all the amatory poems focused on various women. She moves into garret rooms in Max Gate, both to work and to sleep.

1899   Hardy responds to the strife in South Africa (the Boer War, 1899–1902) through a series of poems published in national newspapers.

1901   *Poems of the Past and the Present* published, to great critical acclaim. Further revisions to the novels, especially *Far from the Madding Crowd*, *Tess*, and *Jude*.

1903   Having completed the first part of *The Dynasts*, Hardy decides to publish it rather than wait until he has written the entire epic-drama. Part First of *The Dynasts* published.

1904   Reviewers of *The Dynasts* puzzled by both form and style. Jemima Hardy dies on 3 April. Emma does not attend the funeral.

1905   Meets Florence Emily Dugdale, a teacher and author of children's books.

1906, 1908   Parts Second and Third of *The Dynasts* published, to increasing critical approval.

1909   Hardy and Emma attend the first night of Baron Frederick d'Erlanger's opera *Tess*, not noted for its fidelity to Hardy's novel. *Time's Laughingstocks* published.

1910   Florence Dugdale and Emma begin a close friendship, Hardy receives Order of Merit (June) and the freedom of the Borough of Dorchester (November).

1911   Makes final revisions in most of his novels, for the Wessex Edition (published by Macmillan in 1912).

1912   Receives gold medal from the Royal Society of Literature. Her health declining, Emma publishes *Spaces*, a prose volume describing her religious beliefs. Emma dies on 27 November.

1913   Deliberate immersion in memories and associated emotions of his earliest times with Emma results in an intensely productive period of writing poetry. *A Changed Man and Other Tales* published.

1914   6 February, Thomas Hardy and Florence Dugdale are married. *Satires of Circumstances* published. Hardy depressed by First World War, more so when Frank George, a distant cousin he was considering as his heir, dies at Gallipoli in 1915.

1916   Visit with Florence to St. Juliot and Tintagel, Cornwall, which may have given rise to *The Famous Tragedy of the Queen of Cornwall* (published in 1923).

1917   *Moments of Vision* published. Begins working on the autobiographical narratives that were published posthumously as biographies by Florence.

1919   *Collected Poems* published. Becomes friend and adviser to such post-war poets as Siegfried Sassoon and public figures like T. E. Lawrence.

1922   *Late Lyrics and Earlier* published. Florence and Thomas finish his "biography."

1923   Hardy's old friend and object of romantic interest, Florence Henniker, dies. *The Famous Tragedy of the Queen of Cornwall* published.

1924   Hardy becomes involved in a new dramatic adaptation of *Tess*, in Dorchester. His growing interest in local actress Gertrude Bugler, who plays Tess, moves Florence to persuade Bugler not to perform in the London production planned for the next year.

1925   Successful London production of *Tess*, with another actress in the title role. *Human Shows: Far Phantasies: Songs, and Trifles* published.

1928   11 January, Thomas Hardy dies after several weeks of illness. His body is cremated and buried in Westminster Abbey, while his heart is buried in Stinsford Churchyard in Emma's grave. *Winter Words* published posthumously.

1928   *The Early Life of Thomas Hardy* published.

1930   *The Later Years of Thomas Hardy* published.

1937   17 October, Florence Hardy dies of cancer.

ABBREVIATIONS AND TEXTS

To conserve space in endnotes and citations, the following abbreviations are used in this volume. They designate volumes by Hardy himself; other primary materials such as correspondence, notebooks, and biographies; and a few frequently cited scholarly works.

This section also briefly explains the texts of primary works cited in this volume.

Abbreviations for texts cited

CPW	*Complete Poetical Works*, ed. Samuel Hynes
DR	*Desperate Remedies*
FMC	*Far from the Madding Crowd*
GND	*A Group of Noble Dames*
HE	*The Hand of Ethelberta*
J	*Jude the Obscure*
L	*A Laodicean*
LLI	*Life's Little Ironies*
MC	*The Mayor of Casterbridge*
PBE	*A Pair of Blue Eyes*
RN	*The Return of the Native*
T	*Tess of the d'Urbervilles*
TM	*The Trumpet-Major*
TT	*Two on a Tower*
UGT	*Under the Greenwood Tree*
W	*The Woodlanders* (re-set edition, 1996)
WB	*The Well-Beloved*
WT	*Wessex Tales*

ABBREVIATIONS

Abbreviations for other primary works and scholarly works

Cox — *Thomas Hardy: The Critical Heritage*, ed. R. G. Cox (London: Routledge & Kegan Paul, 1970). Contemporary reviews of Hardy's fiction and poetry, preceded by a historical essay on the reception of Hardy's works.

Letters 1–7 — *The Collected Letters of Thomas Hardy*, ed. Richard Little Purdy and Michael Millgate (Oxford: Clarendon Press, 1978–88), in seven volumes.

LN 1–2 — *The Literary Notebooks of Thomas Hardy*, ed. Lennart A. Björk (London: Macmillan, 1985), 2 vols. (Partially published, Göteborg, Sweden: Acta Universitatis Gothoburgensis, 1974.)

LW — *The Life and Work of Thomas Hardy by Thomas Hardy*, ed. Michael Millgate (London: Macmillan, 1985). See Millgate's essay in this volume for the history of Hardy's autobiography, originally published under the name of his second wife and accepted as a biography for three decades. The original two volumes (1928, 1930) and the one-volume edition (1962; corrected edition, 1972) are often cited in scholarship.

Millgate, *Biography* — Michael Millgate, *Thomas Hardy: A Biography* (Oxford University Press; New York: Random House, 1982).

PN — *The Personal Notebooks of Thomas Hardy*, ed. Richard H. Taylor (London and Basingstoke: Macmillan, 1979).

PW — *Thomas Hardy's Personal Writings: Prefaces, Literary Opinions, Reminiscences*, ed. Harold Orel (London and Basingstoke: Macmillan, 1966).

Purdy — Richard Little Purdy, *Thomas Hardy: A Bibliographical Study* (1954; Oxford: Clarendon Press, 1968, 1978). Much information about the original publication and different versions of Hardy's works.

Texts and editions for citations in this volume

Novels and other works of fiction

Quotations of the fiction are taken from the only series of texts of Hardy's fiction that have been edited in accordance with modern editing theory, the World's Classics Editions; general editor Simon Gatrell (Oxford University Press, 1985–). For the two novels – *Desperate Remedies* and *The Hand of Ethelberta* – and the two collections of stories – *A Group of Noble Dames*

xxiv

and *A Changed Man* – that are not yet part of the World's Classics, this volume employs the Wessex Edition (London: Macmillan, 1912). A brief overview of the state of Hardy's fiction texts: the standard edition is Macmillan's 1912 Wessex Edition, and nearly all modern school and university editions of Hardy reprint the text of the Wessex Edition (with a couple of interesting exceptions; and a few others offer emended readings of random passages). But, although Hardy himself prepared copy for the printers of the edition, and proofread the galleys of individual volumes, the Wessex Edition retains some typographical errors; and, more serious than a few trifling errors, the Wessex Edition retains a very great number of editorial and compositor-imposed readings in every volume that Hardy never tried to identify or remove – mostly, but by no means limited to, punctuation. (Such editorial interference was the standard practice in the nineteenth century.) Thus, although the World's Classics Editions of Hardy are themselves not flawless, they are far more appropriate for serious study than other available versions, and have interesting introductions and excellent explanatory notes.

Simon Gatrell's essay in this volume is a study of the developing concept of "Wessex" in Hardy's fiction; consequently, Gatrell's citations are to the first book editions of Hardy's works. See the second endnote in Gatrell's essay for further information.

Poetry

Samuel Hynes's recently completed five-volume critical edition of *The Complete Poetical Works of Thomas Hardy* (Oxford: Clarendon Press, 1982–95) was chosen for citations of Hardy's poetry, primarily because it includes a critical edition of *The Dynasts*. An equally, if differently, strong edition of the shorter poetry is James Gibson's, which has two presentations – *The Complete Poems of Thomas Hardy*, The New Wessex Edition (London and Basingstoke: Macmillan, 1976) and *The Variorum Edition of the Complete Poems of Thomas Hardy* (London and Basingstoke: Macmillan, 1978; New York: Macmillan, 1979). Hynes's edition is far too expensive for general availability, even for many schools and libraries. Gibson's *Complete Poems*, reprinted in England with corrections in 1978 and in the US in 1989 in Macmillan's Hudson River Editions, has been available from time to time in paperback in both England and the US. The texts of the short poems provided by Gibson and Hynes are often the same. Differences arise because of the editors' varying choice of the texts on which to base their decisions concerning Hardy's final intentions. In the *Variorum Edition*, Gibson bases his text on Hardy's *Collected Poems* (1928 and 1930). In contrast, Hynes takes the first editions of Hardy's individually published volumes of poetry as his basis and modifies the poems published there by identifying Hardy's last revision and his corrections to reprintings, to his own copies, and to the volumes of selected poetry published during his lifetime. Some of Hynes's decisions are necessarily the result of speculation of a well-informed kind.

I

MICHAEL MILLGATE

Thomas Hardy: the biographical sources

Although Hardy was, so remarkably, a twentieth-century poet as well as a nineteenth-century novelist, the date of his birth is now nearly one hundred and sixty years distant, the date of his death already seventy. His immense fame in his own lifetime aroused an inquisitiveness as to his personal life that he sought strenuously to resist, and since his death his continuing, even increasing, reputation and popularity have naturally attracted the attention of biographers. Notoriously, however, Hardy's concern for privacy extended beyond his own death, encompassed the destruction of most of his personal papers and the composition of his own posthumously published official "life," and was endorsed (even though they agreed on little else) by his literary executors.

In these circumstances, and at this distance in time, it seems appropriate to stand back a little from the narrative preoccupations of biography proper and attempt some examination of the sources currently available for the study of Hardy's life and career. Of particular importance are those documentary materials (notebooks, letters, manuscripts) already in print or on microfilm, their wide accessibility enabling students and readers everywhere to approach Hardy directly and establish a "personal" relationship independent of – though not necessarily uninformed by – the published biographies. Such firsthand experiences can be enriching in themselves, and the starting-points of individual scholarship. They can also serve as touchstones by which to assess the tone, temper, and interpretive biases of different biographers and interrogate not only the adequacy and accuracy of their evidence but also the specificity, or absence of specificity, with which the sources of that evidence are identified. At the very least, they sharpen awareness of just how "knowable" a figure Hardy is now or ever can be.

It is necessary to begin near the end, with Hardy's ghosting of his own official biography. Some time in the early summer of 1917, during the darkest days of the First World War and around the time of his own seventy-seventh birthday, he began to collaborate with his second wife, born Florence Emily Dugdale, in the compilation of a record of his life that would be published only after his death and with her name alone on the title page. The hope and expectation was that its rich detail and intimate provenance would constitute a kind of pre-emptive strike and keep other biographers, potentially less sympathetic, effectively at bay. The Hardys evidently envisaged a biography on the "life and letters" model popular during the nineteenth century and not at that date challenged by Lytton Strachey's *Eminent Victorians* (1918), and the two volumes that the widowed Florence Hardy eventually brought out, *The Early Life of Thomas Hardy 1840–1891* (1928) and *The Later Years of Thomas Hardy 1892–1928* (1930), were recognizably in that tradition. They presented their subject in a favorable light, told the story of his life from birth to death, revealed little of a truly private nature, but were diversified by personal anecdotes and previously unpublished observations and reminiscences that were important and fascinating – at least to Hardy's admirers – simply by virtue of their derivation from such an obviously authoritative source.

The omnipresence of Hardy's own hand and voice was evident from the first, and the title page of *Early Life* specifically acknowledged that the volume had been "compiled largely from contemporary notes, letters, diaries, and biographical memoranda, as well as from oral information in conversations extending over many years."[1] But revelation of the full degree and actual character of the subject's own participation came only with Richard Little Purdy's demonstration that the two volumes published in Florence Hardy's name in fact originated in a single composition entitled "The Life and Work of Thomas Hardy" and written in conditions of intense secrecy by Hardy himself (Purdy, pp. 262–73).[2] Florence Hardy, an expert typist, typed up the successive segments of the manuscript as Hardy completed them, and Hardy then burned the original handwritten pages.[3] He was equally ruthless in dealing with his source materials. For both the structure and details of his narrative he drew heavily on the diary-notebooks – full of observations, summaries of old tales told and retold by family and friends, descriptions of people, places, and natural phenomena, plot outlines, verse fragments, and pencil sketches – that he had kept at least from his early twenties onwards. In copying old notebook entries, however, he did not hesitate to rephrase them – perhaps accidentally, he sometimes re-dated them as well – and once the work was finished the notebooks themselves were destroyed, either by Hardy himself or by his executors (his widow and Sydney Cockerell, director of the Fitzwilliam Museum) following his death.[4]

The Life of Thomas Hardy – to use the title under which *Early Life* and *Later Years* were later republished and became generally known – is beyond question a uniquely valuable source. It preserves personal details and comments about life and literature that might otherwise have been entirely lost. On the other hand, its contents and emphases were very largely determined by Hardy himself, many central episodes are mentioned only in passing or altogether ignored, and the transcriptions of notebook entries are always suspect – and always uncheckable, given the destruction of the notebooks themselves. The *Life* has dominated Hardy biography, in short, as simultaneously an indispensable resource and a formidable, sometimes absolute, barrier to knowledge. Biographers, understandably enough, have much deplored this situation, but it seems questionable whether it is one for which either Thomas or Florence Hardy can greatly be blamed.

Long troubled by the misrepresentations of journalistic interviewers and dealers in literary gossip, Hardy in his last decades was additionally distressed by the "impertinences," as he saw them, of Frank Hedgcock's intelligent critical biography of 1911 and Ernest Brennecke, Jr.'s more opportunistically compiled "life" of 1925.[5] The appearance of such material did much to stimulate and sustain Hardy's determination to protect his posthumous privacy by any means available, and while the methods chosen involved concealment and deception they in fact differed little, either in kind or degree, from those often adopted by the subjects of biographies personally "authorized" and subjected to pre-publication review. Final responsibility for the completion, revision, and publication of "The Life and Work of Thomas Hardy" was in any case assigned to his widow, who kept the secret, put together the final chapters, added some characteristic anecdotes and a description of her husband's appearance, and deleted – for his reputation's sake – some lists of people encountered at London parties and a series of bitter comments on the critics of the last novels.

Such alterations have made it difficult to accept without qualification the frequent categorization of the published *Life* as Hardy's "autobiography," but that term can with greater validity be applied to *The Life and Work of Thomas Hardy* (*LW*), the version of the *Life* selected as citation text for the present volume. As signaled by its retention of Hardy's original title and its identification of Hardy as author, the newer edition attempts, by reference to the surviving typescripts in the Dorset County Museum, to reconstruct the text as Hardy left it at the time of his death. Not even Hardy, however, could narrate his own death or determine the precise form of his life's record, and the disappearance of the working diary-notebooks (apart from a few separated leaves) was to some extent offset by the preservation, accidental or otherwise, of several notebooks devoted to specific topics and materials, and most of these have since been published.

The principal manuscripts of the novels and volumes of verse, as sent by Hardy to his publishers, have also for the most part survived, several having been presented in his lifetime to selected institutional libraries. He did not, of course, have the same control over his outgoing personal and business correspondence, but the seven volumes of *The Collected Letters of Thomas Hardy* (*Letters* 1–7) bear witness to the frequency with which – at least during the later years of fame – his letters were preserved by their recipients. Also published, at least selectively, are the letters his wives wrote about him, the impressions left by contemporaries in diaries and memoirs, the interviews by journalists – often eked out with unacknowledged borrowings from earlier interviews – and the more deliberate public pronouncements on a wide range of literary and social topics reprinted in *Thomas Hardy's Personal Writings* (*PW*). Supplementary material, largely unpublished – incoming correspondence, drawings and watercolors, family letters, documents, photographs, artifacts, oral and written testimony gathered from Hardy's relatives and contemporaries by early scholars in the field[6] – can be found in a number of libraries, museums, and private collections in various parts of the world. In Dorchester itself are the evocative childhood items included in the Lock Collection of the Dorset County Library and the supremely important holdings of the Dorset County Museum, extensively (though by no means exhaustively) represented on ten of the eighteen microfilm reels of "The Original Manuscripts and Papers of Thomas Hardy," sold to libraries in Britain and elsewhere by EP Microform from 1975 onwards.

On the basis of such alternative sources, published and unpublished, *Life and Work* can often be amplified and supplemented, questioned and corrected. Its basic authority, however, can less readily be challenged and displaced, and remains especially strong, if especially suspect, for the remoter and obscurer periods of childhood, youth, and early adulthood. Biographers typically depend upon their subject's own reminiscences for details of his or her childhood, and in Hardy's case that dependence is deepened by the paucity of alternative sources. Families such as his, situated towards the lower end of the early-Victorian socio-economic scale, would normally write few if any letters, nor, unless in trouble with the law, would they be named in local newspapers – or anywhere else, indeed, apart from tombstones, census returns, and the stark official records of births, baptisms, marriages, and deaths. It is from just such records, however, that family "trees" can be constructed and their dispersed branches geographically located, and recent research by local and family historians has considerably expanded knowledge of the wider mesh of Hardy's family connections.[7]

Sources other than *Life and Work* can thus readily supply the information that Thomas Hardy was born on 2 June 1840 in the Dorset hamlet of Higher Bockhampton as the eldest of the four children of Thomas Hardy, a stonemason and jobbing builder, and his wife Jemima (born Hand), and that his father's self-employed status gave the family a modest level of economic independence that was still far removed from comfortable affluence. For more detailed insights, however, *Life and Work* is often the first and only resort, and it becomes necessary to read its generally positive retrospections of the childhood years as conditioned by elderly nostalgia and family piety. Hardy always recognized, and cherished, the profound importance of his having grown up within a rural community, participated in its seasonal occupations and festivals, and listened to the tale-telling and music-making of parents, relatives, and friends. Particularly significant were his family's association with Stinsford Church – especially as instrumentalists in the old west-gallery "choir" that was disbanded around the time of his own birth – and his own early religious commitment, acknowledged in *Life and Work* and further witnessed by the survival of heavily marked Bibles and prayer-books.[8] That faith evaporated during his twenties, but he always retained a strong attachment to the hymns and services of the Church of England and to the Church's socializing functions.

The novel *Under the Greenwood Tree* looks back affectionately at that lost world of Higher Bockhampton and Stinsford, as do such poems as "Domicilium," "One We Knew," and "Afternoon Service at Mellstock." But Hardy's childhood was not an Arcadian idyll. He was personally exposed to the exigencies of rural poverty; a surviving notebook fragment (Millgate, *Biography*, p. 34) reveals an early awareness of the more brutal aspects of his neighbors' lives; some of his many cousins were in the laboring class; several relatives were illiterate, or nearly so; and three entire families on his mother's side emigrated to Canada or Australia. At home, his father's easygoing habits and attitudes were more than offset by his mother's tough-minded determination to secure her children's futures in an unkind world. Hardy himself received his first formal schooling, at a newly opened village school, only at the age of eight, but between the ages of nine and fourteen he went on to receive excellent teaching, especially in mathematics and Latin, in schools conducted by Isaac Glandfield Last in nearby Dorchester. Textbooks, school prizes, neatly written exercises in mechanics, a receipt for the supplementary fee for his instruction in Latin, and other such items survive in the Dorchester collections as testimony both to Hardy's youthful diligence and to Jemima Hardy's eagerness to propel him into the middle class. The receipt also survives for the £40 premium the Hardys paid for their elder son to be apprenticed to a local architect named John Hicks,[9] whose office was next to the school run by William Barnes, the Dorset dialect poet.

Six years later, after completing his articles and working for a time as Hicks's assistant, Hardy moved, aged twenty-one, to London and a position (until the summer of 1867) as an assistant architect in the office of Arthur Blomfield, one of the busiest ecclesiastical architects of that period of intense urban expansion and renewal. *Life and Work* is a little thin in its coverage of the years with Hicks. For the years with Blomfield, on the other hand, it is rich in anecdotes, and these can be supplemented, at least for Hardy's working life, by the edition, in photographic facsimile, of his *Architectural Notebook*, containing professional jottings and drawings dating mostly from the 1860s but occasionally from much later periods.[10] The *Collected Letters* also begins to be useful at this point: though little of Hardy's early correspondence survives, the edition does include a handful of lively and informative letters written from London to his sister Mary (*Letters* 1, pp. 1–7), then in the early stages of her schoolteaching career. Documentation remains scarce for his early relationships with women – the silent infatuation with Louisa Harding, the closer associations with Eliza Bright Nicholls and his cousin Tryphena Sparks[11] – and even for the important friendship with the brilliant but unstable Horace Moule, who committed suicide in 1873 (*LW*, p. 98).

It was while he was living in London – at various addresses helpfully located and described by Fran Chalfont[12] – that Hardy finally abandoned a long-cherished scheme of university education and subsequent ordination in the Church of England. Other alternatives to architecture were considered – a little notebook headed "Schools of Painting" has survived (*PN*, pp. 104–14), as have the textbooks he used when studying French[13] – but his hopes and energies were chiefly redirected to literature and especially to the study and practice of poetry. Hardy described several of the poems he published in later years as having been first drafted in the 1860s (e.g., *CPW*, III, pp. 354–56), but no completed drafts from that period are known to be extant, nor is evidence available to support the claim (*LW*, p. 49) that he was submitting verses, unsuccessfully, to magazine editors by 1866. Limited insights into this fascinating stage in Hardy's creative evolution can, however, be obtained from the few surviving verse fragments,[14] from the books – such as Nuttall's *Standard Pronouncing Dictionary*, Walker's *Rhyming Dictionary*, and editions of Shakespeare and the major English poets (now mostly in the Dorset County Museum) – that he bought, used, and often annotated in the mid-1860s, and from the recently edited

"Studies, Specimens &c." notebook,[15] largely devoted to exercises in the generation of poetic language and imagery.

When ill-health – blamed on insalubrious London conditions – brought him back to Dorset in the summer of 1867, Hardy found architectural employment first with Hicks, his former employer, and, following Hicks's death in late 1869, with G. R. Crickmay, the Weymouth architect who had taken over Hicks's practice. He also worked in London again from time to time, remaining almost continuously employed as an architectural assistant until committing himself full-time to literature in the summer of 1872. Nor did he abandon architecture out of any sense of professional or economic failure. His role was almost always secondary – involving the detailed elaboration of other people's designs – but the numerous surviving examples of his work (in Dorchester, at the University of Texas, and in private hands) show that he was a thoroughly competent draftsman, knowledgeable about architectural history and styles, whom his employers did not hesitate to entrust with major responsibilities. Although he later expressed remorse, in "Memories of Church Restoration" (*PW*, pp. 203–17), for having assisted in some of the radical reconstruction of ancient structures typically practiced by Victorian church "restorers," Hardy always valued his architectural background and drew upon it when designing a house for himself, lending practical assistance to the family building business, advising the Society for the Protection of Ancient Buildings, even – in ways perhaps not yet sufficiently understood – in composing his own novels, stories, and poems. C. J. P. Beatty's introduction to the *Architectural Notebook* can in these contexts be supplemented by his *Thomas Hardy: Conservation Architect*.[16]

It was Crickmay who commissioned the inspection of the Cornish church of St. Juliot that led in March 1870 to Hardy's romantic first meeting with the Rector's sister-in-law Emma Lavinia Gifford, whom he married (contrary to the wishes of both their families) in September 1874. That first encounter, so richly evoked many years later in Hardy's "Poems of 1912–13," is recorded in *Life and Work* (pp. 69–78) largely in terms of quotations (perhaps modified) from Hardy's diary and longer extracts from memoirs Emma Hardy left behind her at her death. Since published separately and in their entirety as *Some Recollections*,[17] the memoirs have a certain charm and an obvious biographical interest. Like her travel diaries,[18] however, they throw little light on possible sources of the difficulties by which the marriage was subsequently beset. *A Pair of Blue Eyes*, the novel Hardy wrote with Emma Gifford's assistance during the period of their engagement, does perhaps hint at the Giffords' strong sense of class superiority, and at the Hardys' responsive resentment, but intimate conclusions can only riskily be drawn from Hardy's creating in Elfride Swancourt a character recognizably similar to his fiancée, or from the latter's evidently modeling on Hardy the unprepossessing Alfred During of her own unpublished Cornish story "The Maid on the Shore."[19]

Emma Hardy seems to have destroyed, in a moment of anger, both sides of the correspondence she and Hardy conducted during the four and a half years of their courtship, but her own part in that correspondence is attractively represented by two brief passages quoted by Hardy in his "Memoranda I" notebook (*PN*, pp. 6, 17), used around the time he was writing *Life and Work* to preserve whatever remained potentially "usable" in the old diary-notebooks he was reading through prior to their destruction. In *Letters of Emma and Florence Hardy* these fragments[20] contrast unhappily with the criticisms of her husband and his family Emma Hardy so vehemently voiced during the later stages of her marriage. A passionate letter of February 1896 (pp. 7–8) accuses Hardy's sister Mary of seeking to create divisions between Hardy and herself: "You are a witch-like creature & quite equal to any amount of evil-wishing & speaking – I can imagine you, & your mother & sister on your native heath raising a storm on a Walpurgis night." Visitors to Max Gate sometimes recorded the surfacing of marital antagonisms even on social occasions (Millgate, *Biography*, pp. 451, 481–82), but Hardy himself seems never to have commented on the marriage publicly – other than indirectly in such novels as *Jude the Obscure* and *The Well-Beloved* – or even in private correspondence. Such is the lack of evidence, indeed, that there seems no firm basis for determining what went wrong with the marriage or for discovering the nature of Emma Hardy's evident mental instability, let alone for apportioning blame as between husband and wife.

Emma Hardy certainly sought to assist her husband during the early stages of his career and seems (*LW*, p. 89) to have strongly supported the decision he made in 1872 to exchange the modest certainties of architecture for the headier if riskier possibilities of literature. On returning to Dorset in the autumn of 1867 Hardy had already begun to put aside poetry in favor of the better publication and financial prospects of prose fiction, only to encounter rejection of a first novel, "The Poor Man and the Lady," judged by prospective publishers as too openly hostile to the upper classes and by Hardy himself later on as "socialistic, not to say revolutionary" in tendency (*LW*, p. 63). Hardy reworked various sections of the long manuscript for absorption into other works, notably *Under the Greenwood Tree* and the novella-length story "An Indiscretion in the Life of an Heiress" (1878), but the non-survival of the novel itself has left fascinated Hardy scholars to speculate variously as to its original content and form. What can with confidence now be said about "The Poor Man and the Lady" is drawn together by Pamela Dalziel in introducing the text of "An Indiscretion" included in her edition of Hardy's *Excluded and Collaborative Stories*.[21]

In the instance of "The Poor Man and the Lady" – as on a number of later occasions in Hardy's career – the account given in *Life and Work* can be read alongside surviving correspondence between the author and his actual or prospective publisher. The letters written to Hardy are generally unpublished – to be found in the Dorset County Museum[22] or as copies retained in publishers' archives – but much of what is known about the "Poor Man" derives from John Morley's report on the manuscript and Alexander Macmillan's remarkable letter to Hardy of 10 August 1868, and both were published, together with other letters Hardy received from the Macmillans, in Charles Morgan's *The House of Macmillan*.[23] The history of Hardy's dealings with Tinsley Brothers – publishers of his (partly subsidized) first novel, *Desperate Remedies*, and its immediate successors, *Under the Greenwood Tree* and *A Pair of Blue Eyes* – can similarly be followed through his letters to William Tinsley (in *Letters 1*) and Tinsley's replies at Princeton University. And while Leslie Stephen's commissioning of *Far from the Madding Crowd* for serialization in the *Cornhill Magazine* – perhaps the single most decisive event in Hardy's career – is treated at some length in *Life and Work* (pp. 97–103), the important relationship between the two men receives further illumination from the little group of Stephen-to-Hardy letters printed by Purdy (pp. 336–39).

The development of Hardy's fiction-writing career subsequent to the success of *Far from the Madding Crowd* is well enough known to be surveyed here in broad terms rather than title by title. The compositional and production histories of individual works – what was written and published when and in what circumstances – certainly fall within the purview of literary biography, and in Hardy's case the identification and location of manuscript and other source materials are greatly facilitated by Purdy's bibliography (though some manuscripts have since found different homes) and by the Hardy section of the *Index of English Literary Manu-scripts*, prepared by Barbara Rosenbaum and providing both an introductory survey of the extant manuscripts and a separate listing for each individual document.[24] The manuscripts of *The Return of the Native* and *Tess of the d'Urbervilles* were published in facsimile by Garland Publishing of New York in 1986, having been included earlier – together with the manuscripts of *Under the Greenwood Tree*, *The Trumpet-Major*, *The Mayor of Casterbridge*, *The Woodlanders*, *Jude the Obscure*, and several of the poetry volumes – in the microfilm series issued by EP Microform. Reproduced in that same series, but more accessible in *Personal Notebooks* (pp. 117–86), is the notebook of items about the Napoleonic period that Hardy compiled in preparation for writing *The Trumpet-Major.*

Examples of the construction of specific textual histories on the basis of original documents are provided by the introductions to the Clarendon Press editions of *The Woodlanders* and *Tess* and by John Paterson's and J. L. Laird's genetic studies of, respectively, *The Return of the Native* and *Tess.*[25] Hardy's working methods in general are best described in Simon Gatrell's *Hardy the Creator: A Textual Biography.*[26] Not yet fully explored, perhaps, are the pressures directly and indirectly exerted on Hardy – as a professional writer with no alternative sources of income – by the systems of literary production within which he was obliged to operate. Part of the difficulty here is that the British Library's rich Macmillan archive – no more than lightly skimmed in *The House of Macmillan* – is not matched by the surviving records of the other magazine and book publishers, British, American, or European, with whom Hardy had dealings.

Recent discussion of Hardy's work has rarely involved systematic discussion of his "philosophy" – in part, no doubt, because his thought itself is now seen to have been so little systematic – but a good deal of material is in fact available for the study of his ideas, and especially for the identification of books and articles that may have stimulated his thinking. Central here are the "Literary Notes" notebooks – begun in the mid-1870s, now edited and richly annotated by Lennart A. Björk as *The Literary Notebooks of Thomas Hardy (LN)* – that contain, in the form of notes, summaries, transcriptions, and inserted cuttings and tear sheets, an ample record of books and essays that Hardy read and regarded as important for future intellectual reference or even, as Björk points out (*LN* 1, pp. xxii–xxvii), for possible employment in his own writings. That latter purpose was also served by an as yet unpublished notebook, appropriately headed "Facts, from Newspapers, Histories, Biographies, & other Chronicles – (mainly Local)," which Hardy used primarily for the collection of odd anecdotes and historical details, especially as found in the back files of the *Dorset County Chronicle.*[27]

Observations, perceptions, asserted opinions, and allusions to books and authors appear numerously in *Life and Work*, and quotations from specifically literary texts can be found in the so-called "1867" notebook (*LN* 2, pp. 457–79) and the earlier *"Studies, Specimens &c."* notebook. Other clues as to possible intellectual "influences" can be picked up from the pencil markings and brief annotations Hardy was accustomed to make in the books he owned and read: useful here are William R. Rutland's *Thomas Hardy: A Study of His Writings and Their Background*, Walter F. Wright's *The Shaping of "The Dynasts"*, and Dennis Taylor's *Hardy's*

Literary Language and Victorian Philology.[28] Regrettably, Hardy's library was dispersed in 1938, following the death of Florence Hardy, but some five hundred of the more important volumes were deposited in the Dorset County Museum, significant accumulations exist elsewhere (e.g., the Beinecke Library; Eton College), and information about books currently unlocatable can be found in the Hodgson & Co. sale catalogue for 26 May 1938 or, better, in the catalogues subsequently issued by the booksellers who were the principal purchasers on that occasion.[29]

During the early stages of his life as a professional novelist – and as a married man – Hardy moved somewhat restlessly about, renting accommodation sometimes in London, sometimes in Dorset, once in Somerset. *Life and Work* records these various shifts, the particular vitality of the pages describing the twenty months spent in the small Dorset town of Sturminster Newton tending to confirm that period as indeed constituting what is called, in an uncharacteristic flash of intimacy, the marriage's "happiest time" (*LW*, p. 122). The Hardys' next move, to the London suburb of Tooting in March 1878, is said (*LW*, p. 121) to have been motivated by Hardy's feeling that "the practical side of his vocation of novelist" required him to live in or near London, and he did join the Savile Club at this time and form a number of literary and professional friendships. He was also tempted into the potentially profitable business of writing for the stage, although his experience with a dramatization of *Far from the Madding Crowd* – only glanced at in *Life and Work* (p. 158) – was discouraging enough to be left unrepeated, on anything like the same scale, until the London production of *Tess of the d'Urbervilles* in 1925.[30]

According to *Life and Work*, it was in the Tooting house that the Hardys' "troubles began" (*LW*, p. 128) – a further personal reference that serves, however enigmatically, to posit an earlier beginning to the erosion of the marriage than the scanty independent evidence might suggest. When Hardy fell seriously ill while writing *A Laodicean* in the autumn of 1880, it seems clear (though the manuscript itself does not survive) that Emma Hardy acted as a devoted amanuensis throughout its effortful completion. But problems certainly flowed from the subsequent decision to leave London – which had again proved inimical to Hardy's health – and return to Dorset, first to Wimborne in 1881, then two years later to rented accommodation in Dorchester, and finally, in 1885, to Max Gate, the villa-like house on the Dorchester outskirts designed by Hardy himself and built by his father and brother (see Millgate, *Biography*, pp. 256–64, and *PW*, pp. 191–95). In Dorchester Hardy's newly achieved middle-class status – emphasized by his appointment as a magistrate – was inevitably challenged by local knowledge of his humbler past and suspicion of his faintly raffish profession. Little insight into such difficulties can be gained from contemporary sources or, indeed, from *Life and Work* – apart from the unglossed observation that "removal to the county-town, and later to a spot a little outside it, was a step [the Hardys] often regretted having taken" (*LW*, p. 167). Emma Hardy, however, clearly experienced in Dorchester (*Letters of Emma and Florence Hardy*, pp. 23, 48) a sense of personal ostracism intensified by what she saw as the open and even malevolent opposition of Hardy's family.

Hardy himself, so some of his second wife's comments would suggest (*Letters of Emma and Florence Hardy*, p. 141), seems always to have felt somewhat isolated from Dorchester and its people and largely ignored by the upper-class families living round about. To ask whether such slights were perceived not so much in personal as in social – that is to say, class – terms is indirectly to raise the vexed questions surrounding his annual visits to London and his friendships with people of rank, wealth, and fashion. The evidence here is scarcely in dispute, *Life and Work* itself supplying those lists of people encountered at social occasions that Hardy's sterner critics have invoked as confirmation of his perceived snobbery and social ambition, the obverse, so to speak, of a profound sense of class inferiority and educational deprivation. Critics less stern might want to correlate such evidence with the circumstances of Hardy's working life – the disappointments of his marriage, the cultural limitations of Victorian Dorchester, the still deeper isolation of Max Gate itself, the intensive daily routine of composition and correspondence – and make allowance for his (and his wife's) entitlement to occasional pleasures and indulgences. As a professional novelist, sensitive to the comments of reviewers and largely dependent upon commissions from the editors of magazines, Hardy also found it important to maintain his contacts in the national center of literary life and literary business. The issue is almost entirely one of interpretation, likely to be decided by biographers on the basis of their personal and political preferences and life experiences.

Much the same can probably be said in respect of Hardy's relations with women, both inside and outside of marriage. In 1893 he met and fell in love with Florence Henniker, aged thirty-nine, happily married, well-connected, and an aspiring novelist in her own right. Because most of his letters to her survive, as do a few of hers to him, it is possible to think of their somewhat unequal attachment as adequately documented and understood – especially in light of Pamela Dalziel's authoritative analysis (*Excluded and Collaborative Stories*, pp. 260–82) of their collaboration in the short story called "The Spectre of the Real." But such tidiness depends in part upon the relationship's acknowledged lack of an actively sexual dimension. Where such a dimension is suspected, or not specifically disprovable, biographical prudence sometimes fights a losing battle against biographical prurience.

Just as it was always impossible to prove beyond question that a young man called Thomas Hardy and a young woman named Tryphena Sparks did *not* make love on a Dorset heath one summer afternoon in the 1860s, so it is necessary to entertain the possibility of an early-twentieth-century affair between Hardy and Florence Dugdale, schoolteacher and writer of children's stories, whom he met in 1905, when he was sixty-five and she in her mid-twenties. They were often alone together in London and elsewhere, sexual exchanges of some kind could have occurred, and Florence Dugdale did of course become the second Mrs. Hardy. But no evidence has emerged for the existence of an adulterous relationship, let alone for assigning it specific dates or a particular sexual character. That what is known about Hardy and Florence Dugdale points rather to the unlikelihood of such a relationship is almost beside the essential point – that speculative constructions cantilevered out over evidential voids belong to the genres of fiction and fantasy rather than to biography proper. Unfortunately, what prompts – and is taken as licensing – such excursions is precisely Hardy's reputation for secretiveness, as witnessed above all by the composition of *Life and Work* and the destruction of documents, and Florence Hardy's reputation as a loyal defender of her husband's privacy.

The circumstances in which Hardy wrote the manuscript of *Life and Work* were very different from those of his childhood, even though the Higher Bockhampton cottage was, and is, within easy walking distance of Max Gate (both are now the property of the National Trust and visitable at specified times), and Stinsford Church closer still. Much, indeed, had changed even since his years as a Victorian novelist. He was now financially secure, the late-nineteenth-century shift to a royalty system of literary reimbursement having enabled him to profit handsomely from the continuing popularity of his novels. He enjoyed an extraordinarily high reputation – his successes as a novelist having been reinforced by the publication (1904–08) of his "national" epic-drama *The Dynasts*, much admired if perhaps not so widely read – and in 1910 he had received the exceptional British distinction of appointment to the Order of Merit. His second marriage, in February 1914 (following Emma Hardy's death in November 1912), had materially added to his domestic comfort and, given his new wife's secretarial skills, to his professional efficiency. Above all, perhaps, he was now publicly, even famously, the poet he had always known himself to be, writing in many different meters and stanza forms[31]

on a wide range of subjects, from the most elevated to the most commonplace, and producing new collections with impressive regularity.

The "fair copy" manuscripts of all of Hardy's poetry volumes have been
preserved, essentially in the form in which they were submitted for
publication; the manuscript of *Moments of Vision* has been published in
facsimile, the remainder, excepting only *Human Shows*, were included in
EP Microform's microfilm series. Since these manuscripts show only last-
minute revisions, and since very few of Hardy's working drafts have
survived, the variant readings recorded by Samuel Hynes (*CPW*) and James
Gibson (Gibson, *Variorum Edition*) are chiefly reflective of Hardy's
numerous changes to successive editions. Hynes and Purdy are the best
sources of basic information about poetry volumes and editions, Purdy
and, especially, Rosenbaum the best guides to the existence and location of
individual manuscripts.

Knowledge of Hardy's reading is obviously important to an understanding of his relations with poetic predecessors, and familiarity with the
various notebooks, *Life and Work*, and his own and his wives' letters offers
the surest route to the identification and exploration of events, scenes,
memories, ideas, and images that could have served as starting-points for
particular poems. Much of Hardy's verse contains a strong autobiographical element – most remarkably, of course, the retrospective and remorseful "Poems of 1912–13," written in the wake of Emma Hardy's death.
Clearly, there are real dangers in trying to establish detailed correlations
between finished poems and biographical events, let alone in projecting the
existence of such events on the basis of poetic evidence alone. At the same
time, the poems in their totality constitute a body of evidence – capable of
illuminating ideas, aspirations, emotions, and relationships – that has yet to
be adequately interrogated, evaluated, and integrated into the overall
biographical account.

The sheer quantity of evidence for Hardy's famous last years is greater
than for any other period. He was much visited at Max Gate by admirers,
fellow writers, and friends, many of whom – for example, Edmund Gosse,
Sydney Cockerell, Virginia Woolf, Edmund Blunden, Siegfried Sassoon,
and Robert Graves – recorded their impressions in letters, diaries, and
memoirs. Other, often meaner-spirited, glimpses of Hardy in old age – by
servants, friends, and neighbors – appear, together with much that is useful
(e.g., reprintings of Hardy family wills and sale catalogues of the Max Gate
books and furniture) and some that is not, in the series of pamphlets edited
and published by J. Stevens Cox between 1962 and 1971.[32] Large numbers
of Florence Hardy's letters have been preserved, and although Hardy as he
grew older tended to write fewer letters in his own person, let alone in his

own hand, some sense of the daily burden of correspondence during his last two decades can be obtained from *Letters* 6–7 and the mass of incoming letters in the Dorset County Museum, many bearing his penciled notes for replies to be written and sent by his wife or by her occasional assistant, May O'Rourke – later the author of *Thomas Hardy: His Secretary Remembers* (1965), one of the more substantial of the Cox pamphlets. From January 1921 onwards, Hardy himself kept a day-to-day record of events, interspersed with occasional observations and notes on his reading. Known as the "Memoranda II" notebook (*PN*, pp. 43–102), it formed part of the collection of documents, called the "Materials," that was put together in order to assist Florence Hardy in completing the "Life" – for which, as noted earlier, the working typescripts extensively and (in all the circumstances) remarkably survive.[33]

Hardy in his last decade devoted much time to tinkering with those typescripts – taking out some passages, introducing others – and Florence Hardy, as her letters make clear, became somewhat wearied by the resulting work, as by such other tasks as screening visitors, watching over Hardy's increasingly fragile health, and dealing daily with his business correspondence and with the several personal correspondences she herself kept up essentially on his behalf. She was also understandably if somewhat extravagantly distressed by her husband's infatuation, in his mid-eighties, with Gertrude Bugler, the young and beautiful Dorset actress who took leading parts in local dramatizations of his novels – most significantly, the title role in his own adaptation of *Tess*. But to see Hardy as monolithically mean, melancholy, reclusive, and exploitative of his wives is perhaps to rely too much on evidence generated largely by the depressive aspects of Florence Hardy's own personality and the retaliatory instincts of undertipped servants and disregarded relatives. It is also to endorse the surely questionable tendency, encouraged by the late date of the most accomplished portraits and photographs, to posit the famous final years, subject though they naturally were to many of the familiar frailties and anxieties of old age, as typifying Hardy's entire life and personality.

Some characteristics did of course persist to the end: the habits of thrift and economy inculcated in childhood; the long-established daily rhythms of solitary work. The quiet congeniality that had once made him welcome in London clubs and salons now brought him downstairs at teatime to meet an almost daily influx of visitors. But the challenge, biographically speaking, is somehow to come to terms with what is truly distinctive about Hardy's final years, his extraordinarily, even uniquely, sustained productivity as a poet. It is regrettable that so few working manuscripts of the poems survive, but even their comprehensive availability would not solve the basic mystery of their production. The problem, inherent in literary biography itself, is rather that the central events in the lives of creative figures, their acts of creativity, are precisely those most resistant to exploration and explication. So that if Hardy is at this level indeed unknowable, that neither invalidates the biographical exercise nor diminishes the value and pleasure of sharing actively and independently in its processes.

NOTES

1 Florence Emily Hardy, *The Early Life of Thomas Hardy 1840–1891* (London: Macmillan, 1928), p. [iii]. See *LW*, p. [1].
2 A brief report of Purdy's findings appeared in the *New York Times Book Review*, 12 May 1940, p. 25.
3 For further details of composition and publication, see *LW*, pp. x–xxxvi, and *PN*, pp. [189]–202.
4 For the contents and consequences of Hardy's will, see Michael Millgate, *Testamentary Acts: Browning, Tennyson, James, Hardy* (Oxford: Clarendon Press, 1992), pp. 153–61, 166–68.
5 Frank Hedgcock, *Thomas Hardy: penseur et artiste* (Paris: Librairie Hachette, 1911); Ernest Brennecke, Jr., *The Life of Thomas Hardy* (New York: Greenberg, 1925).
6 See especially Michael Rabiger, "The Hoffman Papers: An Assessment and Some Interpretations," *Thomas Hardy Year Book*, no. 10 (1981), pp. 6–50.
7 See especially Brenda Tunks, *Whatever Happened to the Other Hardys?* (Poole, Dorset: Brenda Tunks, 1990).
8 Dorset County Museum. For the religious contexts of Hardy's childhood and early adulthood, see the opening chapter of Timothy Hands, *Thomas Hardy: Distracted Preacher?* (Basingstoke and London: Macmillan, 1989).
9 Dorset County Museum. As James Gibson observes in *Thomas Hardy: A Literary Life* (Basingstoke and London: Macmillan, 1996), p. 14, the amount would not have been easy for the Hardys to amass.
10 *The Architectural Notebook of Thomas Hardy*, ed. C. J. P. Beatty (Dorchester: Dorset Natural History and Archaeological Society, 1966).
11 For Louisa Harding and Eliza Nicholls, see Millgate, *Biography*, pp. 58–59, 84–85. Tryphena Sparks remains an interesting figure (see the articles by John R. Doheny in *Thomas Hardy Year Book*, no. 12 [1984] and no. 18 [1989]); for the deflation of earlier and more extravagant speculations about her relationship with Hardy, see *Victorian Fiction: A Second Guide to Research*, ed. George H. Ford (New York: Modern Language Association of America, 1978), pp. 313–16.
12 Fran Chalfont, "Hardy's Residences and Lodgings: Part One," *Thomas Hardy Journal*, 8 (October 1992), 46–56.
13 Leonce Stièvenard, *Lectures françaises* (Frederick B. Adams collection); Alphonse Mariette, *Half Hours of French Translation* (Colby College).
14 Millgate, *Biography*, p. 89, quotes some early draft material preserved in Hardy's *Poetical Matter* notebook, compiled like "Memoranda I" (*PN*, pp. 1–40) while Hardy was re-reading the original diary-notebooks and now

known to exist only as a photocopy in the Beinecke Library at Yale. See also Purdy, opp. p. 242.

15 *Thomas Hardy's "Studies, Specimens &c." Notebook*, ed. Pamela Dalziel and Michael Millgate (Oxford: Clarendon Press, 1994).

16 C. J. P. Beatty, *Thomas Hardy: Conservation Architect: His Work for The Society for the Protection of Ancient Buildings* (Dorchester: Dorset Natural History and Archaeological Society, 1995). Beatty's unpublished doctoral thesis, "The Part Played by Architecture in the Life and Work of Thomas Hardy" (University of London, 1963), also remains useful.

17 Emma Hardy, *Some Recollections*, ed. Evelyn Hardy and Robert Gittings (London: Oxford University Press, 1961).

18 *Emma Hardy Diaries*, ed. Richard H. Taylor (Ashington and Manchester: Mid Northumberland Arts Group and Carcanet New Press, 1985).

19 Dorset County Museum; microfilmed by EP Microform. See Millgate, *Biography*, p. 124.

20 *Letters of Emma and Florence Hardy*, ed. Michael Millgate (Oxford: Clarendon Press, 1996), p. 3.

21 Hardy, *The Excluded and Collaborative Stories*, ed. Pamela Dalziel (Oxford: Clarendon Press, 1992), pp. 68–82.

22 Though misnamed and far from perfect, Carl J. and Clara Carter Weber's *Thomas Hardy's Correspondence at Max Gate: A Descriptive Check List* (Waterville, Maine: Colby College Press, 1968) retains its usefulness as a guide to Hardy's incoming letters in the Museum.

23 Charles Morgan, *The House of Macmillan (1843–1943)* (London: Macmillan, 1943), pp. 87–91.

24 Barbara Rosenbaum, *Index of English Literary Manuscripts*. Volume IV: *1800–1900*. Part 2: *Hardy–Lamb* (London and New York: Mansell, 1990), pp. 3–224.

25 *The Woodlanders*, ed. Dale Kramer (Oxford: Clarendon Press, 1981); *Tess of the d'Urbervilles*, ed. Juliet Grindle and Simon Gatrell (Oxford: Clarendon Press, 1983); John Paterson, *The Making of "The Return of the Native"* (Berkeley: University of California Press, 1963); J. L. Laird, *The Shaping of "Tess of the d'Urbervilles"* (Oxford: Clarendon Press, 1975).

26 Simon Gatrell, *Hardy the Creator: A Textual Biography* (Oxford: Clarendon Press, 1988).

27 Dorset County Museum; microfilmed by EP Microform. For examples of Hardy's use of the notebook see Michael Millgate, *Thomas Hardy: His Career as a Novelist* (1971; Basingstoke and London: Macmillan, 1994), pp. 237–43.

28 William R. Rutland, *Thomas Hardy: A Study of His Writings and Their Background* (Oxford: Basil Blackwell, 1938); Walter F. Wright, *The Shaping of "The Dynasts": A Study in Thomas Hardy* (Lincoln: University of Nebraska Press, 1967); Dennis Taylor, *Hardy's Literary Language and Victorian Philology* (Oxford: Clarendon Press, 1993).

29 See Michael Millgate, "The Max Gate Library," in *A Spacious Vision: Essays on Hardy*, ed. Philip V. Mallett and Ronald P. Draper (Newmill, Cornwall: Patten Press, 1994), pp. 139–49.

30 See Pamela Dalziel, "Whose *Mistress?* Thomas Hardy's Theatrical Collaboration," *Studies in Bibliography*, 48 (1995), 248–60, and, for Hardy's theatrical

activities generally, Keith Wilson, *Thomas Hardy on Stage* (Basingstoke and London: Macmillan, 1995).

31 See Dennis Taylor, *Hardy's Metres and Victorian Prosody* (Oxford: Clarendon Press, 1988).

32 Subsequently collected as *Thomas Hardy: Materials for a Study of His Life, Times and Works* (St. Peter Port, Guernsey: Toucan Press, 1968) and *Thomas Hardy: More Materials for a Study of His Life, Times and Works* (St. Peter Port, Guernsey: Toucan Press, 1971).

33 Dorset County Museum; microfilmed by EP Microform.

2

SIMON GATRELL

Wessex

The word *Wessex* was, until the last quarter of the nineteenth century, a purely historical term defining the south-western region of the island of Britain that had been ruled by the West Saxons in the early Middle Ages. But since Hardy unearthed the word and used it in his novels and poems, it has come to mean to more and more people a district – to some degree coterminous with the Saxon kingdom – populated by characters sprung from the novelist's imagination. Indeed, Wessex has come to mean the whole culture – predominantly rural and pre-industrial – found in Hardy's novels and poems. So powerful and widely disseminated has been Hardy's imaginative creation that even during his lifetime, Wessex was being used once again in the traffic of everyday life to denote a region of vague extent in south-western England. Now, at the end of the twentieth century, a glance at a directory to any town to the south and west of Oxford will probably throw up a business or two with Wessex in its name; and this is Hardy's doing.

Wessex as Hardy left it for his readers when he died in 1928 has been the subject of many illuminating critical and descriptive studies, made from a range of points of view.[1] But there is one fundamental truth about Wessex that has scarcely been recognized, nor have its implications been considered: it is that the complex social and environmental organization that readers and critics think of as Hardy's Wessex did not exist in the novelist's imagination when he first began to write, and, as this chapter sets out to show, did not exist in anything like the form we are now accustomed to, until the writing of his last three novels, and more particularly until the publication of the first collected edition of his work in 1895–96. That Wessex the place, and Wessex the culture, are of primary importance in understanding Hardy's work is here taken for granted. What follows will show, in a chronological account, the gradual steps by which the Wessex we are familiar with came into being, and will then examine what Hardy did by way of revision, once his ideas about Wessex had matured, to novels written early in the process. It is because the concern here is with what Hardy *first* wrote, in order to reveal the nature of his increasing sense of what he could do with Wessex, that the illustrative quotations are taken from first editions (contrary to the established practice of this volume). However, references to the World's Classics texts (WC) are also given, and readers will be able to compare the readings with versions they have currently to hand, and note the differences, where there are any, for themselves.

From the start Hardy depended upon the places amongst which he grew up, and upon the people who lived there, for the texture of his novels. This seems to have been more true of the unpublished "The Poor Man and the Lady," written in 1868, than it was of his first published novel, *Desperate Remedies* (1871), a work of sensation and crime. But still, Hardy found it necessary to work out the details of his psychological thriller in an environment with which he was intimately familiar. The seaside resort called Creston in the novel would have been understood as a version of Weymouth by anyone familiar with that Dorset town and its surrounding coastline; the name of the fictional county town, Froominster, was suggested by the river Froom that runs beside Dorchester, the county town of Dorset. The village Carriford – the center of the action – contains elements of Hardy's own birth-parish of Stinsford; the novel's Knapwater House, for instance, is based on Kingston Maurward House. There are also signs, in scenes such as the account of cider-making at the local inn, of pleasure taken in the recreation of a village community. But the main interest of the narrative is elsewhere.

Under the Greenwood Tree (1872), though, offers a quite different case. It is short and simple where *Desperate Remedies* was long and complex, and it has lasted much better, in large part because, though Hardy had not yet formulated Wessex for himself, it is made of elements that would be essential to Wessex. The whole of the action is set in versions of those places I have already named in connection with *Desperate Remedies* – Stinsford, Dorchester, Weymouth – only this time they are called Mellstock and Lewgate, Casterbridge, and Budmouth. Evidently Hardy felt no sense of continuity with the earlier novel, and indeed the narrative draws its strength from his family history and the people and places of his growing up. Aside from the love-story, Hardy's primary concern in the novel is that old customs and habits of the vital village community are under threat; and though by the end of the novel one important custom is done away with, much survives intact, for the time being. This resilient abiding community of mutual interest would become a defining feature of Wessex, even if Hardy was not yet aware of the fact.

While he was writing these novels, Hardy was courting his future wife Emma Lavinia Gifford a hundred miles away in north Cornwall. It is not, therefore, surprising that when put under pressure by the publisher and editor William Tinsley for a serial novel in a hurry, he turned to Cornwall for the environment, and to his Cornish friends for some of the characters. *A Pair of Blue Eyes* (1873) did not on the whole advance the growth of the embryonic Wessex, and might be set aside, were it not for the symbolically significant detail that one of the central characters was sent from remote Endelstow to *Under the Greenwood Tree*'s Casterbridge to school. By the time of its maturity, in the last decade of the century, Wessex had become a system, and this is the first example of a central element in the system, the interconnection of the novels by place and character held in common.

Far from the Madding Crowd (1874) is also linked to *Under the Greenwood Tree* through Casterbridge, but there are several other points of connection. Of particular interest is the reappearance of a character from the earlier novel – Keeper Day – not as a participant in the action, but as one about whom stories are told. Most of the action takes place in a village Hardy calls Weatherbury, based in many particulars on the Dorset village of Puddletown and its vicinity, though with some attempts at disguise. Puddletown is the parish adjoining Stinsford to the north-east, and in *Under the Greenwood Tree* Hardy had offered Mintfield and Yalbury as names of parishes more or less in that direction from Mellstock. Evidently the idea that his novels might be seen as embodying a single culture in part through a common and consistent nomenclature had not yet evolved in Hardy's imagination.

However, it was in *Far from the Madding Crowd* (1874) that Hardy first used "Wessex." He did so in just one chapter: "Greenhill was the Nijnii Novgorod of Wessex; and the busiest, merriest, noisiest day of the whole statute number was the day of the sheep-fair ... The great mass of sheep in the fair consisted of South Downs and the old Wessex horned breeds; to the latter class Bathsheba's and Farmer Boldwood's mainly belonged" (*FMC*, London: Smith, Elder, 1874, II, xx, pp. 228, 230; WC, i, pp. 348, 349).[2] The long history of the Russian fair and the anciently traditional breeds of sheep may have stimulated Hardy's fanciful use of the antique word in this context. What district he actually intended by it, though, is unclear.

A vivid awareness of the strength of the artisan community in rural villages is the power behind *Under the Greenwood Tree*; in *Far from the Madding Crowd* it is the community of interest shared by workfolk on a farm that provides the richness of context that buoys so successfully the love-stories of Bathsheba Everdene, and that establishes the fledgling

Wessex in readers' minds. *Far from the Madding Crowd* also offers the first example of one effect that writing for a middle-class urban magazine-reading public had on Hardy's narratives. Originally Hardy intended to write of a woman-farmer, a shepherd, and a sergeant of cavalry. Fragments of early dialogue in the novel's manuscript show that these characters were once integral parts of the community; but by the time the first edition was published they had been transformed into an elite, and the gentleman-farmer Boldwood had been added. Hardy found that though his instinct was to work within the rural working class, his audience required something different – some sort of gentility, some superiority of social status, something to identify with. Indeed, so late as *The Mayor of Casterbridge* in 1885 a publisher's reader advised turning the novel down because there were no gentry in it.

When critics compared *Far from the Madding Crowd* favorably with George Eliot's work, Hardy saw their comments as a warning-sign. It was not good to be thus labeled. So in his next novel he turned to something quite other – urban gentry and their servants. The admirable qualities of *The Hand of Ethelberta* (1876) have recently been recognized more clearly than used to be the case, but still it is rarely thought of as a Wessex novel; nevertheless Wessex was on Hardy's mind.[3] In this novel it is spoken of as a single county closely the equivalent of Dorset. Wessex life, of which we can now confidently speak, is present in the novel mainly to contrast with London manners and speech, as for example in: "civility stood in town for as much vexation as a tantrum represented in Wessex" (*HE*, London: Smith, Elder, 1876, I, xx, p. 214; Wessex Edition [1912], xviii, p. 144). Or: "It seemed all right and natural to their respective moods and the tone of the moment that free old Wessex manners should prevail, and Christopher stooped and dropped upon Picotee's cheek likewise such a farewell kiss as he had imprinted upon Ethelberta's" (I, xxvi, p. 273; Wessex Edition [1912], xxiv, p. 187).

The novel allowed Hardy to say some of the things about class and gender relationships that he needed to, but he accepted, on reading the reviews and receiving the responses of friends, that it was not what readers were anxious to hear. *The Return of the Native* (1878) was an imaginative return, passionately and deeply felt, to the country just outside the back door of Hardy's birthplace, and to the community it permitted to endure upon it. Egdon Heath has always been acknowledged as a powerful presence in the novel, but the narrative also provides illustrations of the growing sense Hardy had of the nature of Wessex, representing in an imaginative way the realities that lay behind the society in which he grew up. There are several rural rituals enacted in the novel –

the bonfire-making, for instance, or the mumming, or the maypole-dance. Of the maypole Hardy wrote:

> The pole lay with one end supported on a trestle, and women were engaged in wreathing it from the top downwards with wild flowers. The instincts of merry England lingered on here with exceptional vitality, and the symbolic customs which tradition has attached to each season of the year were yet a reality on Egdon. Indeed, the impulses of all such outlandish hamlets are pagan still: in these spots homage to nature, self-adoration, frantic gaieties, fragments of Teutonic rites to divinities whose names are forgotten, have in some way or other survived mediaeval doctrine.
>   (*RN*, London: Smith, Elder, 1878, VI, i, pp. 268–69; *WC*, VI, i, pp. 389–90)

The point of this account and others like it is that Hardy wrote of these rituals as part of his own day-to-day experience as a young man. Their anthropological significance interests him less than their endurance, revealing long human roots in the soil even of haggard Egdon, so indifferent to man; and if the annual flowering of festival was sometimes unspectacular, Hardy would ask whether we should value a hothouse orchid more highly than a heather bell.

Wessex grows through such accounts of community and practice, but so too does Hardy's fear that it was faced with overthrow. In *The Return of the Native* Clym's idealist attempt at transformation through education failed, but practical and efficient men of business were not wanting in rural areas of late-Victorian England: "Reddlemen of the old school are now but seldom seen. Since the introduction of railways Wessex farmers have managed to do without these somewhat spectral visitants" (*RN*, I, ix, p. 172; *WC*, I, ix, p. 74).

Hardy's narrator sees Egdon with the eyes of a child, as limitless. More than any other place he adopted in his writing, the heath on which Hardy played as a child, across which he walked as an adolescent, over which he courted as a young man, is quintessential Wessex – not the Wessex that is simply the surface equivalent of Dorset in *The Hand of Ethelberta*, but something deeper, a place and culture that permeated his life. The heath gives way along its edge to other soils and vegetation, but we have no idea really where the boundaries are, or where in Wessex it is to be found. Southerton, the heathdwellers' market-town in the first edition, is not on any of the maps of the region with which we are now familiar, nor did it occur in any earlier novel. The heath is a vast tract of unenclosed wild merely, and as such representing Hardy's instinctive idea of Wessex more vividly than the carefully researched and plotted place that, as the result of revisions, we now read of.[4] But research was imminent.

In his next novel, *The Trumpet-Major* (1880), Hardy turned to the more distant past, to the Napoleonic wars that had fascinated him from an early age. The conception of Wessex had reached a stage of maturity in his mind that seemed to demand some theoretical basis, and his distinction of two kinds of history in the novel is evidence of the direction his thoughts were taking. In chapter 13, for instance, the heroine is in Weymouth and sees King George on the Esplanade. The narrator observes of her that she "felt herself close to and looking into the stream of recorded history, within whose banks the littlest things are great, and outside which she and the general bulk of the human race were content to live on as an unreckoned, unheeded superfluity" (*TM*, London: Smith, Elder, 1880, I, xiii, pp. 243–44; WC, xiii, p. 108). Unrecorded history, however, also has its stream, and Hardy had begun to discern that part of his fictional enterprise was to record the "unreckoned, unheeded superfluity" of his own small district. His sense of the significance of this unrecorded culture is a substantial part of what lies behind the growth of Wessex, as is the role he cast for himself as a mediator between it and the educated middle classes of his country, who were quite ignorant of the substance and the richness of such remote and rural life. But Hardy still distinguished in the first edition of *The Trumpet-Major* between a historical and a Wessex novel, and so Weymouth remained Weymouth, Dorchester Dorchester, Salisbury Salisbury, and the district a part of southern England.

Wherever his thoughts about Wessex might have been tending, his next two novels did not put them into effect. Both *A Laodicean* (1881) and *Two on a Tower* (1882) are nominally set in Wessex, but it is a matter of location only. However, just at the time when his novels moved away from intense involvement with the society and culture of Wessex/Dorset, Hardy began a steady stream of shorter narratives that did play variations on the themes established in *Far from the Madding Crowd* and *The Return of the Native*. To illustrate this, one might take "The Distracted Young Preacher" (1879) or "The Three Strangers" (1883). The whole of the action of this latter story takes place in and about a vividly imagined, isolated cottage during one stormy night and morning, and yet there is in it as clear and satisfying a representation of what Hardy was beginning to understand by Wessex as in any of his novels. The group of neighbors gathered together to celebrate the birth of Shepherd Fennel's child is a fully realized community, and the action reveals the operation of the spirit of community working through them, the force that binds and sustains Wessex.

There was a gap of four years between the publication of *Two on a Tower* and Hardy's next novel, *The Mayor of Casterbridge* (1886), and during this period Hardy made a considerable imaginative step in his understanding of Wessex, in part stimulated by his return to live in

Dorchester, to build a house there – in effect to settle, for the first time in his married life.

Casterbridge was the capital of the districts in which Hardy had set most of his fiction, and he became determined to embody this significant place as richly as he had Egdon Heath, placing it in a long historical context, from prehistoric earth-works to the Romans and onwards. He also stressed its interinvolvement with the surrounding agricultural countryside, and, most significantly, tied it specifically by place and by character to earlier work. The result is that *The Mayor of Casterbridge* becomes the focus of a circle of previous fictions, stories as well as novels, through Boldwood and Everdene and Darton, through Egdon Heath and Port-Bredy and Overcombe. This development is the earliest attempt on Hardy's part to place much of his fiction in a single historical and topographical context.

For the first time in this novel, also, we observe Hardy acting overtly as local historian for the more accurate information of his readers. He wrote thus in the first edition about the rural suburb of Casterbridge he then called Dummerford, a fictional version of Fordington: "Though the upper part of Dummerford was mainly composed of a curious congeries of barns and farmsteads there was a less picturesque side to the parish. This was Mixen Lane, now in great part pulled down" (London: Smith, Elder, 1886, II, xiii, p. 169; WC, xxxvi, p. 254).

For the first time, too, Hardy focuses on the discontent and poverty of the working people in his narrative. The workfolk in *Far from the Madding Crowd*, for instance, are well-treated by a notably benevolent farmer, and readers were aware that not all farmers were so sympathetic to their laborers. Though John Schlesinger's remarkable 1967 film of the novel, in showing the hiring fair at Casterbridge to be humiliatingly similar to a horse sale or a cattle auction, expresses historical reality, it also expresses much more than Hardy wrote in 1874. The poverty and hopelessness of local workfolk was in fact another of the topics that had occupied Hardy after the completion of *Two on a Tower*. His essay "The Dorsetshire Labourer" had been printed in *Longman's Magazine* in 1883, and his interest in the lives and attitudes to life of the distressed semi-urban inhabitants of Mixen Lane is a fruit of his analysis of the current economic and social situation in Dorset.

It is somewhat surprising, in the light of this substantial contextualizing of Wessex, that Hardy chose imaginatively to return in *The Woodlanders* (1887) to an environment as enclosed and isolated as that of *The Return of the Native*, a world apart of forest and orchard. Hardy was under considerable pressure to produce and complete the work very quickly; the novel has its origin in a draft of the 1870s, which, of its nature, offered little room for him to reshape it in the light of the wider aspects of historical reality and community with other novels opened out in *The Mayor of Casterbridge*. At the same time, in recreating the landscape around Bubb Down, Melbury Bubb, and Melbury Osmond, Hardy was entering another small territory with deep personal associations, the birthplace of his grandmother Betty Swetman, and this may also have influenced the apparent contraction of his horizon.

There is also in the novel direct and indirect evidence that for Hardy Wessex had still not expanded beyond Dorset. The natural market town for the Melburys (in terms of English geography) is Yeovil, but Yeovil is in Somerset, so Hardy has his characters go miles out of their way to Sherton (Sherborne), in order to ensure that they remain within Wessex. Less inferentially, one of the characters tells another that nobody can match him in the whole county of Wessex as a scientist.

In 1888 Hardy collected together most of the short stories he had published in magazines during the last ten years, and called the collection *Wessex Tales*, thus drawing attention to what for some at least of his readers had become a commonplace of thought regarding his fiction. He felt for the first time, in preparing this volume, that the growth of his understanding of Wessex required him to make alterations to established work. The story "Fellow-Townsmen," for instance, takes place in a fictionalized version of Bridport, as anyone familiar with the place would have realized when it first appeared in 1880; but Hardy had then given the town no name, calling it simply "the borough." In 1888 he identified it as Port-Bredy. More significantly, when he turned to "The Distracted Preacher," which dramatized a piece of recorded history, he removed the setting of the story from Dorset (as it had been in the magazine) to Wessex, by altering the names of places – from the Dorset Weymouth to the Wessex Budmouth, and so on. This decision would have its implication for *The Trumpet-Major*, when Hardy came to revise the novel for the first collected edition of his work in 1895.

The following year a new edition of *Desperate Remedies* was issued, and for the first time Hardy had the chance to reconsider a novel written before Wessex had crossed his consciousness. Rather than integrate the narrative with the established Wessex pattern of things, he removed as far as he could all hints of the district upon which he had based the scene of the action – so that, for example, Froominster became Troominster. It would have taken radical rewriting of the environment of the novel to bring it in harmony with that of *Under the Greenwood Tree*, and he was not sufficiently interested in the novel to undertake it. Evidently Hardy did not yet consider all his novels Wessex novels; but this would soon change.

Hardy's next novel, *Tess of the d'Urbervilles* (1891), is in Wessex terms the centrifugal opposite to the centripetal *Mayor of Casterbridge*. Tess in her journeys crosses most of the county, and ends by leaving it. Tess leaves Wessex because she has exhausted community, because there is no room for her by the graves of her ancestors, and there is nowhere else for her to go but to Sandbourne and Stonehenge and her own grave. The state of affairs Hardy outlined in essay form in "The Dorsetshire Labourer" has come to pass in the novel.

On the other hand, the manuscript of the novel shows that *Tess* marks a further and decisive phase in the process of Wessex. Towards the end of the writing of Tess's story, which took from 1888 to 1892, Hardy came to the conclusion that Dorset was only a part of a larger cultural and social region which ought more properly to be called Wessex – that parts at least of Hampshire and Wiltshire and Somerset and Devon were artificially separated from Dorset by county boundaries, in so far as dialect and custom and environment and history and society were concerned. He marked this fundamental expansion of vision when he wrote in the last chapter of the manuscript that Wintoncester – Winchester, the county town of Hampshire – was the ancient capital of Wessex. A few pages earlier in the manuscript, as Angel and Tess walk towards Melchester, Hardy had written of their crossing the boundary between Upper and Mid Wessex. This is the earliest indication anywhere of the expansion of Wessex, and the establishment of a wider county-based geographical system for Hardy's fiction. Earlier references to Wessex in the manuscript were to the familiar Dorset-equivalent, and had to be revised, before the novel saw print, to South Wessex. So we can say with some confidence that in September or October of 1890 Hardy first formulated for himself the idea of Wessex as twentieth-century readers have been accustomed to experience it. The essential qualities of Wessex life did not change as a result, but the range over which their influence was held to be felt was considerably expanded. It is, for instance, a considerably larger claim in the new conception to suggest that Parson Clare was the "earnestest man in all Wessex" (*T*, London: Osgood, McIlvaine, 1891, I, xvii, p. 226; WC, xvii, p. 117) – but Hardy did not choose to diminish Wessex in this instance to South Wessex.

In September 1892 Hardy began arrangements for the publication of the first collected edition of his work, and during the three years that followed, Hardy thought out what effect the conjunction of this larger Wessex with the reissue of all his fiction in one continuous sequence might have on the individual novels. Earlier in his career Hardy had been careful to make it hard for readers to identify with precision the places of his fictional reality, altering distances, directions, relationships. But later, and certainly by the completion of *Tess of the d'Urbervilles*, that had changed. His newly established place-names were for the most part transparent versions of Dorset names, like Port-Bredy for Bridport, and if his mileages were not always precisely accurate, it was rather because he did not possess equipment to measure them, than because he was attempting to disguise anything. In large part, I think, Hardy felt free to do this in the 1890s because he believed that Wessex no longer had a vital equivalent in Dorset – that the culture of his youth had been irreversibly transformed by Victorian technological and social change – by the railway and national schools, by industrialization and the penny press. So no interruption of a living culture could be made by visitors from London wanting to find Egdon Heath or observe a mummers' play, or see the house Bathsheba Everdene inhabited.

Before I go on to consider the Osgood, McIlvaine collected edition, though, I ought to report on a last contribution in novel-form to the literature of Wessex – *Jude the Obscure* – whose first edition was issued as part of that collected edition. As Wessex is conceived in *The Return of the Native* or *The Mayor of Casterbridge*, *Jude the Obscure* is not a Wessex novel at all. Looked at from the angle of vision of this essay, *Jude* resumed where *Tess* had ended. Jude Fawley – born in Mellstock like Dick Dewy (only forty years or so later), orphaned at a very early age, transported to a village whose traditions have been stripped by modernizing Victorianism, a village way outside the old confines of Wessex, though technically within the bounds of New Wessex – Jude thus uprooted spends his whole life unsuccessfully searching for a community to which he can commit himself. The communities in the novel that approach most closely the Wessex village community that readers of Hardy had become familiar with, are based on trade – like the Christminster stonemason fraternity, or the rootless fair-and-circus fellowship – and under pressure of contemporary thought and personal ambitions Jude cannot join them. Hardy wrote the novel, amongst other reasons, to reinforce one of the conclusions of *Tess of the d'Urbervilles*, that the Wessex world given life in his earlier fictions was no longer viable, and where it survived, was living on borrowed time.

One powerful emblem of this is that *Jude the Obscure* is the only one of the "Novels of Character and Environment" in which railways play a significant role.[5] Some – *Under the Greenwood Tree* and *The Mayor of Casterbridge*, for instance – are set in time before the railways came to Dorset, but in an imaginative sense that is only a detail, for railways are irrelevant to Wessex – or at least to Old Wessex, to use the formulation; indeed they are an instrument of the destruction of Old Wessex. Even *The Woodlanders*, which temporally speaking is directly linked to the 1870s by specific changes in the divorce laws, has no railway: when Grace Melbury reaches Sherton from her boarding school, presumably she comes by train, but there is no mention of station or engine; she simply turns up in the center of the town. Railways are imaginatively alien to the Wessex embodied in *The Woodlanders*. Everyone in *Tess of the d'Urbervilles* walks, or rides or drives a horse; when Tess encounters the railway-engine that will carry Talbothays milk to London, Hardy stresses the unbridgeable gap separating the girl from the impersonal machinery. It is only at the end of the novel that Angel Clare actually takes a train out of Old Wessex to Sandbourne. And in this respect as in others *Jude the Obscure* pursues the ending of *Tess* to its inevitable conclusion. *Jude* is a railway novel. From the time that Jude reaches Christminster almost all journeys across this New Wessex are by rail. This means of transport isolates passengers from the country through which they travel, its rails follow no track formed by thousands of years of human travel from village to market, from cottage to church, but merely the line of least resistance between towns of commercial importance. Towards the end of the novel the narrator points out that in fifty years the inhabitants of Stoke-Barehills – Basingstoke – have forgotten completely that the main coach road from London to the south-west passed through their town. (When Hardy came to look at the passage again in 1912 during his revision for the Wessex Edition, he may perhaps, since he was sensitive to such things, have had an intimation of the transformative significance for another generation of inhabitants of the town of the arrival of another mode of transport, the motor-car.)

The issue by Osgood, McIlvaine of all his fiction in a series to be called "The Wessex Novels of Thomas Hardy" provided Hardy with opportunity and problems of a greater magnitude, but not much different in kind, from those he had faced in revising his stories for their collection in *Wessex Tales*. Wessex was the keynote of everything. It was the aspect of his writing that distinguished him most prominently, in the eyes of general readers and critics alike, from the mass of publishing novelists. Hardy knew that had his narratives – strong and satisfying though they mostly were – not been permeated by the social-cultural-economic idea of Wessex, they would not have possessed that rich density of texture for which he was becoming celebrated. Now his fundamental problem, or his greatest opportunity, rested in exactly the process this essay has outlined. When he began writing in the 1870s he wrote of the life of the district he knew best, and disguised his debt as best he could, though the debt was so great that no disguise could be adequate. In the 1890s, with the whole story of Wessex laid out behind him, he had to decide what to do. Was he to accept Wessex as purely his own creation, as a process of vision and interpretation that developed through his novel-writing life; or should he see Wessex as partially at least independent of himself, with a reality beyond his own fiction, with a life of its own which he had borrowed, concentrated, shaped, but which had existed in its random inchoate state in Dorset and surrounding counties and was now dead or dying. Or, to put it in more practical terms, should he leave *Under the Greenwood Tree* as a novel of 1872, or should he regard it as in some ways an inadequate expression of a conception then unrealized, and so alter certain aspects as to adapt it to the New Wessex announced in 1891?

The prefaces that Hardy wrote in 1895 for *Tess of the d'Urbervilles* and *Far from the Madding Crowd* reveal clearly the decision he made. "In the present edition it may be well to state, in response to inquiries from readers interested in landscape, pre-historic antiquities, and especially old English architecture, that the description of these backgrounds in this and its companion novels has been done from the real." Thus Hardy in the preface to *Tess* (*T*, London: Osgood, McIlvaine, 1895, p. xi; WC, p. 6); and he follows this by offering in rather a coy way, some identifications of fictional with real. The preface to *Far from the Madding Crowd* is more revealing: "The series of novels I projected being mainly of the kind called local, they seemed to require a territorial definition of some sort to lend unity to their scene. Finding that the area of a single county did not afford a canvas large enough for this purpose, and that there were objections to an invented name, I disinterred the old one" (*FMC*, London: Osgood, McIlvaine, 1895, p. v; WC, p. 3). Exactly when Hardy decided that his novels were a "series" and when he decided that a single county was insufficient for his purpose is, as I have attempted to show, not absolutely certain. It was a good deal nearer 1896 than 1870, but no one reading the novels in the collected edition would have been able to draw such a conclusion. Even *Desperate Remedies*, which Hardy had through revision excluded from Wessex as recently as 1889, was (as far as possible) brought back into the fold. The revised versions of the novels substantiate Hardy's statements, and if not precisely accurate, proposing as it does that New Wessex sprang fully formed from his forehead in 1874, the passage in the preface to *Far from the Madding Crowd* reflects with clarity the freshly made reality.

In this preface Hardy also described Wessex as "a merely realistic dream-country," though the phrase is better known in its 1912 formulation: "a partly-real, partly dream-country." The strength, in the 1895 version, of "merely" is hard to evaluate, though it seems that Hardy is devaluing realism when set against dream, or imagination. In any case the main thrust of the phrase is to call Wessex wholly a dream-country realistically presented. By the time of the last major revision of all of his fiction, that for the 1912 Wessex Edition (Macmillan), when he again adjusted descriptions and distances and names, he could hardly claim so much with justification, and the phrase was modified. On the one hand the revised version acknowledges the (now more or less consistent) giving of geographical names to geographical features such as hills and rivers, and on the other it also acknowledges the effect of changes of the sort that would allow an investigative reader of the 1912 version of *Under the Greenwood Tree* to recognize in the hero's cottage a fairly faithful reflection of the house in which Hardy was born – something certainly not possible from the description of the place in the first edition of 1872.

Hardy also gives some hints in the preface to *Far from the Madding Crowd* to anyone thinking about the larger scope of Wessex, in his account of the relationship of the novel's Weatherbury with the historical Puddletown. The first point he makes is that the modern "explorer" would find it hard to recognize any resemblance between the two. It is striking that Hardy recognized that his work had generated "explorers," and that in what follows he is at some slight pains to satisfy their needs. He was keenly alive to the commercial potential of this interest in using his fiction as a kind of selective guide to the region, and explained that Weatherbury was a version of Puddletown of thirty or forty years earlier, and that many features had since disappeared.

The preface's final two sentences summarize the root cause of the transformation in custom and architecture:

> The change at the root of this has been the recent supplanting of the class of stationary cottagers, who carried on the local traditions and humours, by a population of more or less migratory labourers, which has led to a break of continuity in local history, more fatal than any other thing to the preservation of legend, folk-lore, close inter-social relations, and eccentric individualities. For these the indispensable conditions of existence are attachment to the soil of one particular spot by generation after generation.
>
> (*FMC*, London: Osgood, McIlvaine [1895], p. vii; WC, pp. 4–5)

And here is the primary reason why Hardy chose to bring all his novels into the New Wessex scheme. He had begun to understand that he was the historian of a Wessex now passed, the recorder of a series of unique micro-environments, ways of life and speech, which together had formed a cultural whole. Thus he chose Wessex as homogeneous historical object over Wessex as subjective process, and undertook the work of bringing *The Return of the Native*, *The Trumpet-Major*, *A Laodicean* – to mention three of the more recalcitrant texts – into the nineties pattern of Wessex.

I have outlined elsewhere the kinds of changes this reworking required; my conclusion was then, and still is, to suggest that after 1896 it was no longer accurate to think of those and several other of Hardy's novels as works of the date of their first publication, for in certain essential aspects their original conception was radically altered.[6] When Hardy's fictional country was shaped out of what was within walking distance of Higher Bockhampton, Wessex was something quite other than the whole of south-western England: in 1896 Hardy asked his readers to see Bath and Mellstock, Southampton and Weatherbury, as places in the same scale of reality. They were all part of a large social and cultural system, an idea graphically represented by the map of Wessex containing these place-names that was attached to every novel for this edition. We are no longer allowed to differentiate *The Trumpet-Major* from the rest as historical novel by its use of English place-names, nor are we allowed to experience Egdon Heath in one of its modes, as an almost mythical place, barely tied to reality at all, as "realistic dream-country."

It will be seen from the choice of verb in the previous sentence, that it is my sense that Hardy lost much when he achieved what I have called New Wessex. His losses included the desire to write more novels. Relative financial security following the success of *Tess*, particularly in America, and the hostility of some critics of *Jude*, somewhat more raucous than usual, made the decision easier. He was no longer content with the requirements the realistic novel imposed on him, and had already begun again to write poetry as a regular thing. But the sense he had of the closure of Wessex as a living culture was central to his slow decision to end his career as a creator of fiction.

In his poetry the idea of Wessex withdraws for the most part into Hardy's own imagination. In what might be thought of as local poems, the collective social and topographical implications of Wessex are often stripped away, to leave what was always there behind it, Hardy's personal response to the realities to hand about him. There is a well-known, often discussed poem in which Hardy reflects on just this issue. "Wessex Heights" was written, the manuscript tells us, in December 1896. The last volume of the Osgood, McIlvaine collected edition had been published in the previous September, and the poem responds to the understanding of Wessex defined by the long process of revision. This is the poem's conclusion:

> So I am found on Ingpen Beacon, or on Wylls-Neck to the west,
> Or else on homely Bulbarrow, or little Pilsdon Crest,
> Where men have never cared to haunt, nor women have walked with me,
> And ghosts then keep their distance; and I know some liberty.
>
> (*CPW*, II, p. 27)

He chose his heights carefully to mark out New Wessex; Ingpen Beacon, the highest chalk down in England, is close to the meeting-point of North

Wessex, Upper Wessex, and Mid Wessex (or, alternatively, Berkshire, Hampshire, and Wiltshire), Wylls-Neck is the highest point in the Quantock Hills of Outer Wessex (or Somerset), Pilsdon Pen rises near the western edge of South Wessex (or Dorset), and "homely Bulbarrow" lies at the center of it all. This ending is an echo with variations of the beginning:

> There are some heights in Wessex, shaped as if by a kindly hand
> For thinking, dreaming, dying on, and at crises when I stand,
> Say, on Ingpen Beacon eastward, or Wylls-Neck westwardly,
> I seem where I was before my birth, and after death may be.
>
> (II, p. 25)

When on the summit of such hills the narrator feels unfleshed, disembodied, pure spirit – one might say a ghost. Free. And what he feels himself free of is all the past complexity of mire and blood in the valleys below that had been the fictional pulse of Wessex. The heights remain Wessex, but they offer liberty where the only necessary audience for his visions is himself. Put crudely, the heights offer poetry as an escape, long desired, from "men with a wintry sneer, and women with tart disparagings."

Perhaps Hardy did not include the poem in *Wessex Poems* (1898) because it was too nakedly autobiographical, and because the experiment of verse was of uncertain success; but also he was aware that the ghostly Wessex of the valleys would have to sustain financially the freed spirit on the hilltops. Perhaps the poem was included in *Satires of Circumstance* (1914) because individuals concerned in the poem had recently died. But in 1911–12 Hardy also found himself constrained to make a last substantial revisitation of the fictional Wessex, for Macmillan's Wessex Edition, the texts of which most people still read. It seems not entirely fanciful to suggest that Hardy was, in finally publishing "Wessex Heights," trying to reassure himself that this time he had given up thinking about Wessex for good. It is not coincidental that in *Satires of Circumstance* and the two following volumes of poetry, *Moments of Vision* (1917) and *Late Lyrics and Earlier* (1922), there are very few poems that could with any justice be called poems of Wessex, and moreover there are some, like "The Choirmaster's Burial" or "Midnight on the Great Western," that are remarkable for the way they avoid making what are clear Wessex connections. In *Human Shows* (1925), however, this is not the case, and the late-flowering in this volume of poems like "A Last Journey," "Winter Night in Woodland," "The Paphian Ball," or "The Sheep-Boy" contributes much to the deep satisfaction the collection gives. Hardy felt again the pull of those elements that had made his novels peculiarly his own:

Life and Death at Sunrise
(Near Dogbury Gate, 1867)

The hills uncap their tops
Of woodland, pasture, copse,
And look on the layers of mist
At their foot that still persist:
They are like awakened sleepers on one elbow lifted,
Who gaze around to learn if things during night have shifted.

A waggon creaks up from the fog
With a laboured leisurely jog;
Then a horseman from off the hill-tip
Comes clapping down into the dip;
While woodlarks, finches, sparrows, try to entune at one time,
And cocks and hens and cows and bulls take up the chime.

With a shouldered basket and flagon
A man meets the one with the waggon,
And both the men halt of long use.
"Well," the waggoner says, "what's the news?"
" – 'Tis a boy this time. You've just met the doctor trotting back.
She's doing very well. And we think we shall call him 'Jack.'

"And what have you got covered there?"
He nods to the waggon and mare.
"Oh, a coffin for old John Thinn:
We are just going to put him in."
" – So he's gone at last. He always had a good constitution."
" – He was ninety-odd. He could call up the French Revolution."

(*CPW*, III, pp. 40–41)

The title invites a reader to expect one of Hardy's little period melodramas
– a duel perhaps; but that is only his joke. In fact the poem reproduces
some of the central elements of Wessex. The landscape is alive with
significance, though on the whole it is only the narrator who sees it. The
range of characters, doctor to laborer, is characteristic of Wessex, but he
manages to make them seem of less significance than the dawn-chorus of
birds or the hills freed of mist. But then the brief exchange places the
environment in a different perspective. Though man may seem a brief-lived
intruder to the Wessex hills, his voice will endure, along with those of the
finches or the larks – Hardy never subscribes to the "Ode to a Nightingale"
(Keats) or "Wild Swans at Coole" (Yeats) comparison of the shortness of
man's life and the apparent immortality of individually indistinguishable
birds. Moreover, man alone has the speech and memory that permit him to

leave, for better or ill, a permanent mark on the permanent hills – so far as anything is permanent. Such a handing-off from death to birth as this poem celebrates is enacted a million times each day, and the whole of human history is symbolized in the French Revolution. But Hardy was also looking back almost sixty years from the vantage point of 1925, when the poem was published, on a fragment of passed community. The doctor in 1925 would perhaps have buzzed down the hill in his small Austin, and the laborer probably would have cycled to work. Would he have stopped to talk to the carter? Who knows?

It may be that Hardy's own gradual removal in class and age from the world of his childhood and youth had as much to do with the growth of his perception that village communities had ceased to be self-sustaining and were moribund, as did the historical reality of agricultural industrialization, or rural marginalization, or universalized education, or the intrusion of railway lines. The question of the accuracy of Hardy's imaginative inter-pretation of the historical realities of his time is of no more importance than that of the accuracy of his equally imaginative interpretation of the topographical realities of Dorset. For all readers of Hardy's Wessex novels and poems, whether familiar with those realities or not, have been stimulated by those imaginative interpretations to recreate their own Wessex of the mind, endowing that place and time with fresh life, again and again.

When I was a teenager, Hardy was the first writer to make me look. *The Return of the Native* made me take a train from London and look at Dorset – first at the places he described, but then everywhere. And now, if I sit, say, on the rampart of the neolithic fort on Eggardon Hill, looking south, all that makes Wessex is in my sight: there are honey buzzards hunting in the valley below, there are iron-age memories on the slopes, there is nothing between you and the sky, there are about you all the downland plants and insects in profusion, there beyond is the sea, there to the right is Golden Cap, there between are farms, hedgerows, cattle and furrowed fields, a tractor glinting in the sunlight, other flashes off cars hurrying between Dorchester and Bridport. There are marks of man on the country every-where, shapes of beauty in all the eye can see, not only transcendent beauty but hand-shaped harmony, in a fair visible pattern, a pattern changed by centuries, but fair in each century. That beauty and that harmony is visible too in a different pattern from the lane that skirts the corn-field and passes the farmhouse, that has been a lane since King Alfred's time, and the one view includes the other. As it happens there is no place visible that Hardy made a part of his fiction, and a hundred years have passed since he finished writing his novels, but nevertheless all I see is within their pages, for he leaves space for the changes he could not know. I would not have seen or understood any of this if Hardy had not helped me; my life would have been measurably poorer if he had not shown me, and left me no choice but to value, the essential Wessex that he knew, transformed in his imagination, and reproduced in his novels and poems.

NOTES

1 See, for example: Andrew Enstice, *Thomas Hardy: Landscapes of the Mind* (London and Basingstoke: Macmillan, 1979); Noorul Hasan, *Thomas Hardy: The Sociological Imagination* (London and Basingstoke: Macmillan, 1982); Denys Kay-Robinson, *The Landscape of Thomas Hardy* (Exeter: Webb and Bower, 1984); Peter Widdowson, *Hardy in History: A Study in Literary Sociology* (London: Routledge, 1989); Merryn Williams, *Thomas Hardy and Rural England* (London and Basingstoke: Macmillan, 1972).

2 All quotations in this chapter are taken from first editions or collected editions, since I am discussing these specific texts, which have, in some instances, different readings from the World's Classics editions. Page references to the latter edition (or, with *HE*, to the 1912 Wessex Edition) are also given, including when the passage being quoted was removed from the novel after the first edition. In the case of *FMC* the first occurrence of "Wessex" in the first edition was changed by Hardy to "South Wessex" in the first collected edition of his work (London: Osgood, McIlvaine, 1896). South Wessex is the name he gave in the 1890s to an area equivalent on his map to the county of Dorset.

3 See especially Widdowson, *Hardy in History*, pp. 155–97. Widdowson, by concentrating on issues of social class, gender relations, and the artifice of realist fiction writing, very effectively removes the novel from its conventionally marginal position in Hardy's *oeuvre*.

4 The effect of simple revisions to names alone in the collected editions of *RN* was transformative: "The town Southerton, which might have been in any direction and at any distance from the centre of the heath as far as the reader of the first edition knew, has entirely disappeared, and in the places where that name occurred are, variously, Casterbridge, Anglebury, and Weatherbury. A place 'about two miles to the right of Alderworth,' unnamed in the first edition, is now defined as Stickleford. Thus the extent of the heath is measured, from Casterbridge in the west to Anglebury in the east, from Weatherbury in the north to Stickleford in the south ... What was once of mysterious extent and of shifting definition is now a limited tract of land any tourist can tramp over" (Simon Gatrell, *Hardy the Creator: A Textual Biography* [Oxford: Clarendon Press, 1988], p. 129).

5 The "Novels of Character and Environment" are seven novels which Hardy in 1912, at the time of the issue of his second revised collected edition, the Wessex Edition, specially distinguished – the novels by which he is now most widely recognized.

6 See Gatrell, *Hardy the Creator*, pp. 118–31.

FURTHER READING

Fowles, John, and Jo Draper. *Thomas Hardy's England*. Boston and Toronto: Little, Brown and Co., 1984.

Williams, Raymond. *The Country and the City*. London: Chatto & Windus, 1973.

3

NORMAN PAGE

Art and aesthetics

Some of Hardy's most striking dicta seem designed to make it difficult to speak of his aesthetics – seem, indeed, to embody a dogged or defiant anti-aestheticism. For, while some of his finest work, including two of his greatest novels and his first volume of verse, appeared in the 1890s, he was decidedly not *of* the nineties; and while he would never have come out in favor of "art for *my* sake" as aggressively as D. H. Lawrence, he would surely have given this stance his quietly firm endorsement. "The beauty of association," he declares in a notebook entry dated 28 September 1877 and quoted in his autobiography, "is entirely superior to the beauty of aspect, and a beloved relative's old battered tankard to the finest Greek vase" (*LW*, p. 124). Such a statement implies aesthetic judgments based on criteria that are subjective, even secret, rather than those shared by any school, movement, period, or culture: as so often with Hardy, solipsism is not far away.

A word that recurs when he is reflecting on his own art is "idiosyncratic": in the spring of 1890 he notes that "Art consists in so depicting the common events of life as to bring out the features which illustrate the author's idiosyncratic mode of regard; making old incidents and things seem as new," and a few months later that "Art is a changing of the actual proportions and order of things, so as to bring out more forcibly than might otherwise be done that feature in them which appeals most strongly to the idiosyncrasy of the artist" (*LW*, pp. 235, 239). What such convictions often amount to is a rejection of representation or "realism" in favor of a highly, even eccentrically personal vision.

One practical result is that moments of quirky, fanciful, almost surrealistic self-indulgence can intrude into passages of the fiction that otherwise observe the canons of high realism. At the beginning of Phase the Fifth of *Tess of the d'Urbervilles*, it is suggested that Tess's confession to Angel not only modifies their relationship but actually effects a transformation in the very appurtenances of the room in which they sit:

But the complexion even of external things seemed to suffer transmutation as her announcement progressed. The fire in the grate looked impish, demoniacally funny, as if it did not care in the least about her strait. The fender grinned idly, as if it, too, did not care. The light from the water-bottle was merely engaged in a chromatic problem. All material objects around announced their irresponsibility with terrible iteration. (*T*, xxxv, p. 225)

There is a similar moment in *The Mayor of Casterbridge*, when Henchard's sense that he has a rival for Lucetta's love is metonymically transferred to Lucetta's house, viewed from outside: "Her windows gleamed as if they did not want him; her curtains seemed to hang slily, as if they screened an ousting presence" (*MC*, xxv, p. 181). In both passages, the character's heightened state of consciousness transforms a banal external world into something dream-like, unexpected and utterly personal, and it seems as though Hardy's own mind often worked in this way. At eighty years old, he reflected that he had "no philosophy – merely a confused heap of impressions, like those of a bewildered child at a conjuring-show" (*LW*, p. 441), and the reference to magical transformations of mundane reality is significant.

The aesthetic implied in such statements as those already quoted is based on individual perceptions and private associations, and is one that takes pride in its own nonconformity, even its own eccentricity. Another notebook entry challengingly asserts that "unconscious Nature" may be as deficient in the indispensable associative power as "the finest Greek vase": "An object or mark raised or made by man on a scene is worth ten times any such formed by unconscious Nature. Hence clouds, mists, and mountains are unimportant beside the wear on a threshold, or the print of a hand" (*LW*, p. 120). Hardy's earliest surviving poem, "Domicilium," is an imitation of Wordsworth, but such a remark compels us to think again about his relationship to the Romantic poets and is itself paralleled in some of his other poems. "The wear on a threshold," for instance, is commemorated in "The Self-Unseeing" – "Here is the ancient floor, / Footworn and hollowed and thin" (*CPW*, i, p. 206) and "the print of a hand" in "Old Furniture" – "I see the hands of the generations / That owned each shiny familiar thing / In play on its knobs and indentations" (*CPW*, ii, p. 227). The notebook jottings cited were made at about the time Hardy was at work on *The Return of the Native*, a novel that contains on its opening pages a disquisition on changing notions of the beautiful.

Hardy, it seems, is as unwilling to accept the idea of Nature as "all in all" (the phrase occurs in Wordsworth's "Lines Composed a Few Miles above Tintern Abbey") as he is to embrace the Keatsian idea of a work of art enshrining beauty and truth – for the "Ode on a Grecian Urn" is surely not far from his mind when he speaks of "the finest Greek vase." But whereas both mountains and classical artifacts are, so to speak, public property, associations largely constitute a private discourse, and one of the curious features of Hardy's career is that one whose instincts led him to construct a system of personal symbols (already evident in a very early poem such as "Neutral Tones") should have found himself working so extensively and for so long in the public discourse of fiction. After all, though, this is only an aspect of the larger mystery that a man so private and secretive by nature should have devoted more than half a century to exposing his deepest emotions to the critical and often hostile gaze of strangers.

The "battered tankard" quotation with which this essay began continues by explaining that "Paradoxically put, it is to see the beauty in ugliness," so that what Hardy is rejecting is less the idea of beauty itself than currently accepted concepts of the beautiful. This is consistent with the passage at the beginning of *The Return of the Native* already referred to, where he speculates that "beauty of the accepted kind" may have had its day: "Indeed, it is a question if the exclusive reign of this orthodox beauty is not approaching its last quarter." The radically changed sensibility of the modern age may, he suggests, turn away from classical and traditional norms and find beauty in, for example, types of landscape hitherto regarded as unappealing; "And ultimately, to the commonest tourist, spots like Iceland may become what the vineyards and myrtle-gardens of South Europe are to him now; and Heidelberg and Baden be passed unheeded as he hastens from the Alps to the sand-dunes of Scheveningen" (*RN*, I, i, pp. 4–5). (The prophecy was accurate as far as at least one admirer of Hardy was concerned, since W. H. Auden shunned the fashionable Mediterranean lands in favor of northern Europe and actually wrote a book about Iceland.)

For Hardy, then, beauty is not an absolute, but is culturally and even individually determined, and as V. de S. Pinto has pointed out, much of his poetry "arises out of his perception of 'beauty in ugliness.' It is important to note that Hardy never advocated a cult of ugliness for its own sake. He rather sought to extend the boundaries of poetic sensibility by an expression of new types of beauty and significance which he found in the ugly and the commonplace."[1] Though true enough as far as it goes, this is perhaps misleading in crediting Hardy with a conscious and dispassionate programme: his experiments, rationalized and articulated after the event, originated in the impulse to express a highly personal vision.

This vision or mind-set informs the whole of his large output, from novels and poems to scattered observations in notebooks and letters, and it is difficult to think of any other writer so productive over so long a period whose work possesses such consistency and integrity. In some of his earliest surviving productions, the poems written in his twenties (but published much later), the distinctive angle on experience is already evident. To trace the sources of this "individual mode of regard" is far from easy, but part of the answer can be put negatively, in Hardy's exclusion from more than a very modest amount of formal education. He started school late, at about eight years old, and left soon after his sixteenth birthday. In his old age he claims that the option was open to him to go to Cambridge, but this knowledge (if indeed it was true) did not neutralize his sense of exclusion, as is evident from his note for a short story that eventually developed into *Jude the Obscure*: "A short story of a young man – 'who could not go to Oxford' – His struggles and ultimate failure ... There is something [in this] the world ought to be shown, and I am the one to show it to them" *(LW,* p. 216; Hardy's square brackets).

It is worth asking how different Hardy's mind-set and culture might have been if he had gone to Cambridge or Oxford at eighteen or even twenty-five, and this is in fact an issue Hardy raises more than once in his autobiography. Stating at one point that he "had at one time as a young man begun reading for Cambridge with a view to taking Orders" (*LW,* p. 407), he explains elsewhere that "his intention in the eighteen-sixties ... was abandoned mainly owing to his discovery that he could not conscientiously carry out his idea of entering the church" (*LW,* p. 390). In yet another passage he reflects that, had the plan been carried out, he might have become a don and a classical scholar – adding, innocently or drily, "But this was not to be, and it was possibly better so" (*LW,* p. 38).

As a don he would hardly have produced the Wessex Novels but might have become a minor poet (a species thick on the ground in Victorian Oxford and Cambridge), somewhat guiltily or defensively cultivating an inaccessible poetic persona in the manner of A. E. Housman. More to the point, he could hardly have developed the highly individual vision and voice that we readily recognize as "Hardyan." For a conventional training would have imposed a discipline and induced a conformity to accepted models. And this in turn might have involved the suppression or repression of whole areas of his personality and sensibility, so that he might have come to resemble Walter Pater, Oxford don and high priest of the Aesthetic Movement, whose manner seemed to Hardy when they met to resemble that of "'one carrying weighty ideas without spilling them'" (*LW,* p. 187).

In the event, his culture was almost entirely a matter of self-cultivation and is notable for its range, its open-mindedness, and what often looks like its indifference to hierarchies and canons. His autodidactic programme started out, conventionally and conservatively enough, with the classics and theology, and in a similar spirit he later put Jude Fawley through a course of reading that, in the generation of Darwin and Huxley, seems curiously out of date, rather than directing his hero's ambitions towards science or engineering. But Hardy's own natural bent was towards eclecticism and encyclopaedism: his real model was not the syllabus of a university department but one of those mass-readership Victorian publications of the kind that invited the knowledge-hungry reader to "enquire within upon everything." As Michael Millgate has shown, many "educational works of the self-help variety," including Cassell's *Popular Educator*, *The Boys' Book of Science*, and John Timbs's *Things Not Generally Known, Familiarly Explained* (1856), were acquired in early youth and remained in Hardy's library at the time of his death.[2]

His intellectual stock-in-trade hence came to incorporate not only Shakespeare and Sophocles, Schopenhauer and Herbert Spencer, but popular works on history and natural history and isolated facts and ideas gleaned from newspapers and journals, often from reviews of books he had not read. He was a lifelong student and in a real sense an intellectual, if the term signifies one who cares deeply and passionately about ideas and the life of the mind: to the end of his days, philosophy, theology, ethics, and scientific thought were among his fields of eager and persistent enquiry. But he also had a collector's eye for the unusual and the bizarre, and was as likely to note down some curious fact of the "believe it or not" variety, or some stranger-than-fiction report from a local newspaper, as he was to store the gleanings of his readings in serious authors and the heavyweight journals. A remarkable intellectual openness, hospitable to all kinds of knowledge, is one of Hardy's most striking characteristics.

This assorted and highly personal culture finds direct and sometimes startling expression in his writings, especially his fiction. As Marlene Springer has said, in an age when allusiveness was a novelistic fashion "Hardy out-alludes virtually every allusionist,"[3] and the abundance as well as the heterogeneity of these allusions raise questions about their *raison d'être* as well as their function and effectiveness. In general they have had a bad press, generations of readers from the contemporary reviewers onwards complaining about their incongruity and intrusiveness. Certainly there are many instances hard or impossible to defend, when the intensity of the fictional moment seems to be injured or even dispelled by the interpolated parade of extraneous knowledge. The early and small-scale novel *Under the Greenwood Tree* is exceptionally short on allusions, but even here the village shoemaker, sitting at work and seen through an open door, is compared to "a framed portrait of a shoemaker by some modern Moroni" (*UGT*, II, ii, p. 70). Not many of Hardy's readers in any period would even have heard of the minor sixteenth-century artist Giovanni Moroni, and even fewer would have encountered or remembered his portrait of a tailor, which Hardy had seen in the National Gallery in London and presumably had in mind. The manuscript and corrected proofs show that the allusion was an afterthought, and even without this evidence one has a distinct sense of embellishment, of a simple narrative being given a rather spurious dignity.

This is not, however, a fair judgment on Hardy's use of allusion in his later novels, where the text is sometimes enriched by the interplay of other texts, more venerated but still familiar. *The Mayor of Casterbridge* is by general consent one of the finest of his mature works and an impressive testimony to his achievement in making the novel a vehicle for tragedy. The text incorporates numerous allusions to the Bible, the Classics (including Greek and Roman mythology and history), Shakespeare and other standard English writers such as Defoe, Gray, Scott, and Shelley, a few French and German writers, as well as folk-beliefs and popular songs. Once or twice we can detect Hardy in the act of raiding his notebooks: when Henchard's circular wanderings in chapter 44 are compared to those of "the Canadian woodsman" (*MC*, xliv, p. 319), this comparison is based on a passage taken from John Rowan's *The Emigrant and Sportsman in Canada* (1876), summarized by Hardy in his notebooks: "Without a compass the best woodsman cannot keep a straight line. Walks in circles, occupying him from 1/2 hour to 2 hrs. & an unobservant person will circumnavigate the same 100 acres of wood all day long" (*LN* 1, p. 100). A rather humdrum observation from a subliterary source has somehow seized Hardy's imagination and he is ready to grant it a place, quite unselfconsciously, among allusions to the masterpieces of world literature. It is also worth noting that the wife-selling incident that sets the story in motion may well have been based on a passage encountered during Hardy's adolescent poring over the work of popular education by John Timbs mentioned above.

Many of the allusions in this novel, like that in chapter 2 to the ancient legend of the Seven Sleepers, make no more than a passing point, but others form significant patterns. There are, for instance, the recurring comparisons, explicit or implicit, between the protagonist and two figures who would be very familiar to virtually all of its original readers: Saul in the Old Testament and Shakespeare's King Lear. If these allusions put a strain on the modern reader, that is a measure of the gulf between the common culture of the late-Victorian age and our own.

Hardy's culture, then, was partly determined by an exceptionally varied reading drawn from a range of sources. But his thinking about art in general and literary art in particular was also informed by a knowledge of, even a passion for, certain non-literary arts. These make many appearances in the fiction and poetry: *Under the Greenwood Tree* (a novel subtitled "A Rural Painting of the Dutch School") opens with music-making and moves to a conclusion in which a wedding is celebrated by dance; Stephen Smith of *A Pair of Blue Eyes* is, like Hardy himself, an architect; the hero of Hardy's *Künstlerroman, The Well-Beloved,* is a sculptor; some characteristic poem-titles are "Heiress and Architect" and "The Choirmaster's Burial." At moments Hardy may even have felt that he had spread his enthusiasms too thinly. The poem "Rome: The Vatican: Sala delle Muse," one of a group inspired by a visit to Italy in the spring of 1887 just after the completion of *The Woodlanders,* expresses some anxiety at the fickleness or instability of his involvements with different art-forms: "I worship each and each; in the morning one, / And then, alas! another at sink of sun" (*CPW*, 1, p. 136). This confession is made to a sort of composite Muse, "an essence of all the Nine," seen in a vision among the more solid sculptures of the gallery, but she is able to reassure him that "'I and my sisters are one'" – in other words, all the different arts, among which the poem cites "Form" (sculpture) and "Tune" (music), as well as all their generic subdivisions (including "'Story, and Dance, and Hymn'"), are no more than aspects of a single entity, Art. In a curious way the poem's argument offers an aesthetic counterpart to the love-story or love-fable that Hardy was to write a few years later, *The Well-Beloved,* in which the artist-hero's quest for an erotic or romantic ideal finds temporary fulfillment in a series of separate embodiments. Long after both poem and novel, Hardy made in his autobiography a remark in a similar spirit: "But probably few literary critics discern the solidarity of all the arts" (*LW*, p. 321), an observation quickly followed by an allusion to the poem just cited.

One manifestation of this belief is Hardy's readiness to draw analogies between, and detect common principles in, different art-forms. At the beginning of 1886, he reflects that "My art is to intensify the expression of things, as is done by Crivelli, Bellini [painters of the Italian Renaissance], &c. so that the heart and inner meaning is made vividly visible" (*LW*, p. 183). Elsewhere, he is ready to recognize that his own practice of metrical forms owes something to his study of Gothic architecture:

> Years earlier he had decided that too regular a beat was bad art. He had fortified himself in his opinion by thinking of the analogy of architecture, between which art and that of poetry he had discovered, to use his own words, that there existed a close and curious parallel, each art, unlike some others, having to carry a rational content inside its artistic form. He knew that in architecture cunning irregularity is of enormous worth, and it is obvious that he carried on into his verse, perhaps unconsciously, the Gothic

art-principle in which he had been trained – the principle of spontaneity, found in mouldings, tracery, and such-like. (*LW*, p. 323)

An earlier passage in the autobiography suggests that a similar principle came to inform his prose: at an early stage of his literary career he accepted the inevitable and found himself (as he rather ruefully puts it) "committed to prose," whereupon he embarked on "a study of style." The conclusion he reached, quoted from a notebook-entry of 1875, was that

> "The whole secret of a living style and the difference between it and a dead style, lies in not having too much style – being – in fact, a little careless, or rather seeming to be, here and there. It brings wonderful life into the writing … It is, of course, simply a carrying into prose the knowledge I have acquired in poetry – that inexact rhymes and rhythms now and then are far more pleasing than correct ones." (*LW*, p. 108)

The principle of calculated "carelessness" implemented in his prose resembles that of "cunning irregularity" in his verse; both experiments, by defying accepted criteria of smoothness and decorum, were to lay him open to criticism and censure. And the dismay or displeasure of many contemporary reviewers and not a few later critics is understandable, while the praise of the Public Orator at Oxford University, who presented Hardy for an honorary degree in 1920, for the "smoothness and elegance" ("'molle atque facetum'") of his writings (*LW*, p. 523) seems peculiarly wide of the mark. For the moment, however, the significant point is that this "cunning irregularity" seems to have been inspired by his early study of Gothic architecture.

It has often been suggested that his architectural experience influenced Hardy on another level, that of plot-making. There is admittedly a rough sense in which the disposition of plots and subplots in constructing a work of fiction can be compared to the disposition of spaces in designing a building, but many Victorian novelists who had not received an architectural training seem to have fashioned their plots on similar principles, and in any case the decisive factor may have been the exigencies of serialization. Hardy wrote *The Mayor of Casterbridge* at the same time that his Dorchester home, Max Gate, was being built to his own designs, but it would not be easy to argue for significant analogies between novel and house; the novel, however, undeniably shows a marked interest in buildings of various kinds, and Hardy's descriptive vocabulary is more technical than that of most novelists.

It is probably, however, the prominent role given to buildings with distinctive architectural features that is the principal legacy bequeathed by Hardy's first career to his second. Notable set pieces include the description of the great barn in *Far from the Madding Crowd*, of Knapwater House in *Desperate Remedies*, and of Endelstow House in *A Pair of Blue Eyes*. In *Two on a Tower* the action moves between the isolated tower (almost as much a symbol as that inhabited by Tennyson's Lady of Shalott), the country house, and the cottage. *A Laodicean* opens with a discussion of changing fashions in architectural styles, and in *Jude the Obscure* Jude and Sue discuss the rival merits of neoclassical and Gothic buildings.

The context in which Hardy's phrase "the solidarity of all the arts" appears is significant. After expressing a somewhat pained surprise at the cool welcome granted by contemporary reviewers to his first volume of verse, he suggests that the nineteenth century offered a precedent for the "modulation from one style into another by a great artist": that precedent is Verdi, with whom Hardy clearly felt he had something in common besides longevity. Not everyone, perhaps, would readily perceive the transition from *Il Trovatore* to *Falstaff* as analogous to that from, say, *Far from the Madding Crowd* to *Wessex Poems*, and in Hardy's case the chronology of the "modulation" was obviously more complex, but it is clear that for him the comparison between an operatic composer and a novelist-poet was a perfectly workable one.

Such a frontier-crossing may have come the more easily because of the love of music that had its origins in his childhood. The early pages of the autobiography devote a considerable amount of space to the tradition of sacred and secular music-making on which the Hardy family prided itself (sometimes, as he admits, at the expense of more worldly considerations). He himself played the fiddle from an early age – an activity commemorated in one of the finest of his short poems, "The Self-Unseeing" – and became a passionately enthusiastic dancer, as another poem, "Reminiscences of a Dancing Man," makes clear. "The Fiddler of the Reels," a short story of considerable power, pays tribute not only to the overmastering power of music and dance but to their aphrodisiac qualities. At the same time, church services gave him an extensive acquaintance with Anglican hymnody and he acquired a lifelong affection for Tate and Brady's metrical versions of the Psalms; again, a poem, "Apostrophe to an Old Psalm Tune," recalls his early church-going, when, "full of wonder, and innocent," he stood "meek-eyed with those of choric bent" (*CPW*, II, p. 163).

As a young man in London he frequented not only such famous dance-halls as the Argyle Room and the Cremorne but also the Italian opera at Covent Garden, forming a taste for popular romantic music that remained with him. Towards the end of his life he told the composer Rutland Boughton, more truthfully than tactfully, that he "had heard no modern compositions," not excluding Boughton's own: the music of such composers as Johann Strauss and Rossini "interested him more strongly, and also church music, mainly on account of the association with his early days" (*LW*, p. 458). As a middle-aged man he enjoyed "going the round of the music-halls" (*LW*, p. 237) in London as well as attending recitals, opera, and ballet. His musical tastes, in short, were, like his literary tastes, highly eclectic, ranging from folksong and traditional church music to the metropolitan and international popular successes of the day, and his fiction, like his poetry, incorporates innumerable allusions to many kinds of music and music-making. There is no exaggeration or apology, indeed there is a kind of quiet pride, in the opening lines of one of his untitled poems: "Any little old song / Will do for me" (*CPW*, III, p. 8).

Such a poem is in fact itself a "little old song," and it is revealing that Hardy has been a favorite among composers looking for words to set to music, for in a sense the task they take up has been begun by Hardy himself. Occasionally, indeed, such settings can seem superfluous or intrusive, competing or even disputing with the genuine musicality of the poems themselves. There is evidence that for Hardy a poem often began as a tune, or at least a rhythmic pattern, such musical elements being anterior to words and "meaning." Virtually all of his poems, moreover, are rhymed, sometimes using the meager rhyme-stock of the English language with considerable ingenuity: "Wagtail and Baby," for instance, introduces the word "drinking" at the end of the second line and then proceeds to find seven rhymes for it in the ensuing quatrains. The effect is of a musical chime, and it is not very surprising that Benjamin Britten should have chosen to set this engaging but relatively unfamiliar poem as one of the items in his song-cycle *Winter Words* (1953).

Hardy's study of the history of British and European painting was lifelong and left many marks, not always entirely happily, on his writings. As a young man working in London he was a constant visitor to the National Gallery, in later years he regularly attended the Royal Academy's annual exhibitions of contemporary art, and on his Continental travels he explored the treasures of Rome, Florence, and other cities. The acres of canvas inspected at the Royal Academy were mostly of a highly conventional kind, and the allusions to artists and paintings in his work draw heavily on the old masters, but there is evidence elsewhere of a certain impatience with tradition and with the representational styles that dominated Victorian art. In 1887 he wrote in his notebook:

"The 'simply natural' is interesting no longer. The much-decried, mad, late-Turner rendering is now necessary to create my interest. The exact truth as to material fact ceases to be of importance in art – it is a student's style – the style of a period when the mind is serene and unawakened to the tragical mysteries of life." (*LW*, p. 192)

Hardy's own perceptions of common objects or scenes often seem to have this transformative quality, and a notebook entry in the following year suggests the way in which his eye and his imagination could be seized by even a banal image: "July 5 [1888]. A letter lies on the red velvet cover of the table; staring up by reason of the contrast. I cover it over, that it may not hit my eyes so hard" (*LW*, p. 219). Letters are almost as common in Victorian genre paintings (for example, Richard Redgrave's well-known "The Governess" and Augustus Egg's "Man and Wife" series) as in Victorian fiction, but their function is narrative or literary: what Hardy is registering here is closer to an impressionistic or surrealistic response, recalling Rosemary Sumner's claim that "his visual images are so close to [those of the Surrealist painters] that often they might almost seem to be a description of their pictures – though they had not yet been painted."[4]

Such images, transforming the quotidian scene by the writer's "idiosyn-cratic mode of regard," occur quite frequently in the fiction. Near the beginning of this essay, I quoted a striking passage from *Tess of the d'Urbervilles* in which, momentarily and disconcertingly, a Victorian domestic interior is transformed into a fantasy-world in which inanimate objects vibrate with consciousness. The narrator's eye at this point is painterly – the water-bottle's "chromatic problem" might also have chal-lenged Cézanne or Van Gogh – but the technique is quite unlike the descriptive method of, say, George Eliot, to whom Hardy owes a great deal in other respects. Nor does it resemble the comic animism of a Dickensian description. Later in the same novel, Tess's murder of Alec is also "announced" visually, through a remarkable image that recalls the note-book entry of 5 July 1888, quoted above. Like the slayings in Greek tragedy, Alec's death takes place off-stage and becomes known through the agency of an insignificant character or "messenger," the landlady: "The oblong white ceiling, with this scarlet blot in the midst, had the appearance of a gigantic ace of hearts" (*T*, lvi, p. 369). The reader shares the landlady's visual shock, if not her housewifely concern, and may also recall that the image strongly resembles (with a simple color-reversal) that recorded in the 1888 diary entry. As Tony Tanner has strikingly demonstrated, the "ace of hearts" image is one of a series constituting an intricate pattern of color symbolism in this novel.[5]

It is in ways such as this, rather than in his numerous but passing (and often perfunctory) allusions to the Old Masters, that Hardy's enthusiasm for painting impinges upon his fiction. As already suggested, such allusions, running all the way from Angelico to Zurbarán,[6] often seem to take for granted an intimate knowledge of the artist's work that most of his readers would be unlikely to possess. (Hardy himself seems to concede this point when he writes, in his first published novel, *Desperate Remedies*, that "Those who remember Greuze's 'Head of a Girl,' have an idea of Cytherea's look askance at the turning" (*DR*, IV, ii, Wessex Edition [1912], p. 61). Thus, references to "the greenish shades of Correggio's nudes" (*DR*, XII, iii, Wessex Edition [1912], p. 245) or "the angry crimson of a Danby sunset" (*FMC*, XX, p. 140) have to be taken on trust, contribute little to the reader's own process of mental picture-making, and may be regarded, without excessive cynicism, as little more than name-dropping. What they do indicate, however, is Hardy's own close familiarity with these artists and his clear visual recollections of their canvases, and there is undeniably something daring and characteristically risk-taking in his infiltration of the name of a painter of, say, classical mythology or the English aristocracy into the world of the Wessex novels.

Hardy's ideas concerning literature and literary style, as well as his more general notions of art, were, then, profoundly influenced by his experience of nonliterary arts. His self-education allowed him to indulge his natural eclecticism: a boy born in 1840 into more privileged circumstances who had taken the well-worn educational route leading to Oxford or Cambridge would have had his aesthetic ideas inhibited by the traditional map of learning with its somewhat arbitrary and tendentious barriers between subjects or disciplines, but an autodidact was at liberty to disregard the imperatives of specialization. For him, mind and sensibility could readily and instinctively conceive as integral areas commonly treated as separate.

Something similar operates in relation to Hardy's attitude to literary forms and genres. Hardy is perhaps unique among English writers in being both a major poet and a major novelist, and the two territories are often in collaboration rather than competition. While many of the poems have a strong narrative element, the fiction is very often poetic not only in local description and imagery but in broader conception. Hardy was sufficiently the inheritor of Romantic convictions about the supremacy of verse to treat his poetry with greater respect than his novels. In his twenties he had, of course, begun as a poet, and failure to secure publication for his poems did not deter him from continuing the writing and reading of poetry. As he recalls, with a touch of wryness, he had formed "the Quixotic opinion that, as in verse was concentrated the essence of all imaginative and emotional literature, to read verse and nothing else was the shortest way to the fountain-head of such for one who had not a great deal of spare time" (*LW*, p. 51). His ranking did not, however, much change with the passage of time, and the letters of his later years frequently advise his correspondents to save their own time by reading his verse rather than his prose, on the grounds that the "essence" of the latter is contained in the former.

Hardy's prefaces, though hardly comparable with those of James or Conrad, contain some revealing statements concerning his attitudes to his own writings. The longest is the 1922 "Apology" that introduces *Late Lyrics and Earlier*, a substantial essay that apparently represents an abridgement of an even longer original version (see *PW*, pp. 58–59); a close runner-up is the important "General Preface to the Novels and Poems" written for a definitive collected edition in 1912. Some, on the other hand, are very brief, running to little more than a dozen lines. In the five prefaces he wrote for his volumes of verse (the other three volumes carry no prefaces), Hardy's tone is unmistakably defensive and self-justifying. The earliest, that to *Wessex Poems*, rather vaguely excuses the use of dialect words ("on what seemed good grounds") and then proceeds to claim that the poems are "in a large degree dramatic or personative in conception." This pretence, as in many instances it surely is, to be writing something akin to Browning's dramatic monologues, is clearly a gambit to discourage their being read as personal or autobiographical statements and as such is entirely consistent with similar claims with respect to the novels (for instance, that there is "not a scrap of personal detail" in *Jude the Obscure* [*LW*, p. 425]), as well as with his firm and sometimes bitter discouragement of biographers. Four years later, the brief preface to his second verse-collection, *Poems of the Past and the Present*, repeats the point almost verbatim("much is dramatic or impersonative even where not explicitly so"), and seven years later still the note introducing *Time's Laughingstocks* informs the reader that the first-person lyrics should be "regarded, in the main, as dramatic monologues by different characters." The attempt to depersonalize his own intensely personal work, and to encourage the reader in the direction of certain kinds of reading while inhibiting other kinds, is deceptive but at least consistent.

One of the most prominent concerns of the much longer and more philosophical preface to *Late Lyrics and Earlier*, and again a familiar one, is the rebuttal of the label of "pessimist" so persistently attached to him. Part of Hardy's strategy is to insist that what is treated by critics and journalists as a coherent philosophy embodied in his writings is no more than "a series of fugitive impressions" (*CPW*, ii, p. 319), and similar disarming claims abound in his published and private writings. The last sentence of his final preface, to the posthumously published *Winter Words* (1928), firmly reiterates the point – a familiar one, but still not easy to take entirely at face value – that "no harmonious philosophy is attempted in these pages – or in any bygone pages of mine, for that matter" (*CPW*, III, p. 167).

The 1912 "General Preface" also takes up the accusations of pessimism and again counters them by an insistence that his work offers "mere impressions of the moment, and not convictions or arguments." With regard to the novels, Hardy is once again on the defensive in responding to criticisms that the narrow boundaries of his fictional world entail damaging limitations. In terms that recall Wordsworth's 1800 Preface to *Lyrical Ballads* (a text he knew well), he maintains that "the elementary passions" can be exhibited in "Wessex nooks" as readily as in "the palaces of Europe" (*PW*, p. 45): as he nicely, and quite relevantly, points out, the extent of the territory across which his characters move is comparable to that in which the tragic drama of the Greeks was set. Behind the light tone of his insistence that "there was quite enough human nature in Wessex for one man's literary purpose," however, is a touchy awareness that he has been categorized as a "provincial" and a sort of gifted peasant who writes of rural life because he has no experience of the sophisticated world. Elsewhere he emphatically rejects Matthew Arnold's attack on provincialism (now, of course, in not merely a geographical or social sense), insisting that "Arnold is wrong about provincialism, if he means anything more than a provincialism of style and manner in exposition. A certain provincialism of feeling is invaluable. It is of the essence of individuality" (*LW*, p. 151).

In that last phrase we are reminded of the stress laid on idiosyncrasy, on a highly personal vision and manner, in some of the statements quoted earlier in this essay. For all the attempts, palpable enough in their motivation, to depersonalize his own work, Hardy remained committed to a Romantic view of art as expressing the uniqueness of its creator's mind and personality. At the same time, the commitment to individuality did not involve the abdication from responsibility for his deeply held convictions, as his references to "fugitive impressions" may seem to suggest. After all, in Shelley, his favorite poet, he had an outstanding example of an artist who reconciled individuality and responsibility.

In his later years Hardy showed an awareness of new developments in literature and sometimes disclosed a wry sense of his own status as a survivor of an almost extinct species: in his preface to *Late Lyrics and Earlier*, published in the year of *Ulysses* and *The Waste Land*, he is somewhat ruefully conscious of himself, "in neo-Georgian days," as a "mid-Victorian" relic (*CPW*, II, p. 317). He read the poems (but not the novels) of Lawrence, corresponded with Pound, talked to Virginia Woolf (though perhaps rather as her father's daughter than as the author of

Mrs. Dalloway), and numbered among his friends such younger writers as Edmund Blunden, E. M. Forster, T. E. Lawrence, and Siegfried Sassoon. He was ready to recognize his own fiction as belonging to a vanished tradition without necessarily being the worse for that. Of the naturalism of such writers as George Moore and Arnold Bennett, he wrote in 1913: "They forget in their insistence on life, and nothing but life, in a plain slice, that a story *must be worth the telling*, that a good deal of life is not worth any such thing, and that they must not occupy a reader's time with what he can get at first hand anywhere around him" (*LW*, p. 391). As a critique of naturalism, this may be less than incisive, but it endorses a point already made more than once in different contexts: that Hardy was as skeptical about representation as he was convinced of the authenticity and validity of the personal, even the eccentric vision.

Earlier, seeking to explain and justify his abandonment of the novel after *Jude the Obscure*, Hardy had commented that the novel was "'gradually losing artistic form, with a beginning, middle, and end, and becoming a spasmodic inventory of items, which has nothing to do with art'" (*LW*, p. 309). The Aristotelian allusion suggests that, for all his traditional placing in the mainstream of realist fiction and his undeniable debt to George Eliot, the significant models for Hardy's fiction included classical tragedy. An Aristotelian concern with probability is likewise evident in his response to Dr. Marie Stopes, pioneer of birth control and aspirant dramatist, who asked for his support in getting her play *Vectia* produced: he wrote to her on 16 April 1926 that "It seems to me that the situation and events are improbable: not too improbable to have happened, but too improbable for art, which must keep far within actual truth" (*Letters* 7, p. 16).

This very late remark is evidence of the consistency of Hardy's belief that art should be governed by its own self-sufficient and demanding rules and conventions. It is a conviction that seems to move in the direction of the aestheticism that this essay began by questioning. Roger Fowler has said that, for the aesthete whose gospel is the conclusion to Walter Pater's *The Renaissance* (1873), "reality amounts to sharp, fleeting impressions, images and sensations arrested by the creative individual from an experience in constant flux."[7] Hardy both knew and had read Pater, as his autobiography and his *Literary Notebooks* attest, and his self-depiction as one preoccupied with "fugitive impressions" rather than a coherent philosophy suggests that he may have more in common with the Aesthetic Movement than has sometimes been supposed. If this line of argument seems to land us in uncertainties and even contradictions, it is at least a familiar experience in trying to come to terms with a writer who, despite his reputation for the homespun and the improvised, constantly challenges us with the complexity of his ideas on art and life.

NOTES

1 V. de S. Pinto, *Crisis in English Poetry 1880–1940*, 5th edn. (London: Hutchinson, 1967), p. 37.
2 Michael Millgate, *Thomas Hardy: His Career as a Novelist* (London: The Bodley Head, 1971), p. 38.
3 Marlene Springer, *Hardy and the Art of Allusion* (Basingstoke and London: Macmillan; Lawrence: University of Kansas Press, 1983), p. 1.
4 Rosemary Sumner, "Some Surrealist Elements in Hardy's Prose and Verse," *Thomas Hardy Annual No. 3*, ed. Norman Page (Basingstoke and London: Macmillan, 1985), p. 39.
5 Tony Tanner, "Colour and Movement in Hardy's *Tess of the d'Urbervilles*," *Critical Quarterly*, 10 (1968), 219–39. For a very early instance of Hardy's acute sensitivity to the color red, see *LW*, p. 20.
6 For a useful list of such allusions, see F. B. Pinion, *A Hardy Companion* (London and Basingstoke: Macmillan, 1968), pp. 193–200.
7 Roger Fowler, *A Dictionary of Modern Critical Terms*, revised and enlarged edition (London and New York: Routledge & Kegan Paul, 1987), p. 2.

FURTHER READING

Bullen, J. B. *The Expressive Eye: Fiction and Perception in the Work of Thomas Hardy*. Oxford: Clarendon Press, 1986.
Grundy, Joan. *Hardy and the Sister Arts*. London and Basingstoke: Macmillan, 1979.
Salter, C. H. "Hardy's Pedantry." *Nineteenth Century Fiction*, 38 (1973), 145–64.
Smart, Alastair. "Pictorial Imagery in the Novels of Thomas Hardy." *Review of English Studies*, n.s. 12 (1961), 262–80.
Vigar, Penelope. *The Novels of Thomas Hardy: Illusion and Reality*. London: Athlone Press, 1974.

4

ROBERT SCHWEIK

The influence of religion, science, and philosophy on Hardy's writings

A consideration of the influence of contemporary religion, science, and philosophy on Hardy's writings requires some prefatory cautions. First, such influences often overlap, and identification of how they affected Hardy's work must sometimes be no more than a tentative pointing to diverse and complex sets of possible sources whose precise influence cannot be determined. Thus in *Far from the Madding Crowd* Gabriel Oak intervenes to protect Bathsheba's ricks from fire and storm, uses his knowledge to save her sheep, and in other ways acts consistently with the biblical teaching that man was given the responsibility of exercising dominion over nature. At the same time, Oak's conduct is congruent with Thomas Henry Huxley's argument in *Man's Place in Nature* that it is mankind's ethical responsibility to control a morally indifferent environment. However, Oak's actions are even more remarkably consistent with details of the philosophical analysis of man's moral relationship to the natural world in John Stuart Mill's essay "Nature" – though its date of publication makes that influence only barely possible.[1] In this and many other such cases, questions of which, and to what degree, one or more possible sources – "religious," "scientific," or "philosophical" – might have affected what Hardy wrote cannot be resolved with any certainty.

It must be emphasized, too, that Hardy was intellectually very much his own man. He was a voracious reader, widely inquisitive, but usually skeptical and hesitant to embrace wholeheartedly any of the various systems of ideas current in his day. Furthermore – as Hardy many times insisted – the views he did incorporate in his texts were unsystematic and inconsistent "impressions," often the utterances of various *personae* in specific dramatic situations. In short, elements of contemporary thought in Hardy's works tend to be embedded in a densely intricate web of imaginative connections and qualifications so complex that a consideration of them can hope only partly to illuminate the manifold ways they may have influenced his writings.

Religion

When Hardy was an architect's apprentice in Dorchester, a dispute with a fellow apprentice and the sons of a Baptist minister on the subject of infant baptism prompted him to more intense study of the Bible and to further inquiry into Anglican doctrine on pedobaptism. Hardy's autobiographical account of his decision to "stick to his own side" (*LW*, pp. 33–34) reveals something of the diverse ways religion could influence his writing. The character of the minister in *A Laodicean* Hardy patterned after the Baptist minister (*LW*, p. 35); his rendering of the issue of baptism in that novel stems partly from his youthful experience but also from later research (*PN*, pp. 180–83); and the phrasing he quoted in his autobiography, "stick to his own side," echoed a phrase from *Far from the Madding Crowd* in a scene where the rustics engage in a memorably comic discussion of differences between Anglicans and Nonconformists (*FMC*, xlii, p. 296) – a scene which itself was probably in part inspired by Hardy's amused recollection of his own youthful decision.

But Hardy's representations of religion were most profoundly influenced by his loss of faith in Christian dogma. He described himself as "among the earliest acclaimers of *The Origin of Species*" (*LW*, p. 158) and recorded that he was "impressed" by *Essays and Reviews* (*LW*, p. 37); one can only guess at what other intellectual and emotional experiences at that time might have contributed to the erosion of his religious beliefs. He had considered the possibility of a career as a clergyman, and as late as 1865, out of deference to his mentor, Horace Moule, wished he could be convinced by the arguments in John Henry Newman's *Apologia*. But Hardy found he could not (*LW*, pp. 50–51), and in that same year he rejected further clerical aspirations, explaining that "he could hardly take the step with honour while holding the views that on examination he found himself to hold" (*LW*, p. 53). By 1888, when a clergyman asked him how to reconcile the absolute goodness and non-limitation of God with the horrors of human existence, Hardy referred him to the life of Darwin and the works of Herbert Spencer and "other agnostics" for a "provisional view of the universe" (*LW*, p. 214). Ten years later, in his poem "Nature's Questioning," he had his speaker respond to Nature's puzzled speculations on the origins of the universe with a flat, "No answerer I ..." (*CPW*, i, pp. 86–87) – a reply that characterized one strain of Hardy's own religious views throughout much of his career.

Yet although Hardy became an agnostic, he remained emotionally involved with the Church: many of his writings dramatize aspects of the pernicious influence of religious doctrines or the ineffectuality of institutional Christianity, but he could also evoke a wistful sense of the loss of an earlier, simpler faith, or affirm the lasting value of Christian Charity. In short, one thing that sets Hardy apart from many of his contemporaries was his capacity to hold the wide variety of "impressions" of religion that inform his writings.

One manifestation of the way Christianity remained a persistent influence on Hardy's writings is that his fiction is saturated with biblical allusions. Critics have disagreed on how effectively Hardy used them, as commentaries on his references to Satan reveal,[2] but scriptural and other religious allusions in Hardy's fiction are distributed unevenly, and in some novels they form patterns that obviously play important roles. In *Far from the Madding Crowd*, for example, many Old and New Testament references enhance the ambiance of timeless antiquity which is one of that novel's most important aesthetic features. For *The Mayor of Casterbridge*, on the other hand, Hardy employed allusions to the biblical story of Saul and David as a major structural element in rendering its plot and character relationships.[3] And in *Tess* and *Jude*, where he was particularly concerned with the inimical relationship of religious mores to human lives, scriptural references repeatedly appear in contexts which suggest that Christianity is a pervasive hindrance to the fulfillment of human aspiration.

Hardy's writings also abound with pejorative characterizations of Christian clergy and other representatives of the Church, as well as with dramatizations of the harmful consequences of Christian teaching: one thinks, for example, of the fanatical text-painter in *Tess*, or of the snobbish and foolishly conventional Felix and Cuthbert Clare, who are ironically called "unimpeachable models" of clergymen (*T*, xxv, p. 162). But Hardy's presentations of representatives of Christianity and his renderings of the impact of Christian belief on both individual characters and on society generally were remarkably diverse and nuanced. In the novels, he tended to treat clergymen and Christianity with increasing hostility. Maybold in *Under the Greenwood Tree* is mildly parsimonious and class-conscious, but Swancourt in *A Pair of Blue Eyes* is a social snob whose prejudices do more serious harm. Hardy's revisions reveal that over the course of time he was increasingly critical of Bishop Helmsdale of *Two on a Tower*,[4] and part of the plot of that novel turns on the cruel choices imposed on the heroine by intolerant Christian attitudes toward human sexuality. By the time he came to write *Tess* and *Jude*, Hardy was even more explicit in dramatizing the way Christian teachings had widespread malign human consequences.

An even more various treatment of the limitations of clerics and Christianity is notable in his short stories and poems. "The Son's Veto," for example, depicts how a clerical education shaped a clergyman's cruel treatment of his mother, while "A Tragedy of Two Ambitions" delineates the plight of brothers who realize that to succeed in the Church of England they must above all be gentlemen rather than scholars or preachers. In Hardy's poems there is the well-meaning but bumbling clergyman of "The Curate's Kindness," the hypocritical preacher of "In Church," the credulous fool of "In the Days of Crinoline," the dully indifferent Mr. Dowe of "An East-End Curate," the disenchanted Parson Thirdly in "Channel Firing," the narrow-minded priest of "The Inscription," the misguided vicar in "The Choirmaster's Burial," and that sincere (but therefore unpromoted) clergyman of "Whispered at the Church-opening." In short, although one generalization which can be made about Hardy's writings is that many involve the limitations of Christian clergy as well as the personal and social harm done by organized Christianity, the ways Hardy handled those themes could scarcely be more diverse.

On the other hand, Hardy from time to time portrayed Christianity as a transient and ineffectual creed based on dubious legends no longer believed. As early as *Far from the Madding Crowd* he had his narrator remark on the durable usefulness of the great shearing-barn as compared to the worn-out purposes of church and castle (*FMC*, xxii, p. 150); similarly, in *Tess* he contrasted the endurance of an ancient abbey mill to the abbey itself which "had perished, creeds being transient" (*T*, xxxv, p. 230). And in *The Dynasts* the Spirit of the Years refers to Christianity as "a local cult" scarcely recognized because it had changed so much (Part First, I, vi, lines 1–12; *CPW*, IV, pp. 53–54). In some poems – e.g., "A Christmas Ghost-Story," "A Drizzling Easter Morning," and "Christmas: 1924" – Hardy rings emotional changes on the theme of Christianity's ineffectualness; in others he fancifully images god as variously flawed – forgetful in "God Forgotten," absent-minded in "By the Earth's Corpse," and error-prone in "I Met a Man." In still others, like "Panthera," he provides secular accounts of biblical stories in the manner of those higher critics who persuaded the speaker of "The Respectable Burgher on 'The Higher Criticism'" to abandon scripture and turn, instead, to "that moderate man Voltaire" (*CPW*, I, pp. 198–99).

There were, however, aspects of Christianity and the Church Hardy treated more positively. Given the testimony in his autobiography of the sincerity he admired in the Baptist minister Frederick Perkins, it is not surprising that some of his more sincere fictional clergymen – Raunham in *Desperate Remedies*, Thirdly in *Far from the Madding Crowd*, Woodwell in *A Laodicean*, Torkingham in *Two on a Tower*, and even old Mr. Clare in *Tess* – are portrayed with greater sympathy. Furthermore, particularly in his earlier fiction, Hardy frequently exploited references to Christian values as a means of influencing reader attitudes toward both character and moral situation. *Far from the Madding Crowd* provides a variety of examples. There Hardy used the revelation that Troy's claim of regular church attendance was false to impugn his character (*FMC*, xxix, p. 204), and he had Bathsheba, in her agitated suspicion of the possibility of Troy's infidelity, see Oak humbly at his evening prayers and be chastened by his calm piety (xliii, p. 306). Near the conclusion of the novel, he used quotations from Newman's "Lead Kindly Light" to underscore Bathsheba's sense of her waywardness (lvi, pp. 402–03) and defined the strength of Oak's and Bathsheba's love by an allusion to the Song of Solomon (lvi, p. 409). Then, too, there are poems like "Afternoon Service at Mellstock," "The Impercipient," "The Darkling Thrush," and "The Oxen" which in their very different ways all convey some sense of regret for a faith now no longer possible. Even in his most anti-Christian novel, *Jude*, Hardy had both Sue and Jude agree with *Corinthians* that "Charity seeketh not her own" (*J*, VI, iv, p. 382), and the speaker of his poem "Surview" also affirms St. Paul's teaching on Charity (*CPW*, II, p. 485).

As late as 1922, Hardy asserted the need for "an alliance between religion, which must be retained unless the world is to perish, and complete rationality, which must come" (*CPW*, II, p. 325). But when he occasionally voiced some dream of a reformed Church, he spoke of it only as dedicated to "the promotion of that virtuous living on which all honest men are agreed" and "reverence & love for the ethical ideal" (*Letters* 1, p. 136 and 3, p. 5 [the latter a quotation from Thomas Huxley]). Not surprisingly, then, in his literary works Hardy did not advance any substitute for the religious faith he had lost. He comically deflated Paula Power's determination at the end of *A Laodicean* to live according to Matthew Arnold's vague formula of "imaginative reason," and, in a far more serious novel, *Tess*, the ultimate norms he invoked involve diverse and conflicting ethical perspectives which at best suggest that human moral worth cannot be reduced to some formula.[5] As David J. DeLaura has persuasively argued in analyses of *The Return of the Native*, *Tess*, and *Jude*, Hardy tended to undercut contemporary optimistic views of achieving some "modern" blend of pagan Hellenic and neo-Christian religion: his treatments of such characters as Clym, Angel, and Sue dramatize in various ways their failures to live by such ideals – and suggest that neither Christianity nor any substitute creed ultimately avails human beings trapped in a blind and morally indifferent universe.[6]

Science

Certainly Hardy's readings in the scientific thought of his day strengthened his sense that the supernaturalism of theological doctrines was an outdated relic hindering development of more rational views of the world. In a letter to Edward Clodd of 17 January 1897, for example, he bitterly complained of "the arrest of light & reason by theology" (*Letters* 2, p. 143). Nevertheless, on the whole, the "light and reason" of science tended not to brighten but to darken Hardy's view of the human condition.

Astronomy and physics

In his poem "Afterwards," Hardy described himself as having an eye for the "mysteries" of the "full-starred heavens" (*CPW*, II, p. 308); yet his was for the most part an eye keen for artistic effects rather than for science, and often Hardy's references to astronomical phenomena are of a distinctly romantic kind. In "The Comet at Yell'ham," for example, the comet serves primarily as a device for making the poetic point that by the time it returns, "its strange swift shine / Will fall on Yell'ham; but not then / On face of mine or thine" (*CPW*, I, p. 189).

Two on a Tower, however, was, at least in intention, different, for Hardy described it as having been undertaken specifically "to make science, not the mere padding of a romance, but the actual vehicle of romance" (*Letters* 1, p. 110). Although he owned a copy of Richard A. Proctor's *Essays in Astronomy*, and a few notes in his *Literary Notebooks* show that he also read other of Proctor's popular expositions of astronomy, it is clear that in preparing to write *Two on a Tower* he took pains to more thoroughly familiarize himself not only with practical details – his research included a visit to Greenwich Observatory – but with the larger implications of current ideas in astronomy and physics. As a consequence, whatever artistic deficiencies that novel may be judged to have – including often clumsy uses of astronomical imagery – it is strikingly indicative of what impact the astronomy of Hardy's day had upon his vision of the human predicament. Among the scientific developments that lie behind *Two on a Tower* are Sir William Herschel's discovery that nebulae are clusters of stars at unimaginably immense distances from the earth and his conclusion that those stars, including the sun, must in time burn themselves out – a conclusion later compellingly confirmed by the research of Lord Kelvin, who in 1851 formulated the second law of thermodynamics. It is a vision of the ultimate consequence of Kelvin's theory of entropy in the universe that Hardy evoked in the words of his "votary of science," Swithin St. Cleeve:

"And to add a new weirdness to what the sky possesses in its size and formlessness, there is involved the quality of decay. For all the wonder of these everlasting stars, eternal spheres, and what not, they are not everlasting, they are not eternal; they burn out like candles ... The senses may become terrified by plunging among them ... Imagine them all extinguished, and your mind feeling its way through a heaven of total darkness, occasionally striking against the black invisible cinders of those stars."   (*TT*, iv, pp. 34–35)

Thereafter, Hardy would occasionally return to such grim prophecies of the future. Some time after 1900 he pasted a cutting in his "Literary Notebooks" of a review which dwelled on Ernst Haeckel's description of the unimportance of man on an unimportant planet doomed to grow cold and lifeless (*LN* 2, pp. 98–101). Hardy incorporated that troubling image in some of his poems: "In Vision I Roamed," for example, dramatizes a wandering by "footless traverse through ghast heights of sky" in a universe "trackless, distant, drear" (*CPW*, I, pp. 10–11), while in "Genitrix Laesa" Hardy's speaker sees no point in curing Nature's ills when "all is sinking / To dissolubility" (*CPW*, III, p. 89).

But the ideas of Herschel, Kelvin, and Haeckel were rooted in eighteenth-century Newtonian physics, and one sign of Hardy's wide-ranging curiosity is that, having lived on into the twentieth century and encountered a radically new physics, he began to ponder its non-Newtonian implications: that time and space are relative to the speed of the motion of an observer, and that time itself is a "fourth dimension." He took notes on popular expositions of Einstein's theories (*LN* 2, pp. 228–29), bought an edition of *Relativity: The Special and the General Theory: A Popular Exposition*, and, in a letter to J. Ellis McTaggart, 31 December 1919, observed that, after Einstein, "the universe seems to be getting too comic for words" (*Letters* 5, p. 353). Predictably, Hardy's readings influenced his poetry. In "A Dream Question" of 1909, for example, Hardy had one of his many imagined gods remark that "A fourth dimension, say the guides, / To matter is conceivable" (*CPW*, I, p. 317). But by the time he published *Human Shows* in 1925, he had absorbed enough of popular expositions of Einstein's theories to subordinate them more fully to his poetic purposes: thus, in "The Absolute Explains" he imaginatively transformed Einstein's "Fourth Dimension" from a concept in physics to a place where, comfortingly, love, song, and glad experience are all "unhurt by age" (*CPW*, III, p. 70, line 45), while the speaker of a companion poem, "So, Time," is consoled by the idea that time is "nought / But a thought / Without reality" (*CPW*, III, p. 72). There is, however, less consolation in *Winter Words*, where, in a drinking song, Hardy had his speaker resignedly toast the way man's apparent importance in the universe had diminished from Thales to Einstein (*CPW*, III, pp. 247–50).

Archaeology

In an "interview" on Stonehenge Hardy wrote for the *Daily Chronicle*, he had thoughtful suggestions for abating its erosion (*PW*, pp. 196–200), and his account of a dig at Maumbury Ring combines evocations of the excitement of its finds with carefully precise details about the excavated site (*PW*, pp. 225–31). It was no doubt partly that interest in archaeology which led him in 1881 to become a member of the Dorset Natural History and Antiquarian Field Club – an organization he imaginatively transformed into the "Wessex Field and Antiquarian Club" whose members narrate the stories of *A Group of Noble Dames*. In 1884, in the course of reading a paper for the Club on "Some Romano-British Relics Found at Max Gate, Dorchester" (*PW*, pp. 191–95), Hardy made a disparaging allusion to a Dorset antiquary, Edward Cunnington, whom he ironically dubbed a "local Schliemann." It is almost certainly his awareness of Cunnington's combination of archaeological incompetence and lack of integrity that lies behind Hardy's short story "A Tryst at an Ancient Earthwork," in which an unscrupulous local antiquary illegally digs at an archaeological site and steals a gold statuette of Mercury.

But it was above all Hardy's imaginative setting of the hopes and fears of the living against archaeological records of the indifferent passage of time that is the most moving consequence of his interest in archaeology. Tess's capture at Stonehenge is certainly his most poignantly effective use of that kind of setting, but only one of many such. Hardy's Wessex landscapes are studded with prehistoric burial cairns: most memorably the "Rainbarrow" of *The Return of the Native*, but also the barrows he compared to the many-breasted Diana of Ephesus that appear in *The Mayor of Casterbridge* (*MC*, xlv, p. 330), in *Tess* (*T*, xlii, p. 273), and, again, in his poem "By the Barrows" (*CPW*, I, p. 317). The inhabitants of Hardy's Casterbridge live against a backdrop of skeletal reminders that ancient Romans before them also once "loved, laughed, and fought, hailed their friends, drank their toasts / At their meeting-times here"("After the Fair"; *CPW*, I, p. 295), and the even more ancient prehistoric originators of Maumbury Ring "mock the chime / Of … Christian time / From its hollows of chalk and loam"("Her Death and After"; *CPW*, I, p. 54, lines 78–80).

In short, just as contemporary astronomy and physics influenced Hardy's imaginative perception of man's trivial physical position in the stellar universe, so his writings reveal a similar preoccupation with the way human aspirations are dwarfed in the vast dimensions of archaeological time. It is worth remembering, then – given the optimistic tone of Darwin's conclusion to *The Origin of Species* and Huxley's visions of prospects for the possibility of human progress – that the sometimes grimmer image of the human condition notable in Hardy's writing was at least in part rooted in discoveries so compelling as the inexorable implications of the second law of thermodynamics and so poignant as those manifold reminders in his Wessex landscape of how fleeting human hopes and desires appear in the long passage of mankind's time on earth.

Biological evolution

Nevertheless, Hardy's letters and notebooks make clear that he had the deepest respect for Darwin and Huxley as representatives of the best scientific thought of his day. It is possible that Darwin's views on heredity (along with those of August Weismann, Herbert Spencer, and William Galton) may have influenced Hardy's treatment of heredity in *The Well-Beloved*,[7] but the chief impact of evolutionary theory on Hardy's writing is notable in two other ways. First, it prompted him to set images of human life against the backdrop of geologic and evolutionary time – a time he would emphasize was incomparably longer than man's archaeological traces. In *The Return of the Native*, for example, his memorable evocation of the timelessness of Egdon Heath ends with a comment on how even its slight irregularities "remained as the very finger-touches of the last geological change" (*RN*, I, i, p. 6), and in *A Pair of Blue Eyes*, when Knight is suspended on the face of a cliff and staring into the eyes of a fossilized Trilobite, Hardy conveyed the immense lapse of evolutionary time that "closed up like a fan" before his eyes by providing a retrospective account, replete with technical terminology, of evolution from man back to that fossil (*PBE*, xxii, pp. 209–10). In his poetry, too, he exploited geology for similar purposes: in "The Clasped Skeletons," for example, an imaginative meditation on the long dead lovers found in a barrow dated about 1800 BC turns on the idea that, in the vast scale of geologic time, they might have been buried only yesterday (*CPW*, III, pp. 209–11).

But Hardy's insights into the implications of evolutionary theory also influenced some attitudes toward human moral responsibility that emerged in his later writings. As Hardy saw it, "The discovery of the law of evolution ... shifted the centre of altruism from humanity to the whole conscious world collectively" (*LW*, p. 373) – a view relatable to those powerful scenes in which Tess mercifully kills wounded game birds (*T*, xli, p. 271) and Jude does the same for a suffering pig (*J*, I, x, p. 64). Similar attitudes underlie such poems as "The Puzzled Game Birds" and "Compassion: An Ode." But Hardy's sense of mankind's new responsibility toward animals also troubled him: in a letter to Frederic Harrison he expressed doubt that humans would accept the new moral duty thrust upon them (*Letters* 3, pp. 230–31), and in "Afterwards" he characterized himself as one who "strove that ... innocent creatures should come to no harm," but did so in vain (*CPW*, II, p. 308).

However, it was the plight of mankind trapped in a universe oblivious to human feelings and ethical aspirations that not only most powerfully moved Hardy but also set him apart from many of his contemporaries who saw some "grandeur" or "progress" in evolutionary change. To one such optimist, he pointedly stressed that "nature is *un*moral" (*Letters* 3, p. 231), and in his autobiography recorded a note to the effect that "emotions have no place in a world of defect, and it is a cruel injustice that they should have developed in it" (*LW*, p. 153). Hardy took up related themes in his poetry: his "Before Life and After," for example, includes the affirmation that before the evolution of consciousness "all went well" (*CPW*, I, p. 333). But it was in his novels that he most plangently rendered the condition of those who futilely aspire to happiness, or fruitlessly strive to achieve ethical ideals, or struggle with painful feelings of moral obligation in a universe otherwise indifferent to such aspirations and feelings. Of his earlier fiction, *The Return of the Native* most distinctly embodies those concerns. Hardy's characterization of Clym Yeobright as bearing evidence "that ideal physical beauty is incompatible with growth of fellow-feeling and a full sense of the coil of things" (*RN*, II, vi, p. 138); his dramatization of Eustacia Vye's frustrated longings for hopeless ideals; his authorial observations on how that "old-fashioned revelling in the general situation grows less and less possible as we uncover the defects of natural laws, and see the quandary that man is in by their operation" (*RN*, III, i, p. 169) – all convey the alienation of thinking and feeling humans in a universe indifferent to human ideals and sensitivities.

In a notebook entry of 1876, Hardy copied the following from an article by Theodore Watts: "Science tells us that, in the struggle for life, the surviving organism is not necessarily that which is absolutely the best in an ideal sense, though it must be that which is most in harmony with surrounding conditions" (*LN*, I, p. 40). The human predicament in those "surrotions" is no more profoundly explored than in *The Woodlanders*, Hardy's most Darwinian novel in the emphasis he placed on the bleak struggle for survival in a woodland setting where "the lichen ate the vigour of the stalk, and the ivy slowly strangled to death the promising sapling" (vii, p. 53). In this context, Hardy's Grace Melbury, Giles Winterborne, Mr. Melbury, and Mrs. Charmond are out of harmony with their surroundings: all rack themselves with futile questions of conscience that, in the end, yield no satisfactory results, while the two characters who do manage to find some "harmony" with an environment indifferent to human moral concerns do so at terrible cost – either by renouncing common human desire, as does Marty South, or by selfishly satisfying desire with no regard for others, as does Edred Fitzpiers. In Hardy's vision of the universe of *The Woodlanders*, there appear to be no acceptable moral choices. *Tess* and *Jude* provide similarly bleak views of the human predicament. In *Jude*, for example, the sensitive and aspiring Jude and Sue are ultimately crushed, while the coarse Arabella and unscrupulous Vilbert are well enough adapted to succeed in satisfying their lower aims.

It was, then, of the consequences of human evolution that Hardy was often particularly pessimistic; in his autobiography, for example, he recorded a note of April, 1889: "A woeful fact – that the human race is too extremely developed for its corporeal conditions, the nerves being evolved to an activity abnormal in such an environment ... This planet does not supply the materials for happiness to higher existences" (*LW*, p. 227). That view Hardy gave most explicit expression to in *Jude*, where he echoed his own ideas in Sue's distraught imagining that "at the framing of the terrestrial conditions there seemed never to have been contemplated such a development of emotional perceptiveness among the creatures subject to those conditions as that reached by thinking and educated humanity" (*J*, VI, iii, p. 361).

Philosophy

While pondering a world which contemporary science increasingly revealed to be indifferent to human feelings and values, Hardy was also reading widely in and about the works of contemporary philosophers, many of whom were responding to that same world view. To the ideas of some – such as Nietzsche and Bergson – he was so hostile (see *Letters* 5, pp. 50–51, 78–79, and 6, p. 259) that any influence they may have had on his writings could only be negative. But in others Hardy found support for his agnosticism, possible alternatives to the supernaturalism of Christian ethics, and various theories of what forces in an uncaring universe might account for the human predicament and conceivably effect its amelioration. Of those writers who most notably influenced Hardy, the chief were Leslie Stephen, François Fourier, Herbert Spencer, John Stuart Mill, Ludwig Feuerbach, Auguste Comte, Arthur Schopenhauer, and Eduard von Hartmann.

Four general influences: Stephen, Fourier, Spencer, and Mill
Hardy stated that the editor and philosopher Leslie Stephen had a stronger influence on him than that of any other of his contemporaries, and "The Schreckhorn," a sonnet celebrating Stephen's personal qualities, testifies to Hardy's respect for him. That they could share a wide-ranging curiosity about philosophical questions is suggested from Hardy's account of how Stephen called upon him to witness his signature on a renunciation of holy orders – after which they talked of "theologies decayed and defunct, the origin of things, the constitution of matter, the unreality of time, and kindred subjects" (*LW*, pp. 108–09). Throughout the rest of his life Hardy cherished the agnostic Stephen's friendship (*LW*, pp. 188), and no doubt his fiction and poetry owe much to the intellectual support Hardy found in such an impressive father-figure.

What influences François Fourier's ideas may have had on Hardy's writings were also of an indefinite kind. In 1863 Hardy was enough impressed to sketch – and thereafter preserve – an elaborate diagram of ideas in Fourier's *The Passions of the Human Soul*, a work he had obviously studied carefully.[8] It is possible that Fourier's view that much of human suffering stemmed from conflicts between intellect and passion, resulting often from Christianity's teachings about marriage, may have influenced some major themes that appear in Hardy's fiction – particularly his hostile portrayal of Christian views on marriage in *The Woodlanders*, *Tess*, and, especially, *Jude*, which Hardy described as dramatizing the "deadly war waged between flesh and spirit" (*J*, Preface, p. xxxv).

Contemporary scientific evidences that man was infinitesimal in the vastness of the universe no doubt made Hardy more receptive to philosophical views that challenged conventional perception of space and time. It is not surprising, then, that he declared Herbert Spencer's *First Principles* sometimes acted "as a sort of patent expander when I had been particularly narrowed down by the events of life" (*Letters* 2, pp. 24–25), for one of Spencer's major arguments was that space and time were incomprehensible. In fact, the question, "What are Space and Time?" with which Spencer opened chapter 3 of his *First Principles*[9] is probably one source (Kant, of course, could be another) of the line, "*What are Space and Time? A fancy!*" in *The Dynasts* (Part Third, I, iii, line 84; *CPW*, v, p. 25). It was in Spencer's writings, too, that Hardy came across the suggestion that there might not be any comprehension underlying the universe (*Letters* 3, p. 244) – an idea that may have influenced his conception of an unconscious Will in *The Dynasts*.

A similar kind of influence is notable in Hardy's response to J. S. Mill.

Hardy claimed that in the 1860s he knew Mill's *On Liberty* "almost by heart" (*LW*, p. 355), and, in fact, in *Jude* he had Sue Bridehead quote from one of Mill's arguments for liberty of thought (*J*, IV, iii, p. 234). Certainly Mill's confident secular individualism, like Stephen's and Spencer's agnosticism, encouraged Hardy in the independent pursuit of his own world view. Then, too, some of the ideas Mill developed in his "Theism" – e.g., that there is no need to postulate a beginning to matter and force in the universe and that consciousness may arise from unconscious causes – might have influenced Hardy's conception in *The Dynasts* of the Immanent Will becoming conscious – though Hardy claimed the latter idea as his own (*Letters* 3, p. 255).

Feuerbach and Comte

The effects of the thought of both Ludwig Feuerbach and Auguste Comte on Hardy's writings are possible to identify with somewhat greater specificity. Feuerbach's idea that the Christian god is the product of man's need to imagine perfection was twice summarized by Hardy in the phrase, "God is the product of man": once in a notebook (*LN* 2, p. 166) and again in a letter to Edward Clodd (*Letters* 3, p. 244). In *The Return of the Native*, the narrator's comment that humans always make a "generous endeavour to construct a hypothesis that shall not degrade a first cause" (*RN*, VI, i, p. 387) may owe something to Feuerbach's influence, but there are poems in *Satires of Circumstance* which almost certainly do. In "A Plaint to Man," for example, one of Hardy's imagined gods asks, "Wherefore, O Man, did there come to you / The unhappy need of creating me[?]" (*CPW*, II, p. 33); in "God's Funeral," the speaker inquires, "Whence came it we were tempted to create / One whom we can no longer keep alive?" (*CPW*, II, p. 35, lines 23–24); and in "Aquae Sulis" the Christian god chides the British goddess of the waters of Bath with the words, "You know not by what frail thread we equally hang; / It is said we are images both – twitched by people's desires" (*CPW*, II, p. 91).

Far more complex influences on Hardy's thought may be traced to the writings of August Comte and his Positivist followers. Hardy marked some passages in the 1865 translation of Comte's *A General View of Positivism* given to him by Horace Moule, and his autobiography includes references to his reading Comte in 1870 and again in 1873 (*LW*, pp. 79, 100); furthermore, his notebooks and letters from 1876 onward show that he read in a *System of Positive Polity* as well as in works by such Positivists as Edward Spencer Beesley, John Morley, Cotter Morrison, and Frederic Harrison. He certainly agreed with Comte's aim to promote human altruism – which he saw as equatable with the Christian "Love your

Neighbour as Yourself" (*LW*, p. 235) – and he acknowledged that "no person of serious thought in these times could be said to stand aloof from Positivist teaching & ideals" (*Letters* 3, p. 53). In his autobiography, he added that if Comte had included Christ in his calendar, it would have made Positivism palatable to people who know it "to contain the germs of a true system" (*LW*, pp. 150–51).

Yet, for all that, Hardy's word *germs* is indicative of the qualified response he took to Comte. For example, in his *Social Dynamics*, Comte described human progress as a "looped orbit," sometimes going backward by way of gathering strength to spring forward again. Hardy's imagination was obviously caught by that metaphor: in one of his notebooks he diagramed it (*LN* 1, p. 76); later he incorporated it in his "Candour in English Fiction," and, again, in his "Apology" of 1922 (*PW*, pp. 126–27, 57–58). But, in that same "Apology," he criticized the Positivists' optimistic view of progress (*PW*, p. 53).

Nevertheless, other influences of Positivist thought can be detected both in Hardy's fiction and in his poetry. For example, Clym Yeobright's "relatively advanced" ideas, based on Parisian "ethical systems popular at the time" (*RN*, III, ii, p. 174), prompted one reviewer to see him as "touched with the asceticism of a certain positivistic school."[10] At least one of Hardy's contemporaries also saw Positivism in *Tess*. In fact, in that novel Hardy probably did adapt notes he made of Comte's division of mankind's "theological" stage into "fetishistic," "polytheistic," and "mono-theistic" parts (*LN* 1, pp. 67, 73–74, 77–78): Tess, Hardy's narrator remarks, is afflicted by "fetishistic fear" (*T*, iii, p. 28) and her rhapsody to nature is described as "a Fetichistic [*sic*] utterance in a Monotheistic setting" (xvi, p. 109). Then, too, the book Angel Clare describes as promoting a moral "system of philosophy" (xviii, p. 120), and the "ethical system without any dogma" he accepts (xlvii, p. 319), both call to mind Comte's *System of Positive Polity*. Furthermore, in 1887 Hardy had taken notes from the Positivist Cotter Morrison's *The Service of Man*, including his argument that primitive religions had no connection with morals (*LN* 1, p. 190) – an argument which Tess repeats to Alec when she tries to "tell him that he had mixed ... two matters, theology and morals, which in the primitive days of mankind had been quite distinct" (*T*, xlvii, p. 320).[11] It was probably such particulars, as well as the final change in Clym from moral rigidity to sympathy and love for Tess, that prompted Frederic Harrison's comment to Hardy that *Tess* reads "like a Positivist allegory."[12]

Comte also argued that poets must promote altruism and "adequately portray the new man in his relation to the new God."[13] Some poems of Hardy's appear to have been influenced by that conception. His "A Plaint to Man," for example, with its theme that humanity must depend on its resources alone for the promotion of an altruistic "loving-kindness" (*CPW*, II, p. 34) sounds very Positivist, as do poems like "The Graveyard of Dead Creeds," "God's Funeral," and "The Sick Battle-God," all of which express some hope for the emergence of altruism in humanity.

Schopenhauer and von Hartmann

What is striking about the impact on Hardy of Stephen, Fourier, Spencer, Mill, Feuerbach, and Comte is that, for the most part, they influenced him by the ways they served as role-models for his repudiation of religious belief, or offered some explanation of Christianity's attraction, or provided an alternative to Christian ethics and values. But, as notes he took on various philosophers ranging in time from Baruch Spinoza to William Clifford reveal, Hardy was also interested in more abstract questions about the nature of what fundamental force or forces might underlie the universe. Of these, his writings were most notably influenced by the central ideas of Arthur Schopenhauer and Eduard von Hartmann, in addition to such concepts as Herbert Spencer's suggestion that there may be no ultimate comprehension in the universe and John Stuart Mill's observation that consciousness may arise from unconscious causes.

In 1907 Hardy undertook to explain to a correspondent that the "philosophy of life" he utilized in *The Dynasts* was a "generalized form of what the thinking world had gradually come to adopt." According to Hardy, its chief features were three: (1) that there is an unconscious and impersonal "urging force" that is immanent in the universe; (2) that man's individual will is subservient to that Immanent Will, but "whenever it happens that all the rest of the Great Will is in equilibrium the minute portion called one person's will is free"; and (3) that the Unconscious Will is "growing aware of Itself ... & ultimately, it is to be hoped, sympathetic" (*Letters* 3, p. 255). Variations on such unsystematic and generalized "impressions" dramatized by Hardy in *The Dynasts* and elsewhere were no doubt in part influenced by the writings of Schopenhauer and von Hartmann.

Hardy's reported comments on Schopenhauer's influence are contradictory: by one account, he denied being influenced at all (Millgate, *Biography*, p. 199); by another, he asserted that his "philosophy" was "a development from Schopenhauer through later philosophers."[14] The latter is more likely. Hardy owned translations of *The World as Will and Idea* (1896) and *On the Four-fold Root of the Principle of Sufficient Reason* (1889) – in which (among others) he marked a passage asserting that "a *will* must be attributed to all that is lifeless."[15] In 1891 he made extensive notebook entries from Schopenhauer's *Studies in Pessimism*, including one emphasizing that "unless <u>suffering</u> is the direct & immediate object of life, our existence must entirely fail of its aim" (*LN* 2, p. 28). Furthermore, some time before 1888 Hardy consulted the *Encyclopaedia Britannica* to take a note on Schopenhauer's pessimistic view of the will to live (*LN* 1, p. 203), and later, no doubt to help clarify Schopenhauer's confusing prose, he turned to *Chambers's Encyclopaedia*, from which he took a note on Schopenhauer's idea of "the unconscious, automatic, or reasonless Will" (*LN* 2, p. 107).

Nevertheless, Schopenhauer's influence on Hardy's writings appears to be limited. His reference in *Tess* to the extremeness of Mr. Clare's "renunciative philosophy which had cousinship with that of Schopenhauer and Leopardi" (*T*, xxv, p. 161), for example, expresses no more than the popular image of Schopenhauer's pessimistic advocacy of renunciation of life – a view which may also have influenced a passage in *Jude* about "the coming universal wish not to live" (*J*, vi, ii, p. 355). Similarly, the concept of an unknowing immanent "Will" in the universe that figures in "He Wonders About Himself," in the "Fore Scene" of *The Dynasts*, and in later spirit choruses, may reflect Hardy's note-taking from *On the Four-fold Root of the Principle of Sufficient Reason*, or from *Chambers's Encyclopaedia*, or from other expositions of Schopenhauer's thought. But, in fact, little Hardy wrote compels attribution to Schopenhauer of influence beyond the level of generality characteristic of popular summaries of his pessimism and of his concept of "Will" as a force underlying the phenomena of the universe.

Specific instances of the influence of Eduard von Hartmann's ideas on Hardy reveal how radically he would modify them. For example, in the late 1890s Hardy took a note on Hartmann's view of the "infallible purposive . . . activity" of an "unconscious clairvoyant" intelligence; he headed that note, "<u>God as super-conscious</u>," and followed it with an excerpted quotation from Hartmann: "We shall ... designate this intell[i]g[ence], superior to all consc[iousness], at once unconsc[ious] & <u>super</u>-conscious" (*LN* 2, p. 111). To this Hardy added "? processive" above von Hartmann's "purposive," and then jotted his observation, "very obscure." Later, Hardy imported a version of that "very obscure" passage into the mouth of the Spirit of the Years in *The Dynasts*, but again changed the word *purposive* to *processive* – a term which conveys a concept markedly different from von Hartmann's:

> In that immense unweeting Mind is shown
> One far above forethinking; prócessive,
> Rapt, superconscious; a Clairvoyancy
> That knows not what It knows . . .
> (Part First, v, iv; lines 184–87; *CPW*, iv, p. 137)

Hence, although Hardy no doubt partly agreed with von Hartmann's concept of the Will as Unconscious, even when almost quoting him he freely made changes that radically altered von Hartmann's views.[16]

What can be said with greatest certainty is that Hardy's readings of and about Schopenhauer and von Hartmann confirmed some ideas he had arrived at independently or that he might earlier have derived from Mill, Spencer, Huxley, and others. Schopenhauer did probably suggest to Hardy the name *Will* for that underlying force in the universe about which he had long ruminated (though Hardy freely used many other names as well), and, by his theory of the "Unconscious," von Hartmann no doubt reinforced what Hardy himself had already conceived – that such a force could be as uncomprehending as those "purblind Doomsters" in his "Hap" (*CPW*, I, p. 10). It is likely, too, that Hardy took from von Hartmann the word *immanent* for his "Immanent Will"; at least the translator of the edition Hardy used more than once speaks of the Will as an "immanent cause."[17] Beyond that, even the most careful efforts to make point-for-point comparisons of what Hardy wrote with Schopenhauer's and von Hartmann's thought are bound to be highly speculative.[18]

But, finally, it is important to note that, as Hardy judged them, Schopenhauer and von Hartmann took a supercilious view of the forlorn hope which (with some lapses) he clung to for an amelioration of the human condition (see "Apology," *Late Lyrics and Earlier* [1922]; *CPW*, II, p. 325). Furthermore they differed greatly from Hardy in the attitudes they adopted toward the human condition. Just as Schopenhauer's claim to take a detached view of life was foreign to Hardy's engaged concern for the suffering of humankind and higher animals, so was von Hartmann's celebration of an Unconscious evolving at the expense of untold human pain. In the end, neither they, nor any other intellectual influences, altered Hardy's conviction, conveyed often both in his poetry and his prose, that human aspiration, human feeling, and human hope, however dwarfed in the cosmic scale of things, were nevertheless more important than all the rest.

NOTES

1 For a consideration of such possible influences on *FMC*, see G. Glen Wickens, "Literature and Science: Hardy's Response to Mill, Huxley and Darwin," *Mosaic: A Journal for the Interdisciplinary Study of Literature*, 14/3 (1981), 63–79.

2 See, for example, J. O. Bailey, "Hardy's Mephistophelian Visitants," *PMLA*, 61 (1946), 1146–84; Frank B. Pinion, "Mephistopheles, Satan, and Cigars," *Thomas Hardy: Art and Thought* (Totowa, N.J.: Rowman and Littlefield,

1977), pp. 57–66; Marilyn Stall Fontane, "The Devil in *Tess*," *Thomas Hardy Society Review*, 1 (1982), 250–54; and Timothy Hands, *Thomas Hardy: Distracted Preacher? Hardy's Religious Biography and its Influence on his Novels* (New York: St. Martin's Press, 1989), pp. 59–60 and 120–21.

3 Julian Moynihan, "*The Mayor of Casterbridge* and the Old Testament's First Book of Samuel: A Study of Some Literary Relationships," *PMLA*, 71 (1956), 118–30.

4 Simon Gatrell, *Hardy the Creator: A Textual Biography* (Oxford: Clarendon Press, 1988), pp. 193–98.

5 See Robert Schweik, "Theme, Character, and Perspective in Hardy's *The Return of the Native*," *Philological Quarterly*, 41 (1962), 554–57, and Bernard J. Paris, "'A Confusion of Many Standards': Conflicting Value Systems in *Tess of the d'Urbervilles*," *Nineteenth-Century Fiction*, 24 (1969), 57–79.

6 David J. DeLaura, "'The Ache of Modernism' in Hardy's Later Novels," *ELH*, 34 (1967), 380–99.

7 See J. B. Bullen's "Hardy's *The Well-Beloved*, Sex, and Theories of Germ Plasm," in *A Spacious Vision: Essays on Hardy*, ed. Phillip V. Mallett and Ronald P. Draper (Newmill, Cornwall: Patten Press, 1994), pp. 79–88.

8 For an analysis of Hardy's diagram, see Lennart A. Björk's *Psychological Vision and Social Criticism in the Novels of Thomas Hardy* (Stockholm: Almqvist & Wiksell International, 1987), pp. 38–42.

9 Herbert Spencer, *First Principles* (1862; New York: The DeWitt Revolving Fund, 1958), p. 60.

10 Robert Gittings, *Thomas Hardy's Later Years* (Boston: Little, Brown and Co., 1978), p. 9.

11 Tess's speech may also have been influenced by the ideas of John Aldington Symonds; see Björk, *Psychological Vision*, pp. 131–32.

12 Letter from Frederic Harrison of 19 December 1891, Dorset County Museum.

13 Auguste Comte, *A General View of Positivism*, trans. by J. H. Bridges (1831; London: Trübner, 1865), p. 252.

14 Helen Garwood, *Thomas Hardy: An Illustration of the Philosophy of Schopenhauer* (Philadelphia: John C. Winston Co., 1911), pp. 10–11.

15 Carl Weber, "Hardy's Copy of Schopenhauer," *Colby Library Quarterly*, 4/12 (November, 1957), p. 223.

16 An instance of how freely Hardy would deviate from von Hartmann's ideas is notable in William Archer's "Real Conversations. Conversation I. With Mr. Thomas Hardy," *The Critic*, 38 (April 1901), p. 316.

17 See, for example, Eduard von Hartmann, *The Philosophy of the Unconscious: Speculative Results According to the Inductive Method of Physical Science*, trans. by William Chatterton Coupland, 3 vols. (1869; London: Kegan Paul, Trench, Trübner, 1893), I, p. 69.

18 Examples of such analyses may be found in J. O. Bailey's *Thomas Hardy and the Cosmic Mind: A New Reading of The Dynasts* (Chapel Hill: University of North Carolina Press, 1956), and Walter F. Wright's *The Shaping of "The Dynasts"* (Lincoln: University of Nebraska Press, 1967).

FURTHER READING

Beer, Gillian. *Darwin's Plots: Evolutionary Narrative in Darwin, George Eliot and Nineteenth-Century Fiction*. London: Routledge & Kegan Paul, 1983.

Collins, Deborah L. *Thomas Hardy and His God: A Liturgy of Unbelief*. London and Basingstoke: Macmillan, 1990.

Gilmour, Robin. *The Victorian Period: The Intellectual and Cultural Context of English Literature, 1830–1890*. London: Longman, 1993.

Jedrzejewski, Jan. *Thomas Hardy and the Church*. London and Basingstoke: Macmillan, 1996.

Orel, Harold. *The Unknown Thomas Hardy: Lesser-Known Aspects of Hardy's Life and Career*. Brighton, Sussex: The Harvester Press, 1987.

Paradis, James and Thomas Postlewait, eds. *Victorian Science and Victorian Values: Literary Perspectives*. New York: The New York Academy of Sciences, 1981.

Rutland, William R. *Thomas Hardy: A Study of His Writings and Their Background*. Oxford: Blackwell, 1938.

5

PETER WIDDOWSON

Hardy and critical theory

Essay titles are an attempt to say much in little, at once synoptic shorthand for the work which follows and for the whole area of intellectual enquiry to which it alludes. As such, they are susceptible to ambiguity and imprecision, and the title of the present essay is no exception. What is meant, we might ask, by "Critical Theory," and is it synonymous with that other cognate phrase – "Literary Theory"? While the commonly made slippage between the terms demands urgent attention, it is way beyond the scope of an essay such as this. Let me clear the ground, therefore, by simply stating that I take "Literary Theory" primarily to be concerned with offering theoretical definitions of the nature of literature, and "Critical Theory" to be the articulation of theorized principles on which critical approaches to the analysis of literature are premised. The latter, at least, will be the working definition deployed in this essay. But even so, in its present formulation, the title remains ambiguous. Are we to be concerned here with Hardy's *own* critical and theoretical writings and *their* relationship to critical theory in general; or is it, rather, the relationship between Hardy's literary *oeuvre* and modern critical theory which is the essay's principal focus? It would be perverse to pretend that it is anything other than the latter; but just for a moment it is worth considering what that former sense might summon up – if for no other reason than to see whether it may have any bearing on the undeniable attraction Hardy's work has had for later critics and theorists of literature.

Hardy was no Henry James in regard to the sustained production of a body of theory about fiction (or, indeed, about poetry). All we have as a self-authenticated theoretical key to Hardy's practice are the short prefaces he wrote for the novels and volumes of poems, themselves so clenched with irony as to be thoroughly diversionary; scattered reflections throughout his notebooks and letters; and "Florence Emily Hardy's" *The Life and Work of Thomas Hardy by Thomas Hardy* (*LW*) – which we know to be Hardy's own attempt to write his "life" as he wanted it to be read. In addition, there are the three essays on fiction he produced, uniquely, between 1888 and 1891,[1] but even these are "occasional" pieces which resolutely refuse to articulate a coherent or systematic theory of fiction. Nevertheless, Hardy was no untutored natural genius, but rather a widely read intellectual closely familiar with the literary debates of the second half of the nineteenth century. For the purposes of the present essay, we may deduce one – albeit crucial – feature of Hardy's involvement in these: one which casts him as ineluctably "transitional" between "Victorian" and "Modern" and which suggests the affinity between his work and late-twentieth-century critical approaches. If we read between the lines of the three fiction essays – verified by jottings in his notebooks and by memoranda quoted in *The Life and Work of Thomas Hardy* – it is apparent that Hardy is actually participating in the pan-European debate about Realism, and that he was opposed to a "photographic" naturalism, favoring instead a kind of "analytic" writing which "makes strange" common-sense reality and brings into view other realities obscured precisely by the naturalized version. Famously, Hardy comments – and we may note here the consonance of his notion of "disproportioning" with the later widely influential Formalist concepts of "defamiliarization" and "denaturalization":

> "Art is a disproportioning – (*i.e.*, distorting, throwing out of proportion) – of realities, to show more clearly the features that matter in those realities, which, if merely copied or reported inventorially, might possibly be observed, but would more probably be overlooked. Hence 'realism' is not Art."
>
> (*LW*, p. 239)

At the same time, however, he can acknowledge Defoe as a mentor, but only perhaps for the latter's ability to "fake" the truth (*LW*, pp. 424–25; see also *The Hand of Ethelberta*, chapters 13 and 16); can himself elevate his Wessex "Novels of Character and Environment" above his "Romances," "Fantasies," "Novels of Ingenuity," and "Experiments";[2] but still close his novel-writing career with *The Well-Beloved*. And he can give up writing fiction at the height of his powers in order to produce the huge "unstage-able" epic verse-drama, *The Dynasts*, and over 950 individual poems – thereafter claiming that poetry was his true art and novel-writing merely a money-making trade. Theorist or not, Hardy surely had a consciously contradictory relationship with Realism – the force of which we shall have cause to return to in surveying the ways in which recent criticism recasts his work.

Just as Hardy himself was not a formulator of literary theory, so his work is not a site on which new critical theory has been formulated in any primary sense. Unlike that of Balzac, say, or Dostoevsky, Wordsworth, Shakespeare, or Joyce, Hardy's work always seems to have a slightly later application as a testing-ground for already defined new theories. Leavis, for example, chose not to deal *in extenso* with Hardy's work; the early New Critics did not cut their teeth on it either, although later related formalistic (including Leavisite) critics did; Marxist and other cultural-materialist (but not yet "new historicist"[3]) criticism took it up quite late; poststructuralist and deconstructive readings only begin to appear in the mid-to-late 1980s; feminist criticism alone takes on Hardy quite early in its post-1960s phase, but even here feminist critical *theory* was not formulated by way of his writings. In this respect again, then, the present essay's title is imprecise, inasmuch as it is not "critical theory" which Hardy promotes, but "theorized criticism": theoretical models applied to his work at once to test their applicability and to see what happens to Hardy read in these new ways. His always protean *oeuvre* seems particularly well suited to being refashioned in the image of the critical approach taken to it.

Two further preliminary equivocations. First, my sketch below of Hardy criticism prior to the late 1960s – when theory took on a highly visible presence within literary studies – must, *de facto*, give an account of *literary criticism* rather than of *critical theory*, simply because the former remained a practice largely unaware that it was based on (subliminally active) theoretical positions. Secondly, a somewhat unbalanced account of "Hardy and Critical Theory" follows, since Hardy's poetry, even now, has not received anything like the same quantity or quality of theoretically engaged critical attention that his fiction has: with a few honorable exceptions, Hardy the Poet awaits his theoretical critics.

Whatever the furor surrounding the publication of *Tess of the d'Urbervilles* and *Jude the Obscure* – after which Hardy effectively gave up writing fiction – the "Wessex Novels" by 1896 represented Hardy's acknowledged achievement in fiction; even more so by 1912, when he himself seems to confirm their status as his "Novels of Character and Environment" (see note 2); and also for most of the twentieth century – including the filmic 1990s. Implicit in this, however, is the exclusion from the received canon of almost half of Hardy's total fictional production: the so-called "minor novels" which abjure his "true" or "characteristic" Wessex mode and exemplify his "faults" as a novelist writ large, and of which *The Hand of Ethelberta* and *A Laodicean* are the most execrated. Taken together with the "flaws" critics have conventionally descried scattered throughout his fiction – "improbable" use of chance and coincidence, "flat" and "stagey" characterization, melodrama, and an obtrusively over-elaborate style – this critical fashioning[4] of the "true" Hardy implies several tacit "theoretical" premises about his work. It tends to see him as *really* a practitioner of humanist realism (the essential mode of the genre as a whole in its finest incarnation) whose work is marred on occasion by a perverse deviation from the characteristic features of such a mode: high moral seriousness, the centrality of human character, verisimilitude. Nevertheless, despite their "faults," the Wessex Novels exemplify these features and justify Hardy's presence in the wider canon of "Great Literature," while the maverick "minor novels" need to be excised in order to sustain this naturalized orthodoxy.

However, it is F. R. Leavis's dismissal of Hardy in *The Great Tradition* (1948) – "by the side of George Eliot – and the comparison shouldn't be necessary" – as no more than "a provincial manufacturer of gauche and heavy fictions"[5] that is the most telling critical intervention in the debate about Hardy's claim to canonic status as tragic realist. It suggests that, in order to promote Eliot as the novelist whose pre-eminent representation of the organic interconnectedness of the "web" of human society places her at the heart of "the great tradition," Leavis surely sensed that he *had to* reject Hardy's fiction because it could so easily be construed as strategically subverting Eliot's humanist-realist project. It is pointedly ironic, then, that the title of Ian Gregor's later, equally formative, contribution to the construction of Hardy as himself a great humanist-realist novelist should be *The Great Web: The Form of Hardy's Major Fiction* (1974).[6]

But two other words besides "web" in Gregor's title indicate a further development in Hardy's critical history. A new interest in the "form" of the "major" novels begins to emerge in the post-Leavisite, post-New-Critical, formalism of the 1950s, 1960s, and 1970s. As their titles suggest, works which offer newly illuminating close textual analysis of the formal proper-ties of Hardy's fiction – language, imagery, symbolism, structure – include Jean Brooks's *Thomas Hardy: The Poetic Structure* (1971), Dale Kramer's *Thomas Hardy: The Forms of Tragedy* (1975), and Peter Casagrande's *Unity in Hardy's Novels: "Repetitive Symmetries"* (1982).[7] What is also apparent, however, is that the theoretical principle driving them is to establish the *unity* and *coherence* of Hardy's vision and practice; that this formal achievement is still premised on the presupposition of a tragic humanist working within an (expanded) notion of realism; and that, *therefore*, the focus must be exclusively on the "major" novels. The informing ideology of the literary criticism, in other words, remains largely unchanged; neither, of course, is it perceived to be an ideology, nor explicitly articulated or questioned. Later, I will suggest how the advent of recent critical theory challenges these positions and opens up Hardy's fiction to analyses which destabilize both that ideology and the fictional texts themselves.

Although early reviewers of Hardy's poetry, shocked by what seemed his treacherous desertion of fiction for another genre in which he had no expertise, commented negatively on his poems,[8] Hardy quite rapidly became accepted and admired as a poetic voice – albeit of a distinctly "characteristic" kind. Certainly, with the volumes *Satires of Circumstance* (1914) and *Moments of Vision* (1917), he was regarded by people of diverse literary persuasions (from Edmund Gosse to Ezra Pound) as a major modern poet; and by his death in 1928, with over 950 individual poems to his credit, his popular, if not his critical, stature was assured. But Hardy's career as poet coincided with the onset of Modernism, and despite Pound's admiration, therefore, by the 1920s Hardy's work was more often aligned with the now enfeebled "Georgian Poetry" movement rather than with the dynamic innovations of the Modernists. Indeed, it was his more "Georgian" characteristics which represented his general appeal – then and, arguably, even now. His celebration of the rural scene, his melancholy love poems, his reinvocation of the lost past, his witty obsession with time, aging, death, and the dead, his downbeat poetic language, and his controlled, rhythmically ever-inventive prosody – all became conventionally associated with the "true" Hardy as Poet. In other words, a frame of recognition was fashioned for his most familiar virtues – what Samuel Hynes was later to christen "Hardy's unique poetic voice" which produced "characteristically Hardyesque" poems.[9]

Harold Orel has divided the history of Hardy poetry criticism this century into three phases.[10] The first is the period up to Hardy's death glanced at above, and continuing till 1940, in which his stature as a poet remained an issue, together with the related question of whether he was really "Victorian" or "Modern." The second is heralded by the publication of the "Thomas Hardy Centennial Issue" of the *Southern Review* (6/1 [1940]), where the principal focus was on his poetry, and where the contributors included, *inter alia*, W. H. Auden, John Crowe Ransom, R. P. Blackmur, F. R. Leavis, Allen Tate, and Bonamy Dobrée. The general thrust of this collection was to celebrate Hardy's technical craftsmanship and poetical prowess, and much of the criticism that follows, down to the 1960s, bears the imprint of this broadly New Critical matrix. Following the publication in the 1960s of a wide array of biographical materials (about Hardy's relationships, views, reading, etc.), Orel suggests the third phase begins, continuing down to the 1990s. Critics were now able to take a diverse range of approaches to the poetry, and Orel's own collection is intended to exemplify this. In the event, the essays he reprints are by such critics as Tom Paulin, Samuel Hynes, Frank Pinion, Paul Zietlow, and U. C. Knoepflmacher – in themselves excellent examples of the kind of humanist formalism practiced on the novels during the same period, but which are neither any more *theoretical* than that was, nor any more fundamentally revisionary in their reading of Hardy's poetry.

The sole explicitly interventionist – and hence arguably "theoretical" – critical work in this whole period was Donald Davie's *Thomas Hardy and British Poetry* (1973). Challenging what he saw as the dominance of Marxist intellectualism and Anglo-American Modernism in the academy, Davie represents Hardy as the originator of an alternative British poetic tradition, whose principal contemporary avatar is Philip Larkin, and whose work promotes an, admittedly "modest" and "limited," but nevertheless "decent," "liberal," and "humanist" poetry. Hardy is for Davie a poet of "integrity" and "social democracy" who allows, albeit minimally, for human choice and freedom, and whose diffidently asserted liberalism thus resists the ideological authoritarianism of late-twentieth-century intellec- tual culture.[11] Davie's position may be rejected on both political and poetic grounds; but at least for once we can acknowledge an engaged reading of Hardy's poetry and of its insertion in contemporary cultural politics.

However, overdetermining the whole history of Hardy poetry criticism is one material (if not "theoretical") factor: the sheer bulk of the material for analysis – 950-plus poems (leaving aside *The Dynasts*) – and the problem of establishing the principles on which a core canon of his "best" work can be selected out. Once again, it is F. R. Leavis who puts down an early marker that there is a crux here. In *New Bearings in English Poetry* (1932), he praises Hardy as the single significant twentieth-century practitioner of an older poetic tradition. But he also notes that amidst "a vast bulk of verse interesting only by its oddity and idiosyncrasy" there are merely "a dozen poems" which are truly "great" and on which Hardy's reputation rests.[12] Leavis typically does not say which they are, but this notion of a limited selection of "true" poems amidst the large mass of his "inferior" poetry recurs constantly in criticism and editing right down to the present. Critics as diverse as William Empson, Mark Van Doren, Samuel Hynes, Donald Davie, and J. Hillis Miller have identified the problem: everyone, says Davie, "complains that nearly 1,000 poems are too much, and asks for a more or less agreed-upon select few, a canon on which Hardy's reputation shall rest." The problem, however – at least in 1973 – was that "one perceives no consensus emerging as to what is centrally significant in Hardy's poetry, still less therefore as to what is the canon of his secure achievements" (Davie, *Thomas Hardy and British Poetry*, pp. 27–28). Editors of modern selections of Hardy's poems still reiterate similar concerns. David Wright identifies his "difficulty" in making a selection as "not least because one man's Hardy is often as not another man's bathos,"[13] and Andrew Motion registers the "alarm" with which even Hardy's "most enthusiastic admirers still respond to the enormous bulk" of the *Collected Poems*, and the perceived impossibility of producing an "adequate selection ... when no one agreed which were [Hardy's] best poems."[14] What is equally striking is the uniformity with which editors give scant indication of the principles on which they have based *their* judgment of what constitutes Hardy's "characteristically" "true," "great," or "finest" work.

In fact, what has happened – in a process of critical and editorial fashioning that has intensified since Davie's effort – is that a fairly small number of Hardy's "familiar" poems have been assumed to define the central core of his poetic achievement, rather as the "major" novels do for his fiction. My own research has shown that around eighty poems are more or less always reprinted in "Selected" editions,[15] together with a variable sampling of less well-known ones depending on the size of the volume and the schema which governs it (biographical, thematic, chronological, etc.). Equally, where critics will on occasion offer a positive reading of an unfamiliar poem, the choice of such will differ from critic to critic. So that while there is a (largely tacit) consensus about Hardy's "best" poems, which seem naturally to select themselves for inclusion and critical appro-bation, there is absolutely no consensus about the virtues or otherwise of the less familiar ones. At neither point, in other words, is there any explicit theorizing of the aesthetic or cultural ideology which shapes Hardy the Poet in this way; rather, many assumptions about the constitution, value, and function of "Literature" are taken for granted there. Hardy's poetry may not yet have been the focus of much theorized criticism, but that does not mean the poet we know and love is not a creature of theoretical presuppositions. Is not the conventional late-twentieth-century image of him still that of ironic rural quietist crafting moving lyrics from the "universal" materials of Nature, Love, Time, and Death?

The "moment" of critical theory arrived around the end of the 1960s, and over the past thirty years "Literary Studies" has been transformed by the incursion of waves of diverse theories about the nature of literature and the function/point (if any) of the academic practice of literary criticism. As a result, and like almost all other "canonic" writers, Hardy has been subject to a variety of the newer critical approaches and has been radically reshaped in the process. Never a primary site for new theory, he has nevertheless proved a fertile testing-ground for theoretical practice. What the remainder of this essay does, therefore, is give a synoptic account of the latter, focusing necessarily but not exclusively on his fiction. In conclusion, it will assess what happens to "Hardy" when such theorized criticism is brought to bear on his work, and speculate on what may still be to come.

Not unexpectedly, the main categories of the newer theoretical perspectives on Hardy are "materialist" (those with a sociological, Marxist, or socialist orientation); feminist; and poststructuralist (the last two also drawing heavily on psychoanalytic theories). The categories are, of course, fluid and over-lapping, so that it is commoner to find socialist-feminist, materialist-poststructuralist, or feminist-poststructuralist approaches than discrete examples of them. What they all have in common, however, is a cultural politics which seeks to subvert the orthodox "Hardy" and to (re)mobilize the "disproportioning" dimension of his work noted above (p. 74).

An ur-text to the first of these is Raymond Williams's early, but recognizably "cultural-materialist," chapter on Hardy in *The English Novel from Dickens to Lawrence* (1970).[16] This has been highly influential in its locating of Hardy's work at a sharply transitional sociological and literary conjuncture, and in its attempt to prise his fiction free of the fashionable cultural pessimism of much modernist literary criticism by emphasizing the positive elements in his "tragedies." Williams also offers some tantalizingly brief comments in *Politics and Letters* (1979) on the subject of why Leavis had to write Hardy out of "the great tradition," and an essay, with Merryn Williams, "Hardy and Social Class" (1980), remains a helpful attempt to define the exact class fraction Hardy derived from (although not from which he wrote as metropolitan novelist).[17]

Terry Eagleton also writes briefly but influentially about Hardy in his "structuralist-marxist" *Criticism and Ideology* (1976), where, influenced by Althusser and Macherey, he emphasizes the formal disjunctions of Hardy's texts and the ideological significance of their resulting "anti-realism." *Jude* then becomes a "calculated assault" on its readership, its "crudities" not a failure of artistic control but "a defiant flouting of 'verisimilitude' which mounts theatrical gesture upon gesture in a driving back of the bounds of realism."[18] Eagleton's most influential concept here is that of "ideology," which allowed for a more complex analysis of the relations between literature and history than did earlier reflectionist notions of "text and context." Now, literary works could be seen to expose, and thus subvert, the ideology within which they were produced, even though they were held within it; and to be historically determined, not just by their moment of production, but also by their *re*production within the cultural and aesthetic ideology of later periods. In *Walter Benjamin or Towards a Revolutionary Criticism* (1981), Eagleton further outlines the modes of production and reproduction in history whereby (the canonic figure) "Thomas Hardy" denotes "the set of ideological practices through which certain texts ... are processed, 'corrected' and reconstituted" so that they can be endowed with the "coherency" of a "readable" *oeuvre* and be found a place in the literary tradition.[19] These processes include the shaping by literary criticism and editing sketched above, and also by education syllabuses, heritage, and tourism, and now by the "classic film" industry. But the particular "correcting" of Hardy's work I want to highlight is how its anti-realist subversiveness has either to be expelled or explained away (hence those "flaws," "minor novels," and never-anthologized "bad" poems) in order to sustain his presence in the English tradition as liberal-humanist novelist and poet.

Eagleton's preparatory insights have been expanded upon most obviously in the work of George Wotton and Peter Widdowson (but see also Penny Boumelha below). In *Thomas Hardy: Towards a Materialist Criticism* (1985), Wotton offers a materialist historical account of "Wessex"; examines the way characters (especially female ones) are "seen" and represented both within and by the novels; extends this to an analysis of the "aesthetic ideology" at work in modern (male) critics' naturalized perception of Hardy's women as sexual objects; and presents a deconstructive reading of the twentieth-century cultural icon Hardy has been fashioned into.[20] Widdowson's book, *Hardy in History: A Study in Literary Sociology* (1989), complements Wotton's by offering an extended analysis (or "critiography") of the way the work of a "major writer" such as Hardy is constructed – in its reproduction at different historical moments by literary-critical and other cultural discourses – and the social and cultural meanings ascribed to it. Here, and elsewhere since, Widdowson has attempted to "re-read" Hardy's fiction against the grain of his conventional critical representation, in terms especially of class, gender, and anti-realism, while his selected edition of Hardy's poetry places in interrogative juxtaposition sections of both the latter's most "familiar" and his least often reprinted poems. It also includes a "critiographical" commentary on the processes by which Hardy has been shaped as a poet for our times.[21]

More recent works of materialist criticism are Joe Fisher's *The Hidden Hardy* (1992) and Roger Ebbatson's *Hardy: The Margin of the Unexpressed* (1993). The ingeniously persuasive theoretical premise of the former is that a distinction can be made in Hardy's novels between his "traded" texts, sold to the bourgeois fiction market – in which "Wessex" and the "Novels of Character and Environment" are the principal commodities – and his "narrated" texts, the "minor" "Novels of Ingenuity," with their subversive narrative strategies. Fisher sees the major novels as representing "an inherently conflictual engagement of the two," in which the expert market "trader" exploits a gap between the man who sells and the narrator who tells, which simultaneously makes the "traded object" acceptable and "corrupts" it. The "hidden Hardy," then, is a "self-subversion ... a sustained campaign of deception which runs through all [the] novels, creating hostile and part-visible patterns" beneath the "surface" of the text.[22] Ebbatson's book is apposite in the context of "Hardy and Critical Theory" because it largely comprises readings which draw directly (if rather formulaically) on the work of major theorists (Derrida, Lacan, Foucault, Kristeva, de Man, Bakhtin) in order to articulate the "not-said" of Hardy's works. It also offers a deconstructive reading of Hardy's admired essay, "The Dorsetshire Labourer," which seeks to show that, rather than being a socially sensitive account of the "real lives" of nineteenth-century farmworkers, it is, in fact, an example of Hardy as successful man-of-letters displacing their poverty, exploitation, and injustice into aestheticized pap for his middle-class metropolitan readership – hence silencing, rather than speaking for, its subject.[23]

To conclude this survey of materialist criticism and pave the way for feminism, it seems fitting to salute the work of John Goode.[24] Informed by, but not predicated on, contemporary theory, Goode's pioneering essays represent a recognition of the subversive textual/sexual politics and performative anti-realism of Hardy's fiction – features which have come to dominate more recent critical analysis. "Woman and the Literary Text" (1976) proposes that texts are not "representations" but processes of signification, and that "we can only see the political implications of a text by attending to its formal identity." Apropos of Tess, Goode suggests that what we witness (and are complicit in) is her "objectification ... by the narrator which is acted out in the novel," so that we too, consuming with our eyes both the text and hence Tess herself, collude in Alec and Angel's patriarchal construction of her as an "object of consumption." As a "character," she is only composed of all the "object images" the novel subjects her to bearing – primarily those of male "gazers" (including the narrator/novelist and the implicated reader). This mode of textual signification means that the novel's discourses *have to be* accepted as unstable and contradictory.[25] Such ideas are extended in "Sue Bridehead and the New Woman" (1979), where Goode suggests that Sue is an "exposing image" in the "taking apart of reality" which *Jude* radically effects – most particularly of the mystifications inherent in conventional heterosexual notions of love and marriage: "the incomprehensibility of Sue ... is one way at least in which the incomprehensibility of the world (i.e., bourgeois ideology) is offered."[26] His later book, *Thomas Hardy: The Offensive Truth* (1988),[27] continues to highlight the disrupted, transformative textuality of Hardy's fiction, registering its self-reflexive obsession with the act of writing as a metaphorical representation of the artifice/iality of "real" social relations and with representation, especially in the patriarchal imaging and silencing of women. But despite the novels' finally unresolvable "incoherence," Goode still sees political force in them, the disjunctions and discontinuities being a reflex of their angry confrontation of conventional ideological discourses: by showing an "offensive truth," truth goes on the offensive.

Feminist critical readings of Hardy abound (as do the earlier essays on "Hardy's Women" they challenge and replace). Mary Jacobus's three essays from the 1970s – on Sue Bridehead, on "Tess's Purity," and on *The Woodlanders*[28] – signal the directions much new feminist work would take: a questioning of Hardy's own attitude to his female characters ("feminist" or chauvinist?) and a gendered close reading of the language of his texts. So, too, does Elaine Showalter's essay, "The Unmanning of the Mayor of Casterbridge" (1979), which proposes that it is in Hardy's understanding of the "feminine spirit in his man of character," of Henchard as "New Man," rather than in his depiction of "New Women," that the case for his "feminist sympathies" may be made.[29] And Patricia Stubbs's chapter on Hardy's fiction in *Women and Fiction: Feminism and the Novel 1880–1920* (1979), while lacking Goode's recognition that the formal tensions and contradictions must in some way "speak" the novels' sexual politics, nevertheless develops a pioneering thesis on Hardy's central "contradiction." This is comprised by his "intensely modern, even feminist consciousness" and his residual acceptance of conventional male literary character-stereotypes for women – thus belying his ultimate containment within patriarchal ideology.[30] While some later feminist critics would agree, others with a less historically constrained poststructuralist perspective would see those "stereotypes" as revealingly fissured and disturbed.

Penny Boumelha, in *Thomas Hardy and Women: Sexual Ideology and Narrative Form* (1982), may be seen as one of the latter. The first critic to offer a full-scale poststructuralist analysis of gender ideology in Hardy, Boumelha is also a socialist-feminist whose work is significantly influenced by Althusser as mediated through the Terry Eagleton of *Criticism and Ideology*. Her conception of ideology, however, is overdetermined by post-1968 feminism, and is thus reinflected in terms of gender: "it will also encode other relations of power and dominance, and principally that of male dominance." Unlike Stubbs, Boumelha does attempt to correlate the "experimentalism" of Hardy's fiction (including, exceptionally, the "minor novels") with its radically subversive presentation of sexual relations, pointing to uncertainty of narrative focus, the "voiding" of "character," textual dislocation, and self-interrogation of the novels' own narrative strategies, as evidence of a "radical break" in which Hardy's texts confront their own informing ideology. The force of his representations of women resides in "their resistance to reduction to a single and uniform ideological position."[31] What remains unclear is whether Hardy's "radicalism" is his own, or whether it is activated in Hardy's *texts* by the radical poststructuralist reading of a modern feminist critic.

Patricia Ingham, a specialist in language as well as a feminist critic, also indirectly challenges Patricia Stubbs. Her *Thomas Hardy: A Feminist Reading* (1989) offers a critique of recent feminist approaches to Hardy – approaches which remain limited by failing to avoid a simplistic reflectionism and by paying inadequate attention to the "multiple voices of the texts" – and then applies an innovative linguistic model of interpretation to Hardy's novels by exploring the "sense of disjunction," the "fault-line," in their narrative languages or "syntax." This "involves the idea that 'the subject' of a novel (in this case usually a female subject) is created by the language, which in turn is a product of ideologies." A close linguistic and gendered reading again reveals the ideological tensions and uncertainties enacted in a late-nineteenth-century male novelist's attempts to find a form and language by which to represent female sexuality beyond the constraints of convention and stereotype. Hardy's figuring of the "pure woman" trope in the language and plot of *Tess*, for example, in fact indicates his desire to transgress the boundaries of his own ideological positioning.[32] A further essay which illustrates that deconstructing Hardy's language is now a primary focus for contemporary critics is Jean Jacques Lecercle's "The Violence of Style in *Tess of the d'Urbervilles*" (1989). Drawing explicitly on the work of linguist and semiotician Gilles Deleuze, Lecercle proposes that violence in the novel's treatment of women and sexuality is its determining characteristic: Tess is at once subjected *to* physical violence in the novel and subjected (i.e., constituted as a subject) *by* the symbolic violence of the language the novel uses to enunciate her. Hardy's achievement lies in his production of a text where different languages clash – giving the "impression of instability, of eruptive violence" – and in his refusal to resolve such linguistic dissonance, but to "let it stand and be perceived." The metaphorical dimension of the novel's language may be a psychological register of Hardy's "rage," but it is the linguistic violence which literally constitutes his style.[33]

Much recent work on Hardy has been by American feminist critics. Rosemarie Morgan's *Women and Sexuality in the Novels of Thomas Hardy* (1988) claims to be a "revisionary" study, and its introduction clearly implies its provenance within deconstruction in registering the need for "an acute sensitivity" to, *inter alia*, Hardy's "contrapuntal narrative voices, his poetic complex of metaphorical structures, his elaborate configuration of points of view."[34] It does attempt to "resurrect" a Hardy not much spoken of these days, whose voluptuous heroines bear witness to his celebration of their robust sexuality and dynamic potential for overthrowing the patriarchal *status quo*. But its failure to engage with the "contradictions" identified by feminist criticism above, combined with surprisingly *un*deconstructionist critical readings, means that it is more revisionist than "revisionary." More sophisticated and persuasive is Kaja Silverman's essay, "History, Figuration and Female Subjectivity in *Tess of the d'Urbervilles*" (1984), which deploys a combination of neo-Freudian (from Lacan and Kristeva[35]) and visual theory (from film studies) to show how the "gaze" constructed by the narratalogical language of the novel – in its complex "processes of colonization, delimitation, configuration and inscription" – represents a gendered power relationship in which the subject of the "gaze" is male and its object female. This leads Hardy subconsciously to negate the potentially redemptive force of female sexuality, which his discourse of representation has itself created, in a final section of the novel entitled (ironically) "Fulfilment."[36]

Also explicitly beholden to Lacanian psychoanalytic theory is Marjorie Garson's *Hardy's Fables of Integrity: Woman, Body, Text* (1991), which reads seven of Hardy's novels as obliquely expressing "somatic anxiety – anxiety about bodily integrity, fear of corporeal dissolution." Both in physical terms and in his "nervously figurative language" and fabular structure, a "mythic subtext" becomes apparent which conveys "anxieties about wholeness, about maleness, and particularly about women." This helps to explain the "instabilities, contradictions, and grotesqueries," the "defensiveness and self-consciousness" about class and gender, in Hardy's texts – or rather, what Garson, in full poststructuralist rig, would always understand as "Hardy": "the wider text" which subsumes both "the life" and the writings.[37] A further collection of cognate work is *The Sense of Sex: Feminist Perspectives on Hardy*, ed. Margaret R. Higonnet (1993).[38] Higonnet's introduction to the volume offers a succinct account of feminist criticism on Hardy; and while the essays are mixed in quality, a number do indeed offer new "perspectives" on Hardy's work. Drawing variously on psychoanalytic theory, film theory, medical history, reader-response, and narratology, those by Kristin Brady on *Tess*, Dianne Sadoff on the film of *Tess*, Judith Mitchell on "Hardy's Female Reader," Mary Rimmer on the chess game in *A Pair of Blue Eyes*, and Penny Boumelha on class and gender in *The Hand of Ethelberta* are to be recommended. One other contribution will help to establish a point I have made in passing on several occasions. It is striking that there is merely a single essay in the entire volume on Hardy's poetry, and that by a male critic, U. C. Knoepflmacher, who offers an interesting (if somewhat shaky) Freudian reading of the sexual-political sub-text of *Wessex Poems*. What is even more striking is that this is one of only three contributions reprinted from a previous publication (in *PMLA*, 105 [1990], 1055–70) rather than written specially for the book, and that it reappears again in the 1995 collection edited by Orel referred to earlier. Now it is quite a reasonable essay, but it is not *that* good; what it shows, rather, is just how little theory-informed criticism there is to date on Hardy's poetry – by feminist critics or by anyone else.[39]

Much of the influence of poststructuralism on Hardy criticism, as will already be apparent, informs the more recent materialist and feminist work surveyed above. But it seems appropriate to conclude this overview with a recognition of one eminent deconstructive critic who has returned time and again to Hardy's writing in both genres: J. Hillis Miller. Such revisiting is itself a central term in Miller's critical project, for every literary text demands an individual "close reading," but because no one reading suffices, "the work of reading must always start again from the beginning, even in a rereading of a work already read."[40] His first major work on Hardy, and his last in phenomenological criticism before shifting to the "Yale" inflexion of Derridean deconstruction, seeks to uncover the "single design in the totality" of Hardy's work: the pervasive formal and thematic mental structures of "distance" and "desire" and the correlation between them.[41] This, of course, is entirely contrary to deconstruction, and Miller later notes that "attempts to survey the whole and organize it thematically, *or phenomenologically*, by noting similarities ... and generalizing on that basis" are "unsatisfactory."[42] Two of his most admired close readings of Hardy's fiction (on *Tess* and *The Well-Beloved*) show, by detailed analysis of the language and formal articulation of the texts, how different forms of repetition lie at the heart of both their structuration and their significa-tion.[43] An earlier version of Miller's penetrating essay on *The Well-Beloved* further sees this "last" novel's "clash of incompatible features" and its overt display of "the fictionality of fiction" as revealing both a radical break with Victorian realism and "an interpretation ... or even ... parody" of Hardy's own previous fiction: "by presenting a schematic and 'unrealistic' version of the pattern they all share," *The Well-Beloved* calls attention to "the geometric artifice" of all his novels and hence to their "covert" rejection of the ideology of humanist-realism.[44]

Miller has also written extensively on Hardy's poetry. *The Linguistic Moment* is "neither a work of pure literary theory nor a work of pure praxis," but a work of "critique," a testing of "the grounding of language in this or that particular text"; and the "self-testing" of this within the poems themselves Miller calls "the linguistic moment": "a suspension ... a breaking of the illusion that language is a transparent medium of meaning" (Miller, *Linguistic Moment*, pp. xviii, xiv). Hardy's 950-plus individual poems are exemplary, with Miller noting the "uniqueness of each moment of experience ... each record[s] in words"; he points out that "each moment, each text, is incommensurate with all the others" and that forms of "discontinuity," "discord," and "irrelation" characterize the *oeuvre* (pp. 270–71, 282). Faced with the fact that the poems are "fugitive glimpses, transient readings of life," the critic "must resist as much as possible the temptation to link poem with poem in some grand scheme" (pp. 289, 283). Miller's own minutely attentive close reading of a "miscellaneous" selection of poems focuses on their recognition of "life's incoherence," which is explained by the irrational, "discordant," and unsystematic properties of language: "for Hardy, between the intention and the deed, between moment and moment, between the self and itself, between mind and landscape, falls the word. This descent of the word is the linguistic moment in Hardy." His ever-renewed "exploration of the consequences for man of the absence of the *logos*" means that there can be no "ontological ground" for the coherence of "collective history or of individual histories," of the "single self" (e.g., "Thomas Hardy"), or of "language" – be it the English language, the language of the "Complete Poems," or that of any individual poem. That is what Hardy's poetry ultimately represents (pp. 290, 303–04). The five essays from various periods collected in *Tropes, Parables, Performatives: Essays on Twentieth-Century Literature* also exemplify such views, as does, especially, Miller's microscopic reading, in *Linguistic Moment*, of the poem "In Front of the Landscape" which shows Hardy "turning perception into language." This represents a process of translation – as all translation must always be – which is a metaphorical transposing, "a misreading or distortion," but one which also protects Hardy's integrity in its refusal of any notion of coherence or system in human life and history. Indeed, the proliferating repetition of such an "act of translation" is what comprises Hardy's "Complete Poems" (Miller, *Tropes*, pp. 208, 212). Miller's deconstructionist work on both genres has quietly and subtly laid the ground for the heteroglossic and unstable "Hardy as Text" which is currently "In Front of the [Critical] Landscape," and which is itself necessarily an "act of translation" in the terms defined above.

We may now ask: what happens to "good little Thomas Hardy" when he is subjected to such theorized criticism? He becomes, I suggest, a terrain of riven textuality whose major landmarks are faultlines which expose the substrata of cultural politics, class, sexuality, and gender, themselves striated by the unstable language of which they are composed. Hardy "Our Contemporary" lurches from the "Heritage Hardy" (which he nevertheless continues to be in popular culture) to a Deconstructionist *avant la lettre*. The ("flawed" but "great") humanist-realist who is properly represented by the "major" Wessex novels is subverted when the "minor novels" are reinserted in the canon, and reappears as a proto-postmodern anti-realist whose own fictional texture is self-deconstructing. Hardy the Poet, once "truly" characterized by only his "finest" poems as the wryly lyrical celebrant of nature, love, time, and mortality or as the ironic liberal-humanist who refuses Modernist cultural despair, is now reconstituted by the undifferentiated mass of his "Complete Poems" in deconstructive proof of the inadequacy of all "grand narratives" – of history, politics, religion, philosophy, and, indeed, of poetry itself.

Now that one of the principal discourses of Hardy's fiction is seen to be class and class relations, readings focus not on the production of an "organic" countryman who gives a "voice" to the rural poor and dispossessed, but on that of a meritocratic, metropolitan man-of-letters who is obsessed, as a bourgeois *arriviste*, with the problems of upward mobility created by a class society in rapid transition. Equally, the foregrounding of sexuality and gender as discourses everywhere encoded in the novels forces us to debate whether Hardy is a proto-feminist, sympathetically exposing the victimization of women in a patriarchal society, or a closet misogynist terrified, like many of his male contemporaries, by the rise of the "New Woman," and whose fiction constantly forecloses on the female aspiration and sexuality it so potently depicts. Does it endorse the pervasively erotic "Male Gaze" it deploys, or deconstruct it? Is Hardy's "true" poetry – most famously in the elegies to Emma of 1912–13 – a movingly remorseful testimony to lost love, or do many less "familiar" poems give a voice to silenced women, whose robust sexuality and strength is counterpoised with male "faintheartedness" and prurient fantasies of "lost prizes"? Central to all this is a recognition that Hardy's language, in both poetry and prose, is not the linguistic medium through which his "vision" is expressed, but the self-reflexive *subject* of all his writing – a language not to be read for its "unifying" and "coherent" systems of imagery and symbolism, but for its contradictory, unstable, and hence revealing, inscription of complex social and sexual tensions.

The fundamental theoretical question *this* "Hardy" poses – and one too seldom asked by even his most sophisticated contemporary critics – is: is Hardy *in control* of his text? Does he *intend* his effects and utterances, whatever we may read them to be, or is his writing merely indeterminate textuality which is made to "speak" – in its decoding by contemporary criticism – the tacit ideological complexities and contradictions of both its moment of production and its moment of reproduction? Is it the *writer* or the *reader* who ultimately determines meaning? Such a question does not, of course, anticipate a definitive answer (nor does it hope to "solve" the problematics of either intentionalism or postmodern relativism): it merely signals that the question should always be *put* – explicitly, and within the critical frame.

In conclusion, we may speculate as to what further critical/theoretical perspectives will be brought to bear on Hardy. First, there is as yet no explicitly "postcolonialist" criticism of his work; but notions of national and racial consciousness surely need to be addressed there, as does Hardy's central place in constructions of "Englishness" and of "English Literature" within twentieth-century national and postcolonial cultures. Secondly, and more surprisingly, there is no gay, lesbian, or "queer" criticism of Hardy's texts so far as I am aware. Overt and covert instances of homoerotic desire feature in the novels (e.g., Miss Aldclyffe for Cytherea in *Desperate Remedies*; Paula Power for Charlotte in *A Laodicean*), but, more importantly, problematized sexuality and the construction of gender are so insistent, diverse, and obsessive in both novels and poems (consider the variously gendered "voices" there, and the many poems which suggest a sexuality ill at ease with itself) that the texts cry out to be explored by a criticism that goes beyond even recent feminist readings. Thirdly, in the absence of one to hand, I am obliged to call for the invention of a theorized praxis which will meet the pressing need for a criticism that can deal with the accelerating reproduction of Hardy's work in the visual media. New generations of "readers" of Hardy will first come to "his" works through film and television versions of them; will need to know how to negotiate the complex relations between written and visually reproduced texts; and how to read the social meanings encoded in them. It is here, as one instance among many in the current intellectual arena, that literary theory and criticism begin to lose definition as discrete activities, and become merely contributory discourses in the more fully comprehensive projects of cultural theory and cultural history.

NOTES

1 "The Profitable Reading of Fiction" (1888), "Candour in English Fiction" (1890), and "The Science of Fiction" (1891) – all rpt. in *PW* and in *Thomas Hardy: Selected Poetry and Non-Fictional Prose*, ed. Peter Widdowson (London and Basingstoke: Macmillan, 1997).

2 The categories Hardy used to group the different kinds of his fiction in the 1912 "General Preface" to the "Wessex Edition" of his works. This preface is reproduced in many modern editions of his novels and poetry.

3 But see n. 39 below.

4 For a more extended discussion of critics' treatment of the "minor novels" and of Hardy's "flaws," see Peter Widdowson, *Hardy in History: A Study in Literary Sociology* (London: Routledge, 1989), chapter 1.

5 F. R. Leavis, *The Great Tradition* (1948; Harmondsworth: Penguin, 1962), p. 140.

6 Ian Gregor, *The Great Web: The Form of Hardy's Major Fiction* (London: Faber & Faber, 1974).

7 Jean Brooks, *Thomas Hardy: The Poetic Structure* (London: Elek Books, 1971); Dale Kramer, *Thomas Hardy: The Forms of Tragedy* (London and Basingstoke: Macmillan, 1975); Peter Casagrande, *Unity in Hardy's Novels: "Repetitive Symmetries"* (London and Basingstoke: Macmillan, 1982). Further examples of this new formalism appear in essays reprinted in *Thomas Hardy: The Tragic Novels*, ed. R. P. Draper (London and Basingstoke: Macmillan Casebooks, 1975, 1991) – especially essays by Tony Tanner and David Lodge.

8 For examples, see the reviews rpt. in Cox; and see *Thomas Hardy: Poems*, ed. J. Gibson and T. Johnson (London and Basingstoke: Macmillan, 1979, 1991).

9 *Thomas Hardy: A Critical Selection of His Finest Poetry*, ed. Samuel Hynes (Oxford University Press, "The Oxford Authors," 1984), pp. xxii, xxi. The identical introduction reappears in a second, different selection by Hynes: *Thomas Hardy: A Selection of his Finest Poems*, also published by Oxford University Press, in the Oxford Poetry Library (1994).

10 *Critical Essays on Thomas Hardy's Poetry*, ed. Harold Orel (New York: G. K. Hall, 1995), pp. 3–11 *passim*. Other useful accounts of Hardy poetry criticism can be found in Gibson and Johnson, "Introduction," *Thomas Hardy: Poems*, and Timothy Hands, *Thomas Hardy* (London and Basingstoke: Macmillan, 1995), chapter 6.

11 Donald Davie, *Thomas Hardy and British Poetry* (London: Routledge & Kegan Paul, 1973), pp. 6, 11–12, 25–26, 39–40.

12 F. R. Leavis, *New Bearings in English Poetry* (1932; Harmondsworth: Penguin, 1963), p. 53.

13 David Wright, "Note on the Selection," in *Thomas Hardy: Selected Poems* (Harmondsworth: Penguin, 1978, 1986), p. 29.

14 Andrew Motion, "Introduction," *Thomas Hardy: Selected Poems* (London: Orion, Everyman Paperbacks, 1994), p. xxvi.

15 Widdowson, "The Familiar Hardy" section of poems, and "Critical Commentary," in *Selected Poetry and Non-Fictional Prose*, pp. 186–217 *passim*.

16 Raymond Williams, *The English Novel from Dickens to Lawrence* (1970; St. Albans: Paladin, 1974), chapter 4. This is largely reprinted as chapter 18 of Williams's *The Country and the City* (London: Chatto & Windus, 1973).

17 Raymond Williams, *Politics and Letters* (London: Verso, 1979, 1981), section IV, chapter 2; and Raymond and Merryn Williams, "Hardy and Social Class," in *Thomas Hardy: The Writer and His Background*, ed. Norman Page (London: Bell & Hyman, 1980), pp. 245–46.

18 Terry Eagleton, *Criticism and Ideology* (1976; London: Verso, 1978),

pp. 131–32. See also Eagleton, "Introduction," Thomas Hardy, *Jude the Obscure* (London and Basingstoke: Macmillan, New Wessex Edition, 1974).

19 Terry Eagleton, *Walter Benjamin or Towards a Revolutionary Criticism* (London: Verso, 1981), pp. 126–27.

20 George Wotton, *Thomas Hardy: Towards a Materialist Criticism* (Dublin: Gill & Macmillan, 1985).

21 Peter Widdowson, *Hardy in History: A Study in Literary Sociology* (London: Routledge, 1989); Widdowson, "Introduction," *Tess of the d'Urbervilles* (London and Basingstoke: Macmillan New Casebooks, 1993); Widdowson, *Thomas Hardy* (Plymouth: Northcote House, Writers and their Work, 1996); Widdowson, *On Thomas Hardy: Late Essays and Earlier* (London and Basingstoke: Macmillan, 1998); Widdowson, ed., *Selected Poetry* (1997).

22 Joe Fisher, *The Hidden Hardy* (London and Basingstoke: Macmillan, 1992), esp. pp. 3, 7.

23 Roger Ebbatson, *Hardy: The Margin of the Unexpressed* (Sheffield Academic Press, 1993). See chapter 6 for the essay on "The Dorsetshire Labourer."

24 John Goode died prematurely in 1994.

25 John Goode, "Woman and the Literary Text," in *The Rights and Wrongs of Women*, ed. Juliet Mitchell and Ann Oakley (Harmondsworth: Penguin, 1976), *passim*, but esp. pp. 253–55.

26 John Goode, "Sue Bridehead and the New Woman," in *Women Writing and Writing about Women*, ed. Mary Jacobus (London: Croom Helm, 1979), pp. 100, 107–08.

27 John Goode, *Thomas Hardy: The Offensive Truth* (Oxford: Blackwell, 1988).

28 Mary Jacobus, "Sue the Obscure," *Essays in Criticism*, 25 (1975), 304–28; Jacobus, "Tess's Purity," *Essays in Criticism*, 26 (1976), 318–38 (rpt. as "Tess: The Making of a Pure Woman," in *Tearing the Veil: Essays on Femininity*, ed. Susan Lipshitz [London: Routledge & Kegan Paul, 1978]); Jacobus, "Tree and Machine: *The Woodlanders*," in *Critical Approaches to the Fiction of Thomas Hardy*, ed. Dale Kramer (London and Basingstoke: Macmillan, 1979).

29 Elaine Showalter, "The Unmanning of the Mayor of Casterbridge," in Kramer, *Critical Approaches*; rpt. in *Thomas Hardy: The Tragic Novels*, ed. R. P. Draper, 2nd edn. (London and Basingstoke: Macmillan New Casebooks, 1991), pp. 114, 102.

30 Patricia Stubbs, *Women and Fiction: Feminism and the Novel, 1880–1920* (1979; London: Methuen, 1981), chapter 4 on Hardy, pp. 58–59.

31 Penny Boumelha, *Thomas Hardy and Women: Sexual Ideology and Narrative Form* (Brighton, Sussex: Harvester Press, 1982), pp. 5, 7. See also Boumelha, ed., *Jude the Obscure* (London and Basingstoke: Macmillan New Casebooks, 1996), and her essay on *HE* in Higonnet, *The Sense of Sex* (see n. 38).

32 Patricia Ingham, *Thomas Hardy: A Feminist Reading* (Hemel Hempstead: Harvester Wheatsheaf, 1989), pp. 6, 7, 71–74. See also her introduction to the Everyman Paperbacks Edition of *T* (London: Orion, 1991).

33 Jean-Jacques Lecercle, "The Violence of Style in *Tess of the d'Urbervilles*," in *Alternative Hardy*, ed. Lance St. John Butler (London and Basingstoke: Macmillan, 1989), esp. pp. 22–23.

34 Rosemarie Morgan, *Women and Sexuality in the Novels of Thomas Hardy* (London: Routledge, 1988), pp. xvi–xvii.

35 An earlier – less feminist and theoretical – attempt to read Hardy's fiction by way of psychology (principally Jung and Freud) is Rosemary Sumner, *Thomas Hardy: Psychological Novelist* (London and Basingstoke: Macmillan, 1981).

36 Kaja Silverman, "History, Figuration and Female Subjectivity in *Tess of the d'Urbervilles*," *Novel*, 18 (1984), 5–28.

37 Marjorie Garson, *Hardy's Fables of Integrity: Woman, Body, Text* (Oxford: Clarendon Press, 1991), pp. 1–5 *passim*.

38 *The Sense of Sex: Feminist Perspectives on Hardy*, ed. Margaret R. Higonnet (Urbana: University of Illinois Press, 1993).

39 One honorable exception to this may be Stan Smith's materialist-historical (but not "theoretical") reading of Hardy's poems in *Inviolable Voice: History and Twentieth-Century Poetry* (Dublin: Gill & Macmillan, 1982), chapter 2. A second will surely be the awaited book on Hardy's poetry by the new historicist critic, Marjorie Levinson.

40 J. Hillis Miller, *Tropes, Parables, Performatives: Essays on Twentieth-Century Literature* (Hemel Hempstead: Harvester Wheatsheaf, 1990), pp. viii–ix.

41 J. Hillis Miller, *Thomas Hardy: Distance and Desire* (Oxford University Press, 1970), esp. p. ix.

42 J. Hillis Miller, *The Linguistic Moment: From Wordsworth to Stevens* (Princeton University Press, 1985), p. 270; my emphasis.

43 J. Hillis Miller, *Fiction and Repetition: Seven English Novels* (Cambridge, Mass.: Harvard University Press, 1982), chapters 5 and 6.

44 J. Hillis Miller, "Introduction" to Thomas Hardy, *The Well-Beloved* (London and Basingstoke: Macmillan, New Wessex Edition, 1975), pp. 13–16.

6

KRISTIN BRADY

Thomas Hardy and matters of gender

From their first publication, the works of Thomas Hardy have been explicitly and obsessively associated with matters of gender. This is the case, not only because these texts confront and perpetuate ideas about sexual difference that were influential in Hardy's own time, but also because his vivid, contradictory, and often strange representations of sexual desire, like a series of cultural Rorschach tests, have continually elicited from his readers intense and revealing responses: the act of interpretation exposes unspoken assumptions that circulate in the historical moment of the interpreter, and Hardy's representations of sexuality are especially effective in making visible those particularized hermeneutical processes. Indeed, to study the changing responses to gender in Hardy's published works from 1871 to the present is, in effect, to trace a fairly detailed history of the ways in which sexuality has been constructed within the British Isles and North America since the late-Victorian period. This essay will offer, therefore, only a schematic summary of what, in my own historical moment, I consider to be the most significant responses to representations of sexual difference in Hardy's texts. To speak of understandings about sexuality is, by definition, to speak of gender: though sexuality may be seen to exist in the "real," the experience of sexuality is always already mediated – and even produced – by culture. As Judith Butler has compellingly argued, gender is the performance of sexuality within culture.[1] So Hardy's texts, as well as the readings of those texts over the last century and a quarter, are themselves gendered performances – continually shifting permutations of ideas about sexual difference.

Victorian notions of sexuality are intriguingly obvious in nineteenth-century reviews of Hardy's fiction, beginning with the 1871 publication of the first novel, which provoked a set of responses that remained roughly consistent at least until the 1891 appearance of *Tess of the d'Urbervilles*. The *Athenaeum* objected to "an occasional coarseness" in *Desperate Remedies*, while the *Spectator* said that the novel was "disagreeable," that it portrayed "no display of passion except of the brute kind" (Cox, pp. 2, 5, and 3). These accusations of coarseness and brutishness – derived partly from Victorian social and scientific discourses about both the lower classes and "primitive" racial groups, as well as about women – were variously echoed, in both negative and positive directions, in reviews of Hardy's work during the ensuing two decades. Repeatedly, reviewers saw Hardy's treatment of sexual desire as sensational, violent, pagan, and bestial. Hardy's female characters especially were seen as manifestations of, to use Julian Hawthorne's quasi-scientific phrasing in the *Spectator*, an "inborn, involuntary, unconscious emotional organism" (Cox, p. 76). What provoked these responses in Hardy's contemporaries was not simply the fact that he offered unusually explicit descriptions of female desire; more unconventional and troubling, perhaps, was his depiction of that desire as inconstant (as *Tess* makes clear, even the fallen woman was expected to remain fixated on her first sexual partner). These heroines were more like rapacious animals than like monogamous ladies, and their behavior digressed in disconcerting ways from the sentimental formula of love-at-first-sight-followed-by-engagement-and-marriage. Five years before Sue Bridehead horrified the British public with her sexual vagaries, James Barrie summarized Hardy's plots in these terms:

> Mr. Hardy seems by the time he began to write to have formed a theory about young women, which ... amounts to this, that on the subject of matrimony no woman knows her own mind ... They think they would like to marry, but are not sure when they arrive at the altar. They hesitate about becoming engaged lest they should then cease to love ... They are seldom sure of their own love unless there is ground for believing that it is not returned, and the only tolerably safe thing to predict of them is, that first they will have two lovers and then marry a third. (Cox, pp. 163–64)

According to Barrie, this instability in Hardy's heroines made them unappealing to a female audience, and he was not the only reader to think of them, in the words of the anonymous reviewer in the *New Quarterly Magazine*, as "men's women" (Cox, p. 62). Indeed, the wavering desire of Hardy's heroines seems to have made them attractive to many male readers, if only because it reassured them about their own comparative stability. Even Coventry Patmore, for example – best known as the author of a much-acclaimed poem about domestic virtue in wives – expressed condescending and self-congratulatory affection for the unvirtuous side of Hardy's heroines: "each has the charm of the simplest and most familiar womanhood, and the only character they have in common is that of having each some serious defect, which only makes us like them more" (Cox, p. 148).

The superior and often clinical tone assumed by Hardy's reviewers may have been a response to the technical language of the fiction itself, which was repeatedly compared to the published discourse of Herbert Spencer, an important popularizer of social Darwinism and of essentialist ideas about gender difference. In the light of this complexly intertextual relationship among post-Darwinian scientific texts, literary works by Hardy, and critical responses to Hardy, it should not be surprising that an important early interpreter of Hardy was Havelock Ellis, whose theories about gender were to become a formative part of the discourse of sexology, the new science of sexual difference during the late nineteenth and early twentieth centuries. In 1883, Ellis placed Hardy's fiction – because of its "minute observation," its "delicate insight," and its "conception of love as the one business of life" (Cox, p. 104) – in the feminine tradition of novel-writing represented by such authors as Jane Austen, Charlotte Brontë, and George Eliot. Ellis summarized an aspect of Hardy's writing that was endlessly intriguing to Victorian readers: here was a male writer offering a style of writing and of plot construction that was considered to be exclusively female. Charles Dickens and William Thackeray, for example, whom Ellis invoked as contrasts to Hardy, did not confine their emphasis so exclusively to the courtship plot, especially to the woman's position within that plot. In Ellis's view, however, Hardy's fiction was also different from that of his female models precisely because his heroines were more "instinct-led" – Ellis repeatedly used this term about them – than concerned with moral questions:

> Morals, observe, do not come in ... Mr. Hardy's heroines are characterized by a yielding to circumstance that is limited by the play of instinct. They are never quite bad. It seems, indeed, that this quality in them, which shuts them out from any high level of goodness, is precisely that which saves them from ever being very bad. They have an instinctive self-respect, an instinctive purity ... Even Eustacia Vye has no impure taint about her. One feels compelled to insist on the instinctiveness of these women. There is, in truth, something elemental, something *demonic* about them. We see at once that they have no souls. (Cox, p. 106)

Implicit in the language of this passage is a linkage of Hardy's women with those racial and social groups defined as "primitive" by Victorian social theories, and later, in a consideration of the Wessex setting, Ellis directly articulated this idea:

> It would almost seem that in the solitary lives on these Dorset heaths we are in contact with what is really a primitive phase of society ... [and] that those qualities which we have found to be distinctive of his heroines, the absence of

moral feeling, the instinctiveness, had a direct relation to the wild and solitary
character of their environment. (Cox, p. 130)

Here Ellis gave expression to the idea, suggested less clearly in many
reviews, that Hardy's construction of gender difference works in terms not
of civilized, Christian codes but of post-Darwinian anthropological theories
about social behavior: the "purity" of Hardy's characters, especially his
women, is that of the rural rustic, of the "instinctive" and amoral
"primitive" races.

Perhaps because his own notion of purity was culturally and racially
rather than morally based, Ellis was later to express impatience with the
debate that ensued among Victorian readers of *Tess* about its heroine as "A
Pure Woman Faithfully Depicted by Thomas Hardy." Yet Ellis's language
often anticipated the terms of that debate, which emerged from the novelty
of applying to a fallen woman the concept of purity in its moral sense.
Indeed, in the characterization of Tess Durbeyfield, Hardy's unorthodox
linkage of ideas about primitivism and about moral purity – perhaps his
own revisionary response to the negative or condescending focus on
paganism in the early reviews – may well have accounted for some of the
fury over *Tess*: the idea of a "primitive" or "pagan" instinctiveness is often
used by the novel's narrator to invoke sympathy for this character who
stands out among Hardy's heroines precisely for her lack of flirtatiousness
and capriciousness, and this fact was a common focus for the reviewers.
Richard LeGallienne was not untypical when he declared Tess to be "the
most satisfying of all Mr. Hardy's heroines. She is by no means so empty-
headed as they are wont to be, but, like her sisters, she is a fine Pagan, full
of humanity and imagination, and, like them, though in a less degree,
flawed with that lack of will, that fatal indecision at great moments" (Cox,
p. 180). So the trait that led Ellis to say that Hardy's heroines are demonic
beings with no souls led LeGallienne to argue that they have the supremely
moral traits of "humanity and imagination." The same kind of thinking, it
seems, led the *Athenaeum* reviewer to see Tess, again in terms of cultural or
racial Otherness, as an "imperfect woman, nobly planned, who, like the
geisha of the Japanese legend, has sinned in the body, but ever her heart
was pure" (Cox, p. 184). Like Hardy's other heroines, but to a much
greater extent, Tess was seen, paradoxically, to be morally "pure" precisely
because she was considered to be physically impure or naturally close to
the earth: to be "instinct-led" was to be both more than and less than
human.

Not surprisingly, Sue Bridehead was often viewed as simply the over-
civilized and therefore hysterical and impure mirror opposite of the

quintessentially natural and pure Tess. In the words of R. Y. Tyrell, Sue's characterization involved a "minute registry of the fluctuations of disease in an incurably morbid organism" (Cox, p. 295). D. H. Lawrence then described Sue's psyche as the battleground for a violent struggle between its primitive and civilized aspects: "One of the supremest products of our civilization is Sue ... And the duality of her nature made her extremely liable to self-destruction. The suppressed, atrophied female in her, like a potent fury, was always there, suggesting to her to make the fatal mistake. She contained always the rarest, most deadly anarchy in her own being."[2] For many nineteenth- and early-twentieth-century readers, then, all of Hardy's women were *organisms* in varying degrees of health, with an unstable relationship between body and mind. Female rather than feminine, they took readers back to the "primitive" roots described by Darwin and other scientific thinkers of the period. So Ellis's analysis of 1896, particularizing in terms of racial groups the standard Victorian response to Hardy's women, declared them to be "a type not uncommon in the south of England, where the heavier Teutonic and Scandinavian elements are, more than elsewhere, modified by the alert and volatile elements furnished by earlier races" (Cox, p. 306). This association of Hardy's women with a primitive nature is found even in Virginia Woolf's more poetic comments, made in 1928, that

> Vain might their beauty be and terrible their fate, but while the glow of life is in them their step is free, their laughter sweet, and theirs is the power to sink into the breast of Nature and become part of her silence and solemnity, or to rise and put on them the movement of the clouds and the wildness of the flowering woodlands.[3]

Woolf also anticipated, however, an important emphasis of much feminist criticism during the last quarter of the twentieth century, for she noted a basic division in Hardy's depiction of female and male characters: "However lovable and charming Bathsheba may be, still she is weak; however stubborn and ill-guided Henchard may be, still he is strong. This is a fundamental part of Hardy's vision; the staple of many of his books. The woman is the weaker and the fleshlier, and she clings to the stronger and obscures his vision" (Woolf, *Common Reader*, p. 250).

Woolf's emphasis on Hardy's subjective "vision," rather than on his fidelity to an objective truth, stands in opposition to much Hardy criticism written during the first three-quarters of the twentieth century, which privileged realism and its premise that good fiction reflected accurately preexisting external facts. Especially during the 1940s and 1950s, with the growing influence of New Criticism and its insistence on the integrity of the text, Hardy's treatment of gender was either silently accepted or praised as an integral part of the organically unified work of art. Historical, social, and generic issues – except when they were invoked as evidence for a work's realism – were generally ignored, and credit for the "truth" of the text was given to the autonomous figure of the author, who was seen to have supreme control over his materials. In this critical climate, at a time when characters were seen as versions of real people, Hardy critics began focusing on intensely personal questions: whether or not Hardy had depicted realistic women, and whether or not he understood them, liked them, or was fair to them. Irving Howe thus confidently declared in 1966 that Hardy had a special knack "for creeping intuitively into the emotional life of women," that "[a]s a writer of novels [he] was endowed with a precious gift: he liked women."[4] Howe's comments were often endorsed by other critics, and many early studies of Hardy's women continued the celebration of Hardy as a man with what Howe had called an "openness to the feminine principle" (Howe, *Thomas Hardy*, p. 109). So in 1976 Anne Z. Mickelson opened her book on *Thomas Hardy's Women and Men* by arguing that Hardy "anticipates much of the thinking in the 1970s on men and women, especially women," and that his approach to "the role of woman in society" is "often searching, sometimes speculative, frequently perceptive, and always compassionate."[5] Three years later, Rosalind Miles praised Hardy for his ability to bring "his female characters so fully to life as women before us." The terms of Miles's praise are almost comical, not only for their excessive enthusiasm and their inconsistent use of metaphor, but also for their seemingly unconscious sexual innuendo: "Hardy suc-ceeded in tapping the vein of trembling wondering love which had originated in him as a child, which had come to fulfilment in his love of Emma Lavinia, and which, though it by-passed her, never ceased to quiver and function."[6] So Hardy's desire for several women, according to Miles, made him supremely understanding of women in general and aided him in the sympathetic and vibrant depiction of his realistic female characters.

This kind of untheorized tribute to Hardy and his characters emerged as recently as 1988 in the judgments of Rosemarie Morgan, who saw Hardy as "transcending" the gender stereotypes of his time in order to create "active, assertive, self-determined women."[7] Acknowledging that Hardy's narrations are sometimes contradictory in their depictions of women, Morgan conveniently isolated and privileged the viewpoint she preferred: "I use the term primary narrator to mean the voice and perspective that, when distinguished from all others, proves to be recognisably coherent, consistent and stable, from the first chapter to the last" (Morgan, *Women and Sexuality*, p. xvii). An even more startling throwback to earlier approaches to Hardy can be found in Robert Langbaum's *Thomas Hardy in Our Time*, published in 1995, which, using Freudian psychology as an unquestioned standard, placed Hardy between George Eliot and D. H. Lawrence for his exploration of "the unconscious and sexuality."[8] The New Critical reading is often tautological, ahistorical, and self-referential in this way: if ideas about gender from Freud or from "the 1970s" can be imposed on Hardy's texts, then Hardy's genius had the remarkable capacity to anticipate those ideas; if portions of Hardy's narrations are objectionable, then these parts of the text can be seen as separate from the primary, stable narration; if certain readers can find versions of themselves in Hardy's fiction, then Hardy somehow had a prophetic vision of those same readers. Hardy, equated with his narrator, is thus given "universal" value, and his characters are seen to be representative of all women and men in all historical periods. Not all New Critical readings of Hardy and his characters were favorable, however. In 1975, Katharine Rogers suggested that Hardy's characterizations of women were negatively biased, and in 1981, Mary Childers confronted Irving Howe by interrogating and complicating his assumption that Hardy *liked* women. Childers offered a salutary corrective to the simplistic notion that Hardy's work could be reduced to the question of whether or not he was fond of women – whatever that might mean – and shifted attention instead to the important issue of masculinity. "In the assertiveness of Hardy's pronouncements about the nature of women," suggested Childers, "the possession of masculinity is secured."[9]

Childers ended her influential article with a caveat that might be seen to mark a crucial shift in studies of Hardy and gender. "One can call this negating gesture [in Hardy's narrative technique] misogyny," Childers commented, or "one can call it male psychology. The possibilities of both social analysis and rapprochement will be increased if we call it male psychology" (Childers, "The Man Who 'Liked' Women," p. 334). Though Childers's language may now appear somewhat dated, her desire to move away from the personal (and ultimately limiting) attack on Hardy's "misogyny" in order to focus on the "social analysis" of his psychological position seems a gesturing away from the New Critical obsession with praising or blaming the author, who is assumed to transcend history and to have absolute control over his text, and toward poststructuralist analysis, with its insistence on both the historicity and the instability of the author, as well as on the cultural production of the text within a system of signs. In any case, such a poststructuralist approach certainly emerged in a sustained form with Penny Boumelha's groundbreaking book, *Thomas Hardy and Women: Sexual Ideology and Narrative Form*, published in 1982.

Boumelha refused to think of Hardy's female characters as mimetic of actual women who are likeable or unlikeable, realistic or unrealistic, positive or negative stereotypes. Instead, aligning herself with Althusserian Marxism and so with an understanding of ideology as a framework of beliefs and social practices "representing as obvious and natural what is partial, factitious, and ineluctably social,"[10] Boumelha saw Hardy's women as cultural signs, representations of historical ideas about women and about gender. Rather than presuming that a fictional representation can be "natural" (or "unnatural"), Boumelha offered a historical analysis of how Victorians understood the "Nature" of "Woman," and she linked this "sexual ideology" to Hardy's use of conventional narrative structures, which themselves embodied particular ideologies. For Boumelha, then, "the radicalism of Hardy's representation of women resides, not in their 'complexity,' their 'realism' or their 'challenge to convention,' but in their resistance to reduction to a single and uniform ideological position" (Boumelha, *Hardy and Women*, p. 7).

This significant move away from concerns with positive or negative readings either of Hardy the man or of his characters has been pursued in recent years by a range of Marxist critics, many of whom include in their analyses ideas about gender. In these studies, attention is given, not simply to female characters, but also to the relationship between understandings of femininity and issues of power. In 1988, for example, John Goode explored the connections between, on the one hand, Victorian understandings of "nature" and gender and, on the other hand, the conditions governing book production; in 1990, Patricia Ingham isolated a "narrative syntax" in Hardy's fiction that used various gendered types – the fallen woman, the New Woman, the poor man, the artist – as its semantic elements; and in 1992, Joe Fisher offered an analysis of Hardy's working-class, and hence "feminine," relationship to the late-nineteenth-century fiction market.[11] That work was followed by Laura Green's recent argument that "Hardy's oblique identification with the ambitions of his heroine is … revealing of the feminized structure of the literary marketplace" and Linda Shires's fascinating analysis of Hardy's anxiety-fraught relationship to the image of George Eliot and her regional fiction.[12] Many of these readings establish important connections between Hardy's class affiliations and his constructions of femininity – an approach that, like that of Ellis, but with different premises and conclusions, connects "Wessex" and Hardy's "rustic chorus" to issues of gender: if a difference of either gender or class can exclude an author or character from the privileges attached to the life of a gentleman, then those same categories can be seen as standing for each other in the fiction; the predicaments of a Cytherea Graye, an

Ethelberta Petherwin, a Bathsheba Everdene, a Tess Durbeyfield, or even a Sue Bridehead might then serve as fictional displacements of the struggles facing a mason's son from Dorset trying to succeed in London's literary marketplace.

Contemporary Marxist criticism has thus been useful in expanding our understanding, to adapt Ingham's metaphor, of how issues of gender might be seen as crucial inflections in the "syntax" of Hardy's fiction. The Marxist emphasis on economies, fiscal and symbolic, has also prodded readers to abandon the ideals of transcendence and universality in order to historicize Hardy, his authorial image, and his fiction. Hardy is no longer the artistic genius actively creating texts that manifest his complete understanding of actual women; he, as well as the texts he produced, is an unstable conduit for the proliferation of various and conflicting discourses about power and gender. This poststructuralist conception of the author is also important for those studies of Hardy that concentrate on his narrative structures, point of view, and voice. Such studies are significant for their potential to focus on issues that affect, both consciously and unconsciously, even the late-twentieth-century reader who is not informed, as a Marxist critic would be, about the position of women in nineteenth-century England, Hardy's class status, or the Victorian literary marketplace. For Hardy's fiction – in large part because its narrative technique both depicts and enacts complicated gendered relationships – still draws fascinated readers, and the dynamic of that fascination is an important topic for literary and cultural analysis.

One of the first critics to look at Hardy's narrative technique in relation to questions about gender was Elizabeth Langland, who argued in 1980 that in *Jude the Obscure* "Hardy lets the perspective of a single character, Jude Fawley, dominate the story. To complicate matters further, it is not clear to what extent Jude's perspective is judged by the narrator, or even ... to what extent Hardy himself is involved in his narrator's and character's perspectives."[13] Though Langland's case might have benefitted from such narratological concepts as focalization and free indirect discourse, which allow for precise analysis of how a supposedly "omniscient" narrator can articulate the visual and ideological perspective of a character, her basic observation, that Sue's notorious inconsistency is a function of the narrator's close identification with Jude, is important and useful, for it leads into a recognition of the extent to which Hardy's narrative technique, however much it may overtly sympathize with women, assumes a male perspective. Characterizations cannot be isolated from narrative technique, in other words, and Hardy's narrative technique is distinctly masculine. Another critic who paved the way for explorations of the gendering in Hardy's narrative technique is Judith Bryant Wittenberg, who in 1983 examined the "almost pathologically voyeuristic" perspective assumed by both Hardy's characters and his narrator in the early novels. She argues of *Desperate Remedies*, for example, that "there is in all of Hardy's fiction no more overtly sexual depiction of the male gaze as a weapon that threatens vulnerable females than in the portrayal of the eye of Aeneas Manston."[14] A similar approach – pursued this time in terms of a complex psycho-analytic understanding of the male gaze – characterizes the influential study of *Tess* by film critic Kaja Silverman, who in 1984 examined the novel's "libidinal economy" in terms of the narrator's contradictory impulses toward fetishization and sadistic control, the two standard responses provoked by male castration anxiety: "The assimilation of [Tess's] form into her surroundings attests to her viewer's or maker's nostalgia for an 'intact state' of things – for a moment prior to differentiation. Her construction as image, on the other hand, speaks to her viewer's or maker's desire for visual control."[15]

Silverman's essay provided the groundwork for an ongoing series of responses to *Tess* that focus on the violence performed by the text on the heroine's body – and, implicitly, on the bodies of women. In 1989, for example, Jean Jacques Lecercle offered a structuralist reading of the novel that saw its style as reinforcing a "violence/woman/language nexus," and in 1993 Elisabeth Bronfen considered the ways in which Tess, as well as other Hardy heroines who die in the text and so become corpses, serves as a trope that "betrays" the ways in which "the inevitable turn to the rhetorical can also engender or be founded on instances of real violation." Also in 1993, Lyn Pykett, providing a valuable historical contextualization for the proble-matic characterizations of both Tess and Sue, theorized the close relation-ship in Hardy's last three novels between the operation of the gaze and their construction of physical bodies: "these works tend both to focus on women as bodies, and to constitute the body (especially, although not exclusively, the female body) as a problem." For Pykett, *Tess*, *Jude*, and *The Well-Beloved* all participate in late-nineteenth-century debates about sexuality, and represent Hardy's own conflicted response to that debate: "Hardy's narrative gaze must, it seems, either look at or away from the female body. It must appropriate the female body, or risk appropriation by it." In the same year, my own essay on Hardy's "Textual Hysteria" similarly saw the responses by Hardy's narrators in both the early and the late fiction as attempting to evade "by a process of projection and dissociation [their] own uneasiness about the body."[16]

These anxieties in Hardy's narrators are not confined to depictions of female characters, or even of human bodies. For in *Hardy's Fables of Integrity: Woman, Body, Text*, an astute and original Lacanian reading of the major novels, Marjorie Garson demonstrated in 1991 that Hardy's anxious concerns "about integrity and wholeness – both psychic and bodily – inform and distort" not only the depiction of "actual human characters," but also the "figurative language which may make the earth, the sky, the heath, the town, the college, the barn, or the house into bodies as well." Garson's analysis uncovered the gendered dimensions of even those seemingly poetic and descriptive passages in Hardy that are generally considered to be gender-neutral. So, for example, the famous "Unfulfilled Intention" outburst by the narrator in *The Woodlanders*, like many other passages in the fiction, contains an "imagery of the exploded body which plays an increasingly insistent role in Hardy's fiction" and "is connected with the eventual disappearance from it of characters like Oak, Clym Yeobright, and Giles Winterbourne, nature's interpreters."[17] Garson's canny observations about the rhetorical effect of Hardy's language lead to the surprising perception that Grace Melbury, in spite of the narrative's overt sympathy with her, can be viewed, in the deep structure of Hardy's plot, as an agent of dismemberment, an exploder of male bodies. All of these readings about Hardyan narration thus have one idea in common: in its focus on women and on female bodies, whether literal or metaphorical, Hardy's fiction manifests a complex combination of arousal and anxiety, of pleasure and unpleasure.

The extent to which a reader is implicated in this conflicted erotic response was confronted directly in 1990 by James Kincaid, who called *Tess* "a titillating snuff movie we run in our minds." Invoking both Havelock Ellis and Algernon Swinburne on the conjunction in sadomasochism of pleasure and pain, Kincaid provocatively asserted that Hardy's novel, by aligning the perspectives of Alec, Angel, Hardy, and the reader, destabilizes the opposition of "normal" and "perverse": "we all wish to create images by distancing, even or especially if that distancing means annihilating. We are all sadists producing images or cadavers to induce sexually titillating pain."[18] Kincaid elided male and female readers in this paradigm, however, a strategy that evaded the problematic position of the female reader in this sadomasochistic model. Does she identify masochistically with Tess, sadistically with Alec and Angel, or both? Or none of these? These are the kinds of questions addressed most directly by Judith Mitchell's clearheaded and informed analysis, published in 1993, of the contradictory position occupied by Hardy's female reader, who, torn between explicit content and the subliminal effects of narrative form, is led to feel "a peculiarly ambivalent kind of pleasure": "Hardy's female reader ... will undoubtedly continue both to applaud his feminism and to deplore his sexism, sensing simultaneously in his novels their 'narrative grammar,' which empathizes so deeply with the plight of the culturally marginalized female, and their 'scopic economy,' in which male consciousness is explored subjectively while female consciousness is quietly and systematically elided."[19] Finally, a reader response that draws together these two possibilities was explored by Margaret R. Higonnet, who suggested in 1993 that a tension in *Tess* between feminine and masculine discourses "exposes the perpetual displacement of woman as figure."[20]

Looking back on this selective history of responses to issues of gender in Hardy, one can see immediately that our terms of analysis increasingly have become both technically and ideologically complex. We no longer have a one-dimensional understanding of Hardy's authorial role, nor do we assume that his texts are perfectly unified. Hardy, his characters, his plots, his language, his images, his narrative devices, his actual and inscribed readers – not to mention his relationships with other texts and with pressing issues of his own time – all are seen to operate in an association of conflict and contradiction: Hardy's texts like women and dislike them; they depict and evoke both pleasure and pain, both arousal and anxiety; they are the source for female readers of frustration and fascination. What more, then, is to be said about Thomas Hardy and matters of gender? Do Hardy's texts continue to function, in Mitchell's words, as "one of the richest and most complex sources of feminist commentary in the realist novel" (Mitchell, "Hardy's Female Reader," p. 186), or have we exhausted their potential (or they ours) to make us think again about sexual difference? My prediction is that they have not, precisely because, as Boumelha argued, they cannot be reduced to any single idea. Hardy's historical position is also a crucial one for our own understandings and performances of gender: publishing his fiction in the years when post-Darwinian theories of sexuality were beginning to take hold, when sexology and then Freudian psychology were being developed, they are an intriguing part of that proliferation of discourses which Michel Foucault saw as helping to form our own late-twentieth-century constructions of sexuality.[21] Where, then, are we headed in our readings of Hardy and matters of gender?

One growing area of concern involves questions about how masculinity is constructed in Hardy's works. Significant attention has always been given to Hardy's central male characters, but only in recent years, with the rise of feminist and queer theory, have critics begun to look at masculinity itself as contingent and changing rather than as normative and stable. A standard work in this new tradition of focusing on masculinity rather than solely on male characters is Elaine Showalter's 1979 essay on *The Mayor of*

Casterbridge, well known partly for its attack on Howe, who, in addition to celebrating Hardy for liking women, also himself *liked* – for reasons that do not celebrate women – the description of Henchard selling his wife:

> To shake loose from one's wife; to discard that drooping rag of a woman, with her mute complaints and maddening passivity; to escape not by a slinking abandonment but through the public sale of her body to a stranger, as horses are sold at a fair; and thus to wrest, through sheer amoral willfulness, a second chance out of life – it is with this stroke, so insidiously attractive to male fantasy, that *The Mayor of Casterbridge* begins.[22]

Showalter quickly demonstrated the extent to which Howe, while bringing "an enthusiasm and an authority to his exposition of Henchard's motives that sweeps us along," in fact "transforms the novel into a male document" (Showalter, "Unmanning," pp. 102–03). Having exposed a characteristic male bias in this *reading* of the text, she then went on to demonstrate how Hardy's novels, and *The Mayor of Casterbridge* in particular, treat issues of masculinity: "Through the heroes of his novels and short stories, Hardy ... investigated the Victorian codes of manliness, the man's experience of marriage, the problem of paternity. For the heroes of the tragic novels ... maturity involves a kind of assimilation of female suffering, an identification with a woman which is also an effort to come to terms with their own deepest selves" (p. 101). Showalter's essay was thus important both for its exposure of sexism in a major work of Hardy criticism and for its insistence that feminist analysis consider the issue of masculinity. Its weakness, however, lay in its New Critical assumption, not altogether unlike that of Howe, that the effectiveness of Hardy's fiction depended on the author's own conscious thoughts about gender issues. Hardy "understood," Showalter argued, "the feminine self as the estranged and essential complement of the male self" (p. 101). In spite, however, of this rather simplistic gender model of essential and balancing opposites, Showalter's essay has had an important impact on Hardy studies: the issue of masculinity is no longer an invisible or neutral one, and, in recent years it has become a crucial topic of analysis.

Since Showalter's essay, Susan Beegel in 1984 presented a New Critical defense of Gabriel Oak's male sexuality in *Far from the Madding Crowd*, and in 1991 Annette Federico offered a historicized reading of Hardy's (and Gissing's) treatments of masculinity as exploring "how notions of masculine identity were beginning to evolve from the solid, monolithic patriarchal role of the mid-1800s to more malleable, less confident styles of manhood." It is also intriguing to see Elizabeth Langland in 1993 building on the perceptions of her 1980 essay about the identification of Hardy's narrator with Jude Fawley's point of view. In "Becoming a Man in *Jude the Obscure*," Langland again saw the characterization of Sue as secondary to the text's obsession with its male protagonist: "This interpretation of *Jude the Obscure* turns attention away from questions of the authenticity of Sue's character – where it has often focused – and queries instead Sue's place in the construction of Jude's masculinity, her role as catalyst for the text's trenchant critique of gender and class paradigms."[23] Again – and here it is on account of Jude's internalization of contemporary ideas about masculinity – inconsistency is seen by Langland to reside in Jude rather than in Sue, who exists in the novel only as a reflection of "Jude's psychosocial investment in her" (Langland, "Becoming a Man," p. 39).

Some of the most adventurous recent explorations of masculinity in Hardy criticism have emerged in relation to the growing and influential field of queer theory. In 1990, for example, Richard Dellamora considered the characterizations of both Jude and Sue in the context of the Wilde trial and the rise of sexology in the 1890s, and in subsequent years he traced the relationship of *Jude* to "Hardy's subliminal inability to deal with the wandering desires of a man like [Horace] Moule," Hardy's mentor who is thought to have made sexual overtures to Hardy and who committed suicide when they were both young men.[24] Dellamora gives particular meaning to a passage, spoken by Jude, which did not appear in the first edition of the novel, but which is part of the holograph manuscript:

> "When men of a later age look back upon the barbarism, cruelty & super-stition of the times in which we have the unhappiness to live, it will appear more clearly to them than it does to us that the irksomeness of life is less owing to its natural conditions, though they are bad enough, than to those artificial conditions arranged for our well being, which have no root in the nature of things!"   (quoted in Dellamora, "Male Relations," p. 471)

These words, according to Dellamora, provide "another instance of the censored and at times self-censored speech of men in nineteenth-century England who realized the need to attend to questions of masculine desire" (Dellamora, "Male Relations," p. 471). Dellamora is not clear, however, about whether or not these "questions of male desire" definitely include homosexual relationships, and Hardy's own reticence on the subject makes certainty impossible. A more productive approach – because it focuses on the effects of Hardy's texts rather than on Hardy's personal thoughts or intentions – was taken by Kincaid, who in 1993 theorized the ways in which *Jude the Obscure* constructs a "reader-as-pornographer/pervert." Kincaid focuses on the scene in which Farmer Troutham beats Jude and argues, as he had in his earlier essay on *Tess*, for a technique that blurs the boundary between "normal" and "perverse": "We are allowed to enjoy the eroticism and also flatter ourselves with our superior sensibility, allowed to identify with and take the pleasure of Farmer Troutham and see him as a beast."[25] Crucial to Kincaid's argument about *Jude* is the fact that Sue is distanced from the reader in a way that Jude is not, and that, as a result, "[i]f Jude is the subject of uninhibited sadism, Sue is caught by the much fiercer monsters of voyeurism" (Kincaid, "Girl-watching," p. 143). Kincaid's analysis, then, finally takes us back to the disturbing dynamic of the sadistic gaze: "We control Sue not with our spanking hand but with our powerful eyes" (p. 145).

The work of Dellamora and Kincaid is opening up valuable new approaches to Hardy's depictions of sexuality. Importantly, both critics point to the ways in which Hardy's fiction simultaneously depicts and elicits sexual responses that are transgressive, not only for their failure to conform with standard rules governing courtship and marriage, but also for their failure to subscribe exclusively to the dictates of compulsory heterosexuality. In this field, however, there remains much to be done. In her groundbreaking book *Between Men: English Literature and Male Homosocial Desire*, Eve Kosofsky Sedgwick makes only brief mention of the Henchard–Farfrae relationship as subliminally erotic,[26] but Hardy's fiction offers great potential for an analysis of a gender framework in which women are the mediating link between men. Homoerotic relationships are pervasive in Hardy, and little has been done with this interesting topic. More ignored still is the subject of female same-sex desire in Hardy, which made an amazingly explicit appearance, complete with a lovemaking scene in bed, in the Cytherea–Miss Aldclyffe relationship of *Desperate Remedies*. Analogous to this is the scene in *The Woodlanders* where Grace Melbury and Felice Charmond, sexual rivals in their respective relationships with Edred Fitzpiers, cling to each other when lost in the woods at night. In these scenes and others (even those involving the milkmaids at Talbothays), Hardy presents physical and emotional ties between women that seem, in the eyes of the twentieth-century reader, startlingly explicit. Yet no one has thoroughly dealt with these relationships or with the broader question of how lesbian desire and/or female same-sex bonds operate in Hardy's sexual economy. A perplexing and intriguing issue is the potential connection between Sue Bridehead and those aspects of the New Woman that were thought to be sexually perverse. Dellamora made the interesting suggestion that in *Jude* the "careful hedging of Sue from intimacy with other women has a valence within the male homosocial economy of the book since Hardy was aware that her wish to retain control of her own body was liable to be construed in contemporary sexology as a sign of sexual inversion. His concern accounts for an imbalance in the sympathy with feminism that one finds in the book" (Dellamora, "Male Relations," pp. 461–62). Yet the very need for Hardy to protect Sue so vigilantly from charges of "inversion" – consider his carefully phrased letter to Edmund Gosse, in which he protests that there is "nothing perverted or depraved in Sue's nature" and that her "abnormalism consists in dispropor-tion: not in inversion" (*Letters* 2, p. 99) – suggests that the book has intertextual connections with a contemporary discourse of lesbian sexu-ality.

Much also remains to be added to the treatment of sexuality in the "minor" fiction and in the poetry;[27] another rich area of investigation is the presence in Hardy's work of a gendered colonial discourse, which has been dealt with most interestingly in Daniel Bivona's fascinating analysis, published in 1990, of "Jude's self-division" as "an arena for cultural conflict between civilization and the primitive past."[28] This sort of study, in fact, might return readers to the original reception of Hardy's work, when his "bestial" women were both celebrated and demonized for their "instinct-led" primitivism. It is Havelock Ellis, after all, who was attracted to Hardy's supposed primitivism and who, some twenty years later, published a book on *Sexual Inversion*, and this strange conjunction once again draws attention to the complex relationship Hardy's texts bear to a whole range of cultural discourses that continue to shape our own constructions of sexual difference. For this reason alone, readers in the twenty-first century will no doubt persist in reading the works of Thomas Hardy for their conflicted and contradictory engagement with matters of gender.

NOTES

1 Judith Butler, *Gender Trouble: Feminism and the Subversion of Identity* (London: Routledge, 1990).
2 D. H. Lawrence, *Study of Thomas Hardy and Other Essays*, ed. Bruce Steele. The Cambridge Edition of the Works of D. H. Lawrence (Cambridge University Press, 1985), p. 109 [originally published in *Phoenix: The Posthumous Papers of D. H. Lawrence*, ed. Edward D. McDonald (New York: Viking; London: William Heinemann, 1936), p. 497].
3 Virginia Woolf, "The Novels of Thomas Hardy," in *The Common Reader*, second series (1932; London: Hogarth, 1965), pp. 250–51.
4 Irving Howe, *Thomas Hardy* (1966; New York: Collier, 1973), pp. 109 and 108.
5 Anne Z. Mickelson, *Thomas Hardy's Women and Men: The Defeat of Nature* (Metuchen, N.J.: Scarecrow, 1976), pp. 1–2.
6 Rosalind Miles, "The Women of Wessex," in *The Novels of Thomas Hardy*, ed. Anne Smith (London: Vision, 1979), p. 26.

7 Rosemarie Morgan, *Women and Sexuality in the Novels of Thomas Hardy* (London: Routledge, 1988), pp. xiii and x.

8 Robert Langbaum, *Thomas Hardy in Our Time* (New York: St. Martin's Press, 1995), p. x.

9 Katharine Rogers, "Women in Thomas Hardy," *Centennial Review*, 19 (1975), 257; Mary Childers, "Thomas Hardy, The Man Who 'Liked' Women," *Criticism*, 23 (1981), 334.

10 Penny Boumelha, *Thomas Hardy and Women: Sexual Ideology and Narrative Form* (Brighton, Sussex: Harvester, 1982), p. 5.

11 See John Goode, *Thomas Hardy: The Offensive Truth* (Oxford: Blackwell, 1988); Patricia Ingham, *Thomas Hardy*. Feminist Readings (Atlantic Highlands, N.J.: Humanities Press International; London: Harvester Wheatsheaf, 1990); Joe Fisher, *The Hidden Hardy* (New York: St. Martin's Press, 1992).

12 See Laura Green, "'Strange [in]difference of sex': Thomas Hardy, the Victorian Man of Letters, and the Temptations of Androgyny," *Victorian Studies*, 38 (1995), 534; and Linda M. Shires, "The Author as Spectacle and Commodity: Elizabeth Barrett Browning and Thomas Hardy," in *Victorian Literature and the Victorian Visual Imagination*, ed. Carol T. Christ and John O. Jordan (Berkeley: University of California Press, 1995).

13 Elizabeth Langland, "A Perspective of One's Own: Thomas Hardy and the Elusive Sue Bridehead," *Studies in the Novel*, 12 (1980), 12–13.

14 Judith Bryant Wittenberg, "Early Hardy Novels and the Fictional Eye," *Novel*, 16 (1983), 155, 159.

15 Kaja Silverman, "History, Figuration and Female Subjectivity in *Tess of the d'Urbervilles*," *Novel*, 18 (1984), 10, 27.

16 Jean Jacques Lecercle, "The Violence of Style in *Tess of the d'Urbervilles*," in *Alternative Hardy*, ed. Lance St. John Butler (New York: St. Martin's Press, 1989), p. 6; Elisabeth Bronfen, "Pay As You Go: On the Exchange of Bodies and Signs," in *The Sense of Sex: Feminist Perspectives on Hardy*, ed. Margaret R. Higonnet (Urbana: University of Illinois Press, 1993), p. 69; Lyn Pykett, "Ruinous Bodies: Women and Sexuality in Hardy's Late Fiction," *Critical Survey*, 5 (1993), 158, 165; Kristin Brady, "Textual Hysteria: Hardy's Narrator on Women," in *The Sense of Sex*, p. 102.

17 Marjorie Garson, *Hardy's Fables of Integrity: Woman, Body, Text* (Oxford: Clarendon Press, 1991), pp. 1 and 93.

18 James Kincaid, "'You did not come': Absence, Death and Eroticism in *Tess*," in *Sex and Death in Victorian Literature*, ed. Regina Barreca (London and Basingstoke: Macmillan, 1990), pp. 29 and 14.

19 Judith Mitchell, "Hardy's Female Reader," in *The Sense of Sex*, pp. 185–86.

20 Margaret R. Higonnet, "A Woman's Story: Tess and the Problem of Voice," in *The Sense of Sex*, p. 28.

21 Michel Foucault, *The History of Sexuality*, Volume I: *An Introduction*, trans. Robert Hurley (1978; New York: Vintage, 1980).

22 Quoted in Elaine Showalter, "The Unmanning of the Mayor of Casterbridge," in *Critical Approaches to the Fiction of Thomas Hardy*, ed. Dale Kramer (London and Basingstoke: Macmillan, 1979), p. 102.

23 Susan Beegel, "Bathsheba's Lovers: Male Sexuality in *Far from the Madding Crowd*," in *Sexuality and Victorian Literature*, ed. Don Richard Cox (Knox-

ville: University of Tennessee Press, 1984), pp. 108–27; Annette Federico, *Masculine Identity in Hardy and Gissing* (Cranbury, N.J.: Associated University Presses, 1991), pp. 15–16; Elizabeth Langland, "Becoming a Man in *Jude the Obscure*," in *The Sense of Sex*, p. 32.

24 Richard Dellamora, *Masculine Desire: The Sexual Politics of Victorian Aestheticism* (Chapel Hill: University of North Carolina Press, 1990), pp. 212–17; and "Male Relations in Thomas Hardy's *Jude the Obscure*," *Papers on Language and Literature*, 27 (1991), 470.

25 James Kincaid, "Girl-watching, Child-beating and Other Exercises for Readers of *Jude the Obscure*," in *The Sense of Sex*, p. 143.

26 Eve Kosofsky Sedgwick, *Between Men: English Literature and Male Homosocial Desire* (New York: Columbia University Press, 1985), p. 113.

27 There has been some valuable work on this material: Jo Devereux, "Thomas Hardy's *A Pair of Blue Eyes*: The Heroine as Text," *Victorian Newsletter*, no. 81 (1992), pp. 20–23; Roger Ebbatson, *Hardy: The Margin of the Unexpressed* (Sheffield Academic Press, 1993); Sarah Davies, "*The Hand of Ethelberta*: Demythologising 'woman,'" *Critical Survey*, 5 (1993), 123–30; Catherine Neale, "*Desperate Remedies*: The Merits and Demerits of Popular Fiction," *Critical Survey*, 5 (1993), 115–22; Mary Rimmer, "Club Laws: Chess and the Construction of Gender in *A Pair of Blue Eyes*," in *The Sense of Sex*, pp. 203–20; Penny Boumelha, "'A Complicated Position for a Woman': *The Hand of Ethelberta*," in "*The Sense of Sex*," pp. 242–59; U. C. Knoepflmacher, "Hardy's Ruins: Female Spaces and Male Designs," in *The Sense of Sex*, pp. 107–31.

28 Daniel Bivona, *Desire and Contradiction: Imperial Visions and Domestic Debates in Victorian Literature* (Manchester University Press, 1990), pp. 108–09.

FURTHER READING

Beer, Gillian. "Finding a Scale for the Human: Plot and Writing in Hardy's Novels." In *Critical Essays on Thomas Hardy: The Novels*. Ed. Dale Kramer, with the assistance of Nancy Marck. Boston: G. K. Hall, 1990, pp. 54–73.

Casagrande, Peter J. "A New View of Bathsheba Everdene." In *Critical Approaches to the Fiction of Thomas Hardy*. Ed. Dale Kramer. London and Basingstoke: Macmillan, 1979, pp. 50–73.

Dalziel, Pamela. "Hardy's Sexual Evasions: The Evidence of the 'Studies, Specimens &c.' Notebook." *Victorian Poetry*, 31 (1993), 143–55.

Gribble, Jennifer. "The Quiet Women of Egdon Heath." *Essays in Criticism*, 46 (1996), 234–57.

Levine, George. "Shaping Hardy's Art: Vision, Class, and Sex." In *The Columbia History of the British Novel*. Ed. John Richetti. New York: Columbia University Press, 1994, pp. 533–59.

Morgan, William W. "Gender and Silence in Thomas Hardy's Texts." In *Gender and Discourse in Victorian Literature and Art*. Ed. Antony H. Harrison and Beverly Taylor. DeKalb: Northern Illinois University Press, 1992, pp. 161–84.

Nunokawa, Jeff. "*Tess*, Tourism, and the Spectacle of the Woman." In *Rewriting the Victorians: Theory, History, and the Politics of Gender*. Ed. Linda M. Shires. New York: Routledge, 1992, pp. 70–86.

Rooney, Ellen. "'A Little More than Persuading': Tess and the Subject of Sexual Violence." In *Rape and Representation*. Ed. Lynn A. Higgins and Brenda R. Silver. New York: Columbia University Press, 1991, pp. 87–114.

Sadoff, Dianne Fallon. "Looking at Tess: The Female Figure in Two Narrative Media." In *The Sense of Sex: Feminist Perspectives on Hardy*. Ed. Margaret R. Higonnet. Urbana: University of Illinois Press, 1993, pp. 149–71.

Scarry, Elaine. "Work and the Body in Hardy and Other Nineteenth-Century Novelists." *Representations*, 3 (1983), 90–123.

Shires, Linda M. "Narrative, Gender, and Power in *Far from the Madding Crowd*." In *The Sense of Sex: Feminist Perspectives on Hardy*. Ed. Margaret R. Higonnet. Urbana: University of Illinois Press, 1993, pp. 49–65.

7

JAKOB LOTHE

Variants on genre: *The Return of the Native*, *The Mayor of Casterbridge*, *The Hand of Ethelberta*

According to Peter Szondi, a crisis in European drama occurs around 1880. The reason for this crisis is essentially generic: drama is no longer absolute and primary (unfolding as a linear sequence in the present), but relies for its effect on narrative elements incorporated into the dramatic structure. Szondi's main example is Henrik Ibsen, in whose plays – such as *Ghosts* (1881) and *The Wild Duck* (1884) – the thematic significance of the actions, dreams, and desires of the main characters is inseparable from their past histories as unravelled through the playwright's sophisticated retrospective technique. "Here the past is not, as in Sophocles' *Oedipus*, a function of the present."[1]

Like most turning-points in literary form, the crisis Szondi identifies in European drama in the late nineteenth century is productive in that it precipitates the formal experimentation of twentieth-century drama. Szondi's notion of crisis also implicitly accentuates the link between various forms of generic interplay and the ways in which the characteristic features or sub-genres of one particular genre can be combined. In the genre of drama, Ibsen's dramaturgic use of the past is partly motivated by his understanding of tragedy. In the genre of the novel, Hardy's extensive use of classical tragedy cannot be separated from the ways in which he attempted to achieve tragic effects through narrative technique and through the form of the novel. If Ibsen's rejuvenation of dramatic form is inseparable from his incorporation of "genre-alien" narrative elements, Hardy's achievement as a novelist is also closely related to, though not solely dependent on, experiments in genre – adapting for example features of tragedy to the narrative fiction he produced. To make this point is not to minimize the differences between Ibsen and Hardy (or between drama and the novel), but it is interesting to note how, at the same time in the history of European literature, two major authors exploit features of other genres as they experiment with their own genre. Thus, the dispute whether tragedy can be written in any literary form other than drama will not constitute a large part of this essay. Rather, it aims to show how variants on genre form an integral part of Hardy's fiction. Widening rather than delimiting the thematic range of the major novels, Hardy's variations of genre blend with modulations of plot, imagery, and narrative structure. In Hardy, generic variations are incorporated into the processes of structuration which the plots of the novels appear to reenact; seen thus they are integral to, rather than superimposed on, narrative form as well as content.

I

As briefly indicated above, it does not follow that all of Hardy's experiments in genre are wholly or unproblematically successful. *The Return of the Native* is a case in point, but before discussing this first example some comments need to be made on the concept of genre in general and on tragedy and the novel in particular.

Genre can usefully be thought of as a means of sub-dividing and ordering different forms of literature. However, although the definition of a given genre is often typological (i.e., presenting itself as being generally valid), genre definitions are not wholly stable but are subject to change in accordance with historical and cultural alterations. A clarifying account of this problem is Mikhail M. Bakhtin's "Epic and Novel." Comparing and contrasting the novel with the epic – which is characterized by national tradition and an absolute epic distance – Bakhtin stresses the novel's dynamism, flexibility, and its formal and thematic range.[2] This characteristic elasticity and generic versatility, which at the same time contribute to and complicate definitions of the novel, derive in part from its tendency to exploit and incorporate elements of other genres into its own. Bakhtin's main example is Dostoevsky, but his point is just as persuasive if applied to the modernist or post-modernist novel. An illustrative example is Franz Kafka's *The Trial*, which, though commonly referred to as a novel, could also be described as a fragment (it has different endings) or a parable (the incorporated parable "Before the Law" is in one sense a condensed version of the whole text).

Hardy's novels provide rich illustrations of Bakhtin's theoretical notions about the genre. With a view to Bakhtin's theory, the experiments in genre which Hardy conducts within the formal framework of the novel corroborate, rather than call into question, essential characteristics of the novel. To discuss such variants is the main critical objective of this essay, but we should not forget that in actual fact they constitute a pattern of variations not just within the genre of the novel but also in Hardy's work as a whole. For Hardy worked in a variety of genres; and the best illustration of his mastery of other genres than the novel is the lyric poetry he wrote subsequent to *Jude the Obscure*. Very few other European authors (Goethe would be one) have made a similarly sustained effort at working in genres as different as the novel and lyric poetry; and if considerations of artistic quality are added to quantitative ones, Hardy's achievement becomes all the more remarkable. The variants on genre observable in Hardy's novels, then, need to be considered in the context of his understanding of literature as art and as a blend of genres. "Novel-writing as an art cannot go backward," he notes on 4 March 1886 (*LW*, p. 183); and on 5 August 1890 he reflects that "art is a disproportioning ... of realities, to show more clearly the features that matter in those realities" *(LW*, p. 239). By "disproportioning" Hardy means that art can and should distort, throwing events and characters out of proportion, and one of the ways in which the novel can achieve this is by adapting and exploring elements of tragedy.

Although Hardy's understanding of tragedy derived in large part from his reading of classical and Shakespearean tragedy, it was colored by notions about the genre prevalent in his own time. Hardy was inclined to see his own work as the writing of tragedy, and numerous nineteenth-century reviewers assumed that his fiction was closely related to this genre. One essential reason for this assumption was the centrality of tragedy in Hardy's times. Characteristically, however, the Victorians – who held tragedy to be a reflector of essential qualities of their culture – understood the genre inclusively, relating it not just to drama but to various facets of Victorian literature and culture. For example, Tennyson's *Idylls of the King* has tragic features, Browning's knowledge of tragedy shaped several of his early dramas and poems, and "the tragic spirit of uncompromised resolute-ness in the face of basic conflict distinguishes the analytical method of Walter Pater's prose."[3]

By the time Hardy began writing, comparisons of the novel with tragedy were common. There was a growing awareness that the novel was becoming the dominant genre, and that it was attempting to achieve, in its own way, many of the things that the older genre of tragedy had done. But what did the word "tragedy" mean in relation to the novel? Jeannette King finds that

> It was frequently used, as it is today, to mean an extremely sad and unexpected event. In fiction, as in life, it usually meant death or some equally final disaster. For many writers, however, this single event illustrated the nature of life in general, a pattern of continuous and inevitable – *not* unexpected – suffering. For them "tragedy" suggested a vision of life, a tragic philosophy, and it is in just such philosophical and moral terms that the comparison between tragedy and the novel is most often made.[4]

In spite of the example of Shakespeare, tragedy still made many Victorian critics think of Greek tragedy. Typically, however, Greek tragedy meant not just the actual drama of Aeschylus, Sophocles, or Euripides but also Aristotle's *Poetics*. If Aristotle almost always has a role to play in any modern discussion of tragedy, his understanding of tragedy is also reflected in that of Victorian critics and, albeit in a different way, in Hardy's notion of the genre. Defining tragedy as "an imitation of an action that is serious, complete, and possessing magnitude,"[5] Aristotle's discussion is predominantly structural, thus contrasting with the increasingly normative and scholastic tradition which extends from Racine's drama (and Boileau's theory of drama) to the neoclassical drama of Swinburne, Arnold, and Tennyson. One distinctive feature of this tradition was the emphasis put upon such supposedly Aristotelian concepts as the noble hero, the cathartic effect, and the rejection of "low" characters; and the failure of a novel to meet these criteria would often make Victorian critics skeptical about its tragic pretensions.

More central to Aristotle's conception of tragedy, however, is the dynamic interplay of key elements such as *hamartia* (infamous tragic error), *peripeteia* (reversal), and *anagnorisis* (recognition). Asserting that "tragedy exhibits a state of things in the life of an individual which unavoidably causes some natural aim or desire of his to end in a catastrophe when carried out" (*LW*, p. 182), Hardy indirectly comments on all of these elements and on their interdependence for cumulative tragic effect. His response is very much that of a novelist, adapting Aristotle's theoretical observations to his own needs and ambitions as a writer of fiction. In a note dated April 1878, for example, he relates his notion of tragedy to aspects of the novel, observing that "a Plot, or Tragedy, should arise from the gradual closing in of a situation that comes of ordinary human passions, prejudices, and ambitions, by reason of the characters taking no trouble to ward off the disastrous events produced by the said passions, prejudices, and ambitions" (*LW*, p. 123).

This note pinpoints several constituent factors in Hardy's fictional use of tragedy. First, the juxtaposition of tragedy and plot suggests, especially if we adopt Peter Brooks's critically stimulating understanding of plot as "the dynamic shaping force of the narrative discourse,"[6] that Hardy conceives tragedy as partaking of narrative form as well as content. For Hardy, as for Brooks as a modern theorist and Aristotle as an ancient one, plot is crucially important for literary structure. Second, the word "ordinary" is interestingly related to "situation," which can be uncommon and challenging. This suggests a latent conflict: "Tragedy arises out of the gap between what the character is – his true self – and what he does – the identity he presents to the outside world" (King, *Tragedy in the Victorian Novel*, p. 99). The word "disastrous," finally, signals that more often than not situation emerges as the stronger of the two factors. Hardy underlines the interplay of situation and character, however: disastrous events happen, yet characters can also produce them. Characters are trapped in history, yet they contribute to its formation from within. Thus Hardy's understanding of tragedy is affiliated with his sense of history. At this level of abstraction too, form and content are interrelated, and they are both associated with the complex issue of representation. As Forest Pyle has observed, "throughout Hardy's work, history functions both as an object of representation and as the condition of representation itself."[7]

II

The titles of Hardy's tragic novels give the reader the first indications of the close, and potentially disastrous, affinity of situation, event, and character. In *The Return of the Native*, the key word "native" not only characterizes Clym but also – though more strongly on a second reading than on a first – provides a first description of Eustacia which is ironic yet strikingly succinct. Moreover, "native" also signals the great significance of the environment where the events take place: the topography of Egdon Heath presents an all-encompassing situation which, appearing boundless spatially and unchangeable temporally, is peculiarly stable and self-sufficiently isolated, and which exerts a powerful influence on the characters throughout. In this novel setting is not just a spatial marker. It topographically delineates and furthers the novel's characteristic unity of place which provides an interesting, if somewhat mechanical, link to classical tragedy. Part of the function of the novel's remarkable first chapter is to elevate the heath from setting to situation in a tragic sense; mapping the field of human activity, it indicates an area superseding and extending beyond such activity.

In the genre of the novel it is highly unusual to devote an initial chapter exclusively to a description of place. In the Hardy canon too this is exceptional; as regards the narrator's positioning of character in the landscape the novel's *second* chapter resembles the beginnings of texts such as *The Mayor of Casterbridge* and *Tess of the d'Urbervilles*. Yet if the absence of characters in chapter 1 does not entail a corresponding lack of tragic elements, the reason is suggested by the way in which the third-person narrative operates: accurately describing the heath as if from the vantage point of a distant observer (e.g., the opening of chapter 3), the narrator tends to generalize – and these generalized statements increasingly indicate the possibility, perhaps inevitability, of tragedy in the setting of the heath: "Every night its Titanic form seemed to await something; but it had waited thus, unmoved, during so many centuries, through the crises of so many things, that it could only be imagined to await one last crisis – the final Overthrow" *(RN,* I, i, p. 4). Affirming the first chapter's status as prologue, key words such as "crisis" and "final Overthrow" point to events which, the reader is invited to infer, will follow the narrator's preamble. The description of the heath's form as "Titanic" lends further support to a reading of the prologue as a prolepsis of tragedy. Suggesting its immense, and potentially destructive, power, the heath's titanic form contrasts markedly with the frailty and vulnerability of human "form" (I, ii, pp. 11, 12). In some ways Hardy's description of the heath resembles, indeed adumbrates, Virginia Woolf's presentation of human absence in Part 2 of *To the Lighthouse.* This modernist novel too has tragic features of loss and isolation, and just as Woolf as it were in the absence of human beings tends to personify the wind and the waves, so Hardy's heath is endowed with distinctly anthropomorphic qualities.

For all its influence on the characters within its boundaries, however, the heath's "face" (I, i, p. 3) is enigmatic. So is, according to the narrator's introductory presentation, one of the main characters, whose "form was ... like an organic part of the entire motionless structure" (I, ii, p. 12). Only gradually (Hardy makes effective use of delayed decoding here) do we infer that the form is that of Eustacia. But whereas the awesome, elemental mystery of the heath suggests a cohesive force with great tragic potential, Eustacia is enigmatic in a more problematic sense: there is a disturbing incongruity between the majestic heath with which she is associated and her limited intellect and imagination. "She desires greatness, but does not know what greatness is" (King, *Tragedy in the Victorian Novel,* p. 103). Hardy's characterization of Eustacia in the famous "Queen of Night" chapter makes the problem conspicuous. On the one hand, a sense of tragedy is evoked through its imagery and by affirming the affinity of Eustacia and the heath; on the other hand, her intellectual shortcomings, her mundaneness and social aspirations, undermine the possibility of tragic action in the classical sense. Yet as Jeannette King has noted, "It is this gap between the world of high tragedy and reality which is the source of her tragedy" (p. 103). Like Gustave Flaubert's Emma Bovary, Eustacia aspires towards something which is attractive because it is unknown. She differs from Emma, however, in the grandeur which follows from her association with the heath she detests. The lasting impression Eustacia makes on the reader derives in part from the third-person narrator's choice to modify the kind of attitudinal distance from her which Flaubert (via his narrator) meticulously observes in his presentation of Emma, and which Eustacia's later dreams and actions seem to demand.

To make this point is to suggest that although the descriptions of Eustacia are partly ironic, the function of irony as an integral part of characterization can be difficult to ascertain. If, as Dale Kramer has suggested, "Eustacia's tragic authority is limited exactly because her own perspective is so myopic,"[8] this shortsightedness involves a prevailing authorial uncertainty about her essential character traits. The features of the tragic hero which Aristotle identifies and discusses are more easily illustrated by referring to Clym than to Eustacia. Thus, while it is uncertain whether Eustacia experiences a peripety (i.e., reversal in her fortunes) in the Aristotelian sense, Clym's main peripety revolves round his sense of guilt after his mother's death: precipitating Eustacia's flight, it has disastrous consequences for his wife and changes his own life completely. Yet in the case of Clym too, Hardy's presentation of the relationship between tragic experience and tragic order is problematically inconsistent. Jeannette King relates this problem, which is formal as well as thematic, to conflicting concepts of tragedy: in *The Return of the Native* Hardy superimposes, more noticeably than in *The Mayor of Casterbridge*, "images of classical tragedy onto a portrait of contemporary life" (King, *Tragedy in the Victorian Novel*, p. 105).

The novel's ending offers a good illustration of how difficult, given the basic conflicts of the plot and its dynamic development, this kind of ambitious combination is to achieve. Hardy's original plan was to organize the novel into five books, like the five acts of Shakespearean tragedy, but he was obliged to add a sixth book of "Aftercourses" to satisfy the wish of his magazine editor for a (more) happy ending. Although critically interesting, and although unquestionably a part of the novel as we now have it, Book VI is distinctly anticlimactic if compared to the account of the deaths of Eustacia and Wildeve at the end of Book V. In Bakhtin's terminology, the narrative discourse of Book VI is predominantly monologic; it is not possessed of the "dialogic tension"[9] which informs Books I to V. Monologism in this case involves a dominance, in "Aftercourses," of narrative statement over narrative presentation of characters in action; it refers to a movement towards harmony which goes against the grain of the novel's narrative thrust, and which also makes the action less unified and problematically extends its temporal span. Moreover, the tragic implications of the deaths of two of the protagonists at the end of Book V are reduced by Hardy's decision to turn Clym into an itinerant preacher and to arrange the marriage of Thomasin and the reddleman.

To draw attention to such imperfections is not to say that *The Return of the Native* fails artistically, nor is it to suggest that Hardy's experiments with tragedy are unproductive. Flawed as it is, this novel is distinguished by an effective narrative rhetoric which goes far towards overriding its inconsistencies, and criticism of its defects must therefore be combined with appreciation of what it achieves as it ambitiously and experimentally plays on the genre of tragedy within the elastic framework of the novel. One of the artistic strengths of *The Return of the Native* resides in the manner in which the sense of tragedy is implemented, sustained, and reinforced by the light/dark and north/south imagery which permeates the novel,[10] and which is inseparable from Egdon Heath. Suggesting a sense of doom, it indicates that there is no escape – in time or space – from the plot sequence in which the characters are inextricably involved.

III

If *The Return of the Native* shows us Hardy in the process of learning how to appropriate the genre of tragedy for his own creative writing, in *The Mayor of Casterbridge* he is able to handle tragedy in a more self-assured way. There is no need to decide which of the two novels is "better" (both are major works in the Hardy canon), but we can note two significant variations. First, although in the former novel too the sense of tragedy is heightened by the interplay of past and present actions, in *The Mayor of Casterbridge* this interaction is crucial and takes the form of a repetitive pattern of irony and reversal, connecting it more closely with Greek tragedy. Second, while the plot of *The Return of the Native* seems to further a problematically imprecise notion of tragedy, partly because it needs to accommodate character features and character experiences as different as those of Eustacia and Clym, *The Mayor of Casterbridge* is distinguished by the centrality of the novel's protagonist and by his great tragic potential.

That Henchard's unique position in this novel bears a close relation to tragedy becomes apparent from a summary of the action; and it is confirmed by the novel's full title: *The Life and Death of the Mayor of Casterbridge: A Story of a Man of Character*. "Character" is a key word: it signals the author's respect for his main character and can be related to the concept of *ethos*, the Aristotelian term under which essential qualities of the tragic hero can be subsumed. In Aristotle's understanding of tragedy, *hamartia* forms an essential part of the main character's *ethos*. However, and this is relevant to our understanding of Henchard as a tragic character, as *hamartia* is a kind of flaw in a character who is "good," it takes the form of a weakness or blind spot within a range of good qualities. Compare

Henchard's two decisive acts at the beginning of the novel: first he sells his wife for five guineas to a sailor, then he says the oath aloud "and seemed relieved at having made a start in a new direction" (ii, p. 20). The first act is central to Henchard's *hamartia*, but it typically describes effect rather than cause. Obliquely illustrating Aristotle's definition of *hamartia*, it actualizes Hegel's notion of tragedy as the site of a conflict between two incompatible but equally valid laws, embodied in two individuals or in the collision between what the protagonist has "knowingly done ... [and] what he was fated by the gods to do and actually did unconsciously and without having willed it."[11] Yet if Hegel's theory of tragedy is not as different from that of Aristotle as some critics have argued, this is partly because an Aristotelian concept such as *hamartia* is *productively* imprecise. We do not understand why Henchard sells his wife, but Hardy makes us sense that he could have done it (and that alcohol is the catalyst of the event rather than its primary cause).

Opposed as they appear to be, Henchard's decisive acts of selling his wife and taking the oath are, from the perspective of tragedy, curiously interlinked. As Robert Heilman has observed of tragic form, "there is a pulling apart within the personality, a disturbance, though not a patholo-gical one, of integration. The character is not 'one,' but divided."[12] Thus, Henchard's contrastive acts are both commensurable manifestations of the tragic *ethos*; as a character he is tragic rather than melodramatic. His character is divided, invaded: "All the great characters in tragedy are invaded, made to house the alien in our midst and thus, like Lear, made 'houseless.'"[13]

The thematic effect of Henchard's acts at the beginning of *The Mayor of Casterbridge* depends crucially on their narrative presentation. For Hardy as novelist, experiments in the genre of tragedy involve a further develop-ment of a third-person narrative characterized by the narrator's detached, and often strikingly visual, observation of his characters. There are, however, notable variations of narrative distance, and these are further combined with modulations of perspective, generalized statements, and interspersed dialogue. Throughout the novel dialogue functions not only as basis for dramatic action but also as the foundation of, as well as a narrative variant on, the third-person narrator's informative statements and reflections. Although the transitions between these narrative situations can be jerky, the interplay of the two modes constitutes a vital aspect of the text's narrative method. Furthermore, considering Hardy's exploration of tragedy through the form of the novel, it is striking how much the dialogue can reveal, and how characteristic it is of the text's broad narrative move-ment. An example from chapter 11:

"I like the idea of repeating our marriage," said Mrs. Henchard after a pause. "It seems the only right course, after all this. Now I think I must go back to Elizabeth-Jane, and tell her that our kinsman Mr. Henchard kindly wishes us to stay in the town." (xi, p. 74)

The passage illustrates how closely the sense of tragedy is associated with repetition, which permeates *The Mayor of Casterbridge*. Considering the novel as a tragedy, the concept of repetition may usefully be diversified by means of J. Hillis Miller's distinction between two forms of repetition. The first form, what the French philosopher Gilles Deleuze calls "Platonic" repetition, is grounded in an archetypal model which is untouched by the effects of repetition and of which all the other examples are copies. "The assumption of such a world gives rise to the notion of a metaphoric expression based on genuine participative similarity or even identity."[14] Positing a world based on difference, the other, Nietzschean mode of repetition assumes that each thing is unique, intrinsically different from every other thing. Similarity arises against the background of fundamental difference, and there is, finds Miller, "something ghostly about the effects of this second kind of repetition" (*Fiction and Repetition*, p. 6).[15]

The frequently paradoxical manner in which these two forms of repetition co-exist in *The Mayor of Casterbridge* reinforces the novel's tragic dimension. In the quoted passage an illustrative paradox is embedded in the interpretation of Susan's words as a sudden move towards the second form of repetition, or at least as a modification of the first form which the opening of her speech seems to comply with. That this change cannot be observed prior to a second reading itself tells us something about the sophistication of Hardy's third-person narrative. The crucial phrase is "our kinsman," which to the informed reader is, of course, a lie (since Elizabeth-Jane is the daughter of Newson, not Henchard). Why then does Susan "like the idea of repeating our marriage" when she knows of this fact? Perhaps not just because she wants Henchard to believe that Elizabeth-Jane is his child but also because of her surprisingly resigned attitude – a resignation which in Hardy is so often connected with, indeed prompted by, understanding (compare Clym's reaction to his failing eyesight). But if, contrary to the surface meaning of her words, Susan senses that remarrying Henchard may prove ominous, then she has achieved an insight comparable to that of the third-person narrator, and then the form of repetition extractable from her words is the second rather than the first.

Suggesting that the dominance of Henchard as protagonist does not preclude the possibility of character development on the part of the minor characters, this interpretation stresses the tragic potential of the two forms of repetition as they co-exist, in peculiarly alogical fashion, in *The Mayor of Casterbridge*. Henchard's decisions and acts are variously repetitive throughout; and a number of these repetitions can be related to the concepts of *hamartia*, peripety, and *anagnorisis* (recognition). Though hard to pinpoint exactly, Henchard's *hamartia* has an element of hubris, accentuating the interrelationship between character on the one hand and fate or chance on the other. Acting impulsively and then regretting his actions, Henchard makes decisions the consequences of which he cannot possibly foresee, and which therefore become, especially on a second reading of the novel, subject to irony. Like Sophocles' Oedipus, Henchard invites danger as he attempts to escape it. For example, although the eagerness with which he implores Farfrae to stay on in Casterbridge suggests hope (of a competent assistant in the corn business), it is accompanied by a vague sense of fear. Reinforcing the third-person narrator's distance from the protagonist, this fear is more obviously associated with the narrator rather than with Henchard. It is characteristic of Hardy's experiments with tragedy in this novel that the vantage point of the third-person narrative tends to approximate the position of a helpless spectator who, like the chorus in Aeschylus' *Oresteia*, expresses not just hope but also impotence and a fear of inevitable disaster.

Henchard's peripety is closely linked to his *hamartia*. One of the means by which we are led to suspect that Henchard's hopeful reunion with his wife may in fact lead to his delayed punishment is the ellipsis (the temporal anachrony of eighteen years between chapters 2 and 3) which signals that the narrative's focus is not on Henchard's spectacular rise to the office of mayor but on its reversal: his slowly spiralling decline which, towards the end of the novel, involves a painful *anagnorisis*. Henchard's sense of having arrived at his life's end is very strong in the two last chapters of *The Mayor of Casterbridge*. The distance between narrator and character is here primarily one of knowledge, presenting a picture of Henchard as vulnerable, disoriented, and fundamentally alone. For example, when he thinks he has identified the site where he committed his crime twenty-five years ago, he mistakes similarity for identity: "it was not really where the tent had stood, but it seemed so to him" (*MC*, xliv, p. 319). As often during the process of Henchard's decline, the irony activated here is tragic as well as dramatic: there is a marked contrast between the individual and his actions, wishes, and hopes on the one hand, and the workings of the unyielding power of fate or chance on the other.

For Miller, this example illustrates how the first form of repetition (associated with Henchard) is contradicted by the second form (associated with the narrator). However, a significant narrative variation emerges through the interspersed, descriptive passages that portray a changed

Henchard, and that show how the distance between narrator and character decreases. Two paragraphs further on it is as though the protagonist – unconsciously, through his actions – has fathomed the paradoxical impossibility of returning to Casterbridge as well as of leaving the town for good. Instead, his tragedy is sealed as he performs a repetitive, circular movement: "his wandering, like that of the Canadian woodsman, became part of a circle, of which Casterbridge formed the centre" (p. 319). Moreover, refusing to make "another start on the upward slope" (p. 320), he reveals an insight comparable to, and probably exceeding, Susan's, and approaching that of the narrator. As Henchard, through this subtle narrative variation, shows an affinity with the second form of repetition, the ending of *The Mayor of Casterbridge* presents a complex, essentially tragic thematics generated by the way in which Hardy's narrative exploits both forms of repetition simultaneously.

IV

Broadly, then, Aristotle's description of the characters of tragedy as good, appropriate, lifelike, and consistent applies to Henchard, whose *ethos* conforms to, indeed seems to be constituted in accordance with, the most central notions of tragedy expounded in the *Poetics*. Yet, although Hardy's fictional exploration of tragedy predominates in *The Mayor of Casterbridge*, and although tragedy is the most important single variation in his novels, several of his works explore the possibilities of the novel by activating genres such as comedy and pastoral. An example is *The Hand of Ethelberta* (1876), a novel with distinctly comic features which was written between *Far from the Madding Crowd* and *The Return of the Native*. That Hardy regarded *The Hand of Ethelberta* as a comedy is evident from the subtitle: "A Comedy in Chapters"; and in his Preface to the novel he describes it as a "frivolous narrative" (*HE*, Wessex Edition, p. v). Its plot centers on Ethelberta's spirited efforts to maintain her social position after she is left a widow at twenty-one; as she eventually secures an old peer for her husband (while her admirer Christopher Julian is left to marry her sister Picotee), the reader may get the impression of an old-fashioned novelette rather than a searching, innovative novel.

The faults of *The Hand of Ethelberta* have been identified and discussed by several critics; they include a partly unconvincing plot, a similarly unengaging mix of minor characters, and extended passages of cumbersome and ineffective narrative discourse. To agree that *The Hand of Ethelberta* is a relative failure, however, is not to say that it is critically uninteresting. Remarkably different from the novels it succeeds and precedes, it suggests that Hardy's career as a novelist might easily have taken other directions than it actually did. Briefly indicating the variations of genre in this text, we first note that by moving the action from a rural to an urban environment (London and Sandbourne) Hardy not only introduces a new setting but also establishes a town–country, London–Wessex opposition which is central to his treatment of London society. Although the urban setting predominates (and the rural side of the opposition remains largely implicit), the contrast gives edge to Hardy's presentation by introducing a satirical element into the overall comedy. As Michael Millgate has observed, "If *The Hand of Ethelberta* is very obviously a Comedy of Society, deliberately satirical and contemporary, it is also an ambitious exploration of social and moral values – not an aberration in Hardy's career but rather an experiment with techniques and areas of subject-matter which he had not previously exploited in print."[16]

Combined with the urban setting, characterization contributes considerably to the formation of comedy in *The Hand of Ethelberta*. Two constituent factors of characterization are variations of narrative perspective and the use of narrative counterpoint. An example of this method is the central scene where Ethelberta is a guest at a fashionable dinner party (Wessex Edition, xxix, pp. 165–73); here the third-person narrator's perspective approximates to that of the servants (especially Picotee), who eavesdrop and comment on the upper-class company. The main reasons why Ethelberta appears to be exempted from satirical contempt are suggested by her status as attractive heroine and, perhaps more importantly, by the link which her modest origin provides with the lower classes and with country life. Her complexity as a character is enhanced by the way in which she emulates upper-class attitudes from the perspective of an outsider. Yet, although the combination of her humble background and London career as a professional story-teller may suggest an autobiographical resemblance between the main character and Hardy as author, critics have tended to overemphasize the novel's autobiographical element (which is observable, as an integral part of the fiction, in all of Hardy's novels – most notably in *Tess of the d'Urbervilles*).

If we ask what makes the novel's scenes and characters comic, a partial answer is provided not so much by the theory that laughter is generated by a sense of superiority (a notion of comedy associated with Hobbes, Bergson, and Meredith), but rather by the theory (associated with Kant, Baudelaire, and Freud) that it is produced by a sudden sense of the ludicrous and the incongruous. Aristotle briefly comments that comedy imitates "persons worse than the average ... [because of their] ridiculousness" (*Poetics*, p. 49); and although it would be misleading to claim that

The Hand of Ethelberta portrays English upper-class society as simply "ridiculous," this quality is not wholly absent from the novel's satirical exposure of contemporary social phenomena – especially if these are compared to the typical way of life in rural Wessex. More than a hundred years on, a number of the novel's observations on class, and class distinctions, remain acute; and thus *The Hand of Ethelberta* dramatizes, as Edward Blishen puts it, "some persisting English discomforts."[17]

Broadly speaking, however, Hardy's variations on the pastoral are more convincingly integrated into his overall experimentation with genre, and better attuned to his idea of Wessex as a fictional universe uniquely his own, than is the comedy evinced by a text such as *The Hand of Ethelberta*. This said, the notion of comedy as a generic variant in Hardy needs to be diversified. *A Pair of Blue Eyes* and *Two on a Tower* both combine comedy and tragedy; and the tragic novels can incorporate comic elements. In *The Return of the Native*, for instance, such elements add vitality to the description of rustic country life on Egdon Heath. If the effect of this kind of comedy is quite different from the social satire of *The Hand of Ethelberta*, this is largely because, as becomes obvious already in the introductory description of Egdon Heath, comic elements are repeatedly qualified by tragic and pastoral ones. Qualification, though, is not elimination, and the fact that comedy is not altogether absent from the discourse of the tragic novels is a reminder that some of Hardy's minor characters fare better in life than do Eustacia, Henchard, Tess, or Jude. This kind of interplay of tragic and comic features conforms to a tradition which goes right back to Aristophanes (some of whose comedies have been seen as inversions of Euripides' tragedies).

The thematic effects of Hardy's uses of pastoral can be similarly ambiguous, qualifying or reasserting distinctive parts of both comedy and tragedy. As pastoral characteristically blends with the topography and thematic texture of Wessex, however, it is arguably essential to his achievement in a way comedy is not. In order to make this suggestion, which posits a productive linkage between Hardy's fictional creation of Wessex and his uses of pastoral, the genre needs to be understood quite inclusively as a fictional imitation of rural life as related to, though by no means solely defined by, an imaginary Golden Age. The genre is commonly seen as beginning with Theocritus' *Idylls* (third century BC); and in *Don Quixote* Cervantes ingeniously employs pastoral as he inserts narratives about shepherds into the main narrative, and also draws on the genre when he concludes the novel.

In Hardy as in Cervantes, two of the most intriguing facets of pastoral are the sense of peaceful interlude it provides and the sense of loss it provokes. In Hardy these two facets are often interlinked, though obviously the sense of loss is stronger in a tragic novel such as *Tess* than it is in, say, *Far from the Madding Crowd*. In conjunction with a distinctive strand in the genre's tradition, an elegiac tone obtains in Hardy's use of pastoral. Like most nineteenth- and twentieth-century authors, Hardy, to use Friedrich Schiller's concepts, is a sentimental writer in that he is conscious of being distanced from the nature he describes.[18] For Hardy as for Schiller, "nature" is both a spatial and temporal marker; and part of the significance of Hardy's fictional incorporation of pastoral is suggested by the way in which his exceptional knowledge of one particular topography (Wessex) combines with his appreciation of a disappearing era (early to mid-nineteenth century) to specify his sentimental attitude. Its sense of loss is integral to Hardy's understanding of history, which, though it does not romanticize the past, is skeptical about the far-reaching effects of mechanization and urbanization.

Reinforcing the historical dimension of the novels, and endowing "primitive" rural life with vitality and dignity, pastorals in Hardy's use of the genre also create idyllic interludes which effectively contrast with the tragic endings of many of the plots. This observation applies to the broad narrative movements of texts such as *The Return of the Native*, but Hardy can also draw on pastoral in order to contrast different ways of life, and different attitudes to nature, in one narrative situation. Chapter 47 of *Tess of the d'Urbervilles*, for example, opens with a descriptive, remarkably visual, first paragraph: "It is the threshing of the last wheat-rick at Flintcomb-Ash Farm. The dawn of the March morning is singularly inexpressive, and there is nothing to show where the eastern horizon lies" (*T*, p. 315). However, as Tess and Izz Huett arrive in this beautiful setting, the kind of work awaiting them is not of the habitual, manual sort described earlier in the novel, but instead work conditioned by the newly introduced "red tyrant that the women had come to serve ... the threshing-machine, which, whilst it was going, kept up a despotic demand upon the endurance of their muscles and nerves" (p. 315). A sense of pastoral is evoked by the suggested affinity of the scenery and traditional, manual work, whereas the contrastive metaphor of "red tyrant" not only introduces the threshing-machine but also adumbrates the characterization (in the fourth paragraph) of the engineer as an intruder ("He was in the agricultural world, but not of it").

To stress the thematic significance of Hardy's uses of pastoral is to reaffirm the importance of Wessex for his fictional achievement. Hardy's Wessex is, in Michael Millgate's phrase, "located somewhere in a vague, unspecifiable past, seeming all the more elusive of historical definition because of the very success with which it evoked a remote and almost timeless rural world" (Millgate, *Career*, p. 248). The constellation of three constitutive elements in this accurate description – the past, timelessness, and rural world – suggests that the description of Egdon Heath at the beginning of *The Return of the Native* emblematically delineates Hardy's fictional universe. As J. Hillis Miller has observed, this description takes the form of "an extended prosopopoeia. The heath is personified as a great brooding creature, neither male nor female, beyond sexual difference."[19] Thus two genres are productively combined: while the pastoral aspect is retained, the heath is personified as "titanic" and potentially dangerous, evoking a sense of tragedy as history.

A first concluding point of this discussion, then, is that in Hardy's fiction variants on genre occur not just successively and cumulatively from work to work: there are also structurally sophisticated combinations of genre within several of the major novels, and such generic modulations considerably extend the thematic range of the texts. They make the novels' thematics more conflicting and diverse, juxtaposing characteristics of different genres and activating various facets of their long traditions.

Second, Hardy's variations of genre are conducted within, and by means of, the narrative and structural register of the novel. As Bakhtin has shown, the novel's generic flexibility makes it eminently well-suited to this kind of fictional exploration. The novel allows, for example, for "the full exploitation of subjectivity as an index to tragedy ... in *Tess of the d'Urbervilles*" (Kramer, *Forms of Tragedy*, p. 113). Since subjectivity here, as Kramer suggests, reveals the influence of Ibsen, we can see how, in one and the same text, Hardy's understanding of the genre of tragedy in general blends with his response, as a writer of fiction, to the work of one particular dramatist. Although Hardy's narrative method may seem quite traditional, it is more complex and nuanced than it appears at first sight. Proving highly congenial to generic variation, it involves the use of an unidentified third-person narrator (who is part of the fiction but located outside and subsequent to its action), variations of narrative distance and perspective, complex (frequently paradoxical) combinations of the first and second forms of repetition, and clusters of imagery and metaphor. In one sense, Hardy's narrative method is a generic variation in its own right, as it serves to engender and shape a set of highly original novels at a crucially transitional stage of European literary history. At the same time, Hardy's narrative enables him to explore other genres as well.

Third, although this discussion has been dealing with significant variants on genre in Hardy's work, it does not follow that these are the only genres Hardy uses. In addition to comedy and tragedy, Hardy plays on a number of the novel's sub-genres; and although pastoral is one of the most interesting, his novels can also, as Marjorie Garson has demonstrated, be read "as fables about the constitution of the self and about its inevitable dissolution."[20] Moreover, there are intriguing elements of oral narrative in Hardy – legend, ritual, fairy-tale, even parable. At this point too, aspects of genre are related to issues of narrative. The historical dimension of both concepts is striking in Hardy; for him, as for Walter Benjamin, the movement of history involved a gradual transition from the (essentially rural and simple) community of which oral story-telling was an integral part to the situation of the novelist as a lonely writer.[21]

Finally, for Hardy generic experimentation is not an aim in itself, but is integral to his investigation of the possibilities of the novel as a genre. Not just playing on literary genres, Hardy productively exploits other art-forms – painting, sculpture, architecture, music – in his creative work as a novelist. If the exploration of tragedy is the most significant single variant on genre in Hardy's fiction, part of the reason is that the novels forcefully present tragic features which include a sense of doom, contingency, and hopelessness, yet also incorporate a deep respect for human passion, stamina, and moral integrity. Hardy's tragic thematics defy attempts at summarized statements. If there is a thematic core or center in Hardy's universe it is vast, boundless temporally as well as spatially. It is perhaps best described by Hardy himself as he, concluding the poem "In a Museum," situates the song of an ancient bird and the voice of a choir boy

In the full-fugued song of the universe unending.

NOTES

1 Peter Szondi, *Theory of the Modern Drama*, ed. and trans. Michael Hays (Minneapolis: University of Minnesota Press, 1987), p. 16, and see also pp. 8–9. Originally published as *Theorie des modernen Dramas: 1880–1950* (Frankfurt a.M.: Suhrkamp, 1956).
2 Mikhail M. Bakhtin, "Epic and Novel," in *The Dialogic Imagination: Four Essays by M. M. Bakhtin*, ed. Michael Holquist (Austin: University of Texas Press, 1981), pp. 3–40.
3 Dale Kramer, *Thomas Hardy: "Tess of the d'Urbervilles"* (Cambridge University Press, 1991), p. 72.
4 Jeannette King, *Tragedy in the Victorian Novel: Theory and Practice in the Novels of George Eliot, Thomas Hardy and Henry James* (Cambridge University Press, 1978), p. 2.
5 *Aristotle's Poetics*, trans. James Hutton (New York: Norton, 1982), p. 50.
6 Peter Brooks, *Reading for the Plot: Design and Intention in Narrative* (Oxford: Clarendon Press, 1984), p. 13.

7 Forest Pyle, "Demands of History: Narrative Crisis in *Jude the Obscure*," *New Literary History*, 26 (1995), 359.

8 Dale Kramer, *Thomas Hardy: The Forms of Tragedy* (London and Basingstoke: Macmillan, 1975), p. 64.

9 Mikhail M. Bakhtin, "Discourse in the Novel," in *The Dialogic Imagination*, p. 314.

10 J. B. Bullen relates such contrasts to Hardy's "verbal portraiture"; see his *The Expressive Eye: Fiction and Perception in the Work of Thomas Hardy* (Oxford: Clarendon Press, 1986), pp. 88–117.

11 G. W. F. Hegel, *Aesthetics: Lectures on Fine Art*, II, trans. T. M. Knox (Oxford: Clarendon Press, 1975), p. 1214.

12 Robert B. Heilman, *Tragedy and Melodrama* (Seattle: University of Washington Press, 1968), p. 7.

13 Adrian Poole, *Tragedy: Shakespeare and the Greek Example* (Oxford: Blackwell, 1987), p. 38.

14 J. Hillis Miller, *Fiction and Repetition: Seven English Novels* (Oxford: Blackwell, 1982), p. 6. See also Gilles Deleuze, *Logique du sens* (Paris: Les Éditions de Minuit, 1969).

15 For more extended discussion, see my "Repetition and Narrative Method: Hardy, Conrad, Faulkner," in *Narrative: From Malory to Motion Pictures*, ed. Jeremy Hawthorn (London: Edward Arnold, 1985), pp. 118–23.

16 Michael Millgate, *Thomas Hardy: His Career as a Novelist* (1971; London and Basingstoke: Macmillan, 1994), p. 115.

17 Edward Blishen, "Hardy, *The Hand of Ethelberta*, and Some Persisting English Discomforts," in *Celebrating Thomas Hardy: Insights and Appreciations*, ed. Charles P. C. Pettit (London and Basingstoke: Macmillan, 1996), p. 177.

18 Friedrich Schiller, "On Naive and Sentimental Poetry," in *German Aesthetic and Literary Criticism: Winckelmann, Lessing, Hamann, Herder, Schiller, Goethe*, ed. Hugh B. Nisbet (Cambridge University Press, 1985). Originally published as "Über naive und sentimentalische Dichtung," *Die Horen* (1795–96).

19 J. Hillis Miller, *Topographies* (Stanford University Press, 1995), p. 26.

20 Marjorie Garson, *Hardy's Fables of Integrity: Woman, Body, Text* (Oxford: Clarendon Press, 1991), p. 1.

21 See Walter Benjamin, "The Storyteller" (trans. Harry Zohn), in *Illuminations*, ed. Hannah Arendt (London: Fontana, 1979), pp. 83–109.

8

PENNY BOUMELHA

The patriarchy of class: *Under the Greenwood Tree, Far from the Madding Crowd, The Woodlanders*

Central to all of the novels under discussion here is a story of love, courtship, and marriage. More particularly, for the central female character in each case, this central fable takes the form of an erotic or marital "double choice," to use Franco Moretti's phrase;[1] the woman is first attracted to the "right" partner, then distracted by one or more "wrong" partners before confirming – whether emotionally or formally – the "rightness" of the original choice. Also central to all three, though, is a perhaps less familiar story of class mobility and social allegiance, focused through the narrative structures of fluctuating economic fortunes, ownership of property, the accumulation of financial or social capital, trading, and inheritance. These two central points of concern are, of course, deeply interconnected, thematically and in narrative terms. The triangulated relationships of potential lovers represent marital choice as the primary mode of class transition for women; it is evident that, though Fancy, Bathsheba, and Grace have all received a good education, in each case it functions rather as a marital asset than as an alternative path for class mobility. So, the vicissitudes of the lovers display the panoply of social possibilities for the heroine, and the eventual choice of husband is at the same time the choice of class position, or at least of economic and/or social status. The choice turns out slightly differently in each case. In the simplest of the three texts, *Under the Greenwood Tree*, Fancy Day only mildly flirts with the possibility of accepting a richer or more educated suitor before confirming her choice of Dick Dewey the carter. In *Far from the Madding Crowd*, Bathsheba Everdene over time accepts all three suitors – the penurious half-aristocratic Troy, the wealthy landowner Boldwood, and the (variously) farmer, shepherd, and bailiff Gabriel Oak; the "right" choice can only be confirmed by the melodramatic elimination of the rivals. In the complex and self-consciously sardonic *The Woodlanders*, Grace Melbury is never allowed (or obliged) to sacrifice her social rise for the confirmation of her original choice, Giles Winterborne, though the rightness of the attachment is nonetheless allowed a brief and consolatory *post mortem* confirmation. In each case, the presence of differences of class serves at some point to stimulate romance, to merge ambition and desire, and to thwart fulfillment.

Of course, the choice to be made is never *only* about class position. In each case, the first-presented suitor represents a certain sturdy, faithful worth apparently associated with his being native to the locality, while the other possibilities may include a sexually compelling but faithless new-comer such as Troy or Fitzpiers, and a wealthy but unattractive older man such as Shiner or Boldwood. What might be called moral merit seems to be related directly to occupation: in each case, the "good" suitor is engaged in manual labor, the feckless suitor is as far from it as can be imagined, and the wealthiest option is a landowner. It would be easy to deduce from this a kind of sexual pastoral, in which the unshowy virtues of the hero represent the timeless qualities of a stable rural society in the heart of nature, disrupted by the influence of city-dwellers and outsiders who bring with them inappropriate ideas, aspirations, and values threatening the survival of the locality. This is a view that has often been argued, and indeed all three of the texts draw upon the conventions of the pastoral mode in a way that might appear to endorse it: the use of the seasonal cycle to structure the time-span of events, for example, or the association of the hero with fruitful labor, or the references to fertility rites and folk rituals, or the use of resonantly symbolic and allusive rural phenomena such as flocks of sheep or apple-trees. But in my view, such elements are self-consciously used to question as well as to evoke the values of the pastoral, and it would be a great mistake to settle for seeing in these novels a representation of country life as an idyllic and timeless enclave, sheltered from the pressures of contemporary life.

Rural society, for Hardy, is just that: a *society*, in which exploitation, solidarity, and the struggle for survival are experienced quite as keenly as they are in urban settings. Mellstock, Weatherbury, and Little Hintock are not simply backdrops for the sympathetic engagement of nature with human activities, but places of work and unemployment, financial loss and gain, social hierarchy and economic transaction. Economic and social detail is precise and significant: such episodes as the twopence Oak pays so that Bathsheba can pass through the turnpike gate, Marty's sale of her hair for two sovereigns to supplement her meager piecework earnings, or Mrs. Day's anxiety to make known to the neighbors the quality of her tablecloths and cutlery are constant reminders of the determining power of economic and class relations, even when they also carry other kinds of figurative weight. Work is taken in a serious and specific sense; in the symbolic set piece of the storm scene of *Far from the Madding Crowd*, for example, the reader is still always made aware of *how* Gabriel's experience of work enables him to predict the weather or *how* he goes about saving the ricks. We know how money is acquired and lost, how much things cost and laborers are paid, what domestic as well as agricultural labor supports the local economy. Clearly then, interpretation of these novels will need to focus on their realism as well as their obeisances to pastoral convention.

The plot of marital choice that I have outlined above combines the issues of gender and class in making clear the extent to which the social fate of the heroine depends upon the class and economic position of her husband; as Mr. Melbury puts it, "a woman takes her colour from the man she's walking with" (*W*, xii, p. 86). Class position and economic position may be at variance, of course; Fitzpiers is clear that he has "stooped to mate beneath" himself (*W*, xxxv, p. 251) even though he is supported by the money of the Melburys. Nevertheless, whereas a hero can marry "up" or marry "down" without significantly transforming his own position, the social status of the heroine is secondary and derivative as soon as she marries. This combination of class and gender in the marital plot is important, and will be further discussed in the accounts of the individual texts below, but there are also other issues to be considered in relation to Hardy's mapping on to one another of the social discourses and facts of class and gender.

Hardy's concern with cross-class romance could almost be described as obsessive, and it persists virtually throughout his writing career. Indeed, his first (unpublished and now lost) work bore a title that could almost serve as an epigraph to his fiction: "The Poor Man and the Lady." This continuing concern is fueled, I think, by an eroticization of class difference, in which the "otherness" of the other class is conceived through a kind of melancholic desire. That this cross-class desire is not simply a transposition into other terms of social ambition is evident, because it appears to be the *difference*, and not the class position in itself, that carries the erotic charge. In any case, it traverses the divisions of class in all directions (doctor for working girl, or educated woman for laborer, as well as shepherd for farmowner or maid for aristocratic soldier), so that it by no means always implies any form of social gain. At the same time, the prevalence of class-disparate romance in Hardy also means that the representation of gender difference is shot through with an alertness to questions of power, status, and inequality. The love relationship is, in a sense, perceived as inherently politicized, and antagonisms and rivalries of class are installed at the heart of desire. Gender difference and class difference, working in the space between antagonism and desire, are both represented as relations of power, and their intersections can take various forms. The different distributions of power are not necessarily singular and uni-dimensional, though; gender privilege and class privilege may reinforce one another (as in, say, Fitzpiers's casual appropriation of Suke Damson), but they may just as easily be in conflict (as in Bathsheba's dismissal of Oak from her employ for the way he speaks to her as a woman) or in other complex forms of overlap. Exploitation, patronage, and solidarity can function together or contradictorily within the social relations of class and those of gender.

Further, the mapping on to one another of issues and relations of class and gender has an important role to play in denaturalizing the differences upon which both forms of social organization are predicated. The differences come to be seen as contingent and arbitrary rather than as inherent and fixed, as they were presumed to be in much of the ideology of the period. For instance, the concern of the novels with actual or potential *changes* of class position makes it impossible to see social status as fixed once and for all by birth or descent. Nor is it only the plot of sexual choice that rests upon class mobility; the novels are full of characters who are (in the terminology of the time) self-made or of decayed aristocratic stock, and Gabriel Oak demonstrates the volatilities of class position in his migrations between landowner and wage-laborer status. Change, mobility, and choice are to the fore in the representations of class difference. At the same time, these novels combine – often rather unsettlingly – numerous voices of conventional wisdom about the nature of women and their difference from men with other moments that destabilize the certainties of the nineteenth-century gender polarity. The scenes of shared labor crucial to the representation of fulfilled love between Gabriel Oak and Bathsheba Everdene and of the thwarted love of Marty South for Giles Winterborne stress likeness and commonality rather than difference. Bathsheba's fear that her social and economic power may have made her "mannish" is answered decisively but unexpectedly in Liddy's positing of gender convergence rather than polarity: "not mannish; but so almighty womanish that 'tis getting on that way sometimes" (*FMC*, xxx, p. 209). At moments such as those I have cited, differences – whether of class or of gender – are clearly shown as products of history rather than of nature.

Although the representation of class and gender differences and alliances is not confined to the heterosexual love relationship, it is there that Hardy locates their pains and pleasures at their sharpest. Difference itself is often powerfully erotically charged. There is, I think, something fetishistic about Hardy's textualization of sexuality, and it is often expressed in a slightly disturbing way through the disembodied gender significations of clothes; the scene in which the gazes of the members of the Mellstock Quire all "converge ... like wheel-spokes" upon Fancy's boot, lovingly exploring its "flexible bend at the instep" and "rounded localities of the small nestling toes" (*UGT*, I, iii, pp. 25–26) is echoed by the scene of the assembled wives and mistresses of Fitzpiers staring at his abandoned nightshirt, or by Boldwood's secret amassing of a hoard of silk and satin dresses, sable and ermine muffs, all carefully labeled "Bathsheba Boldwood" as if they substituted for the woman herself. Perhaps it is because of this erotic dimension to his understanding of difference that Hardy so notably conceives and represents the intensely social discourses of gender and class in almost entirely individual terms. Certainly, both class and gender shape and color the experience and relationships of individual characters, but the novels are almost devoid of any sense of collectivity. The rises and falls of class position happen through and to individuals; Oak's catastrophic loss of his investment, for instance, is due to his foolishness in leaving his freshly lamb-fed dogs unattended, rather than to changes in market prices.

Where gender is concerned, matters appear rather different. Though there is little of female friendship in the novels, both *Far from the Madding Crowd* and *The Woodlanders* contain important moments in which a recognition of commonality of experience between women overcomes the way in which their own emotional interests place them at odds; in the first, Bathsheba takes responsibility for Fanny's burial and grave initially because it is her role as employer, but then out of fellow-feeling, while in the second, Grace Melbury and Felice Charmond cling together in the woods in a mutual acceptance of the suffering of the other. Nevertheless, in each case that commonality rests upon the private experience of the love relationship, and then only because the man (and not just the situation) is in each case shared. It is striking, too, that none of the central female characters in these texts has a mother; Fanny and Grace have stepmothers, Bathsheba has (if only briefly) an aunt, Marty South has only a father. The effect is to heighten the sense of isolation in which these characters live out their common dilemmas.

This absence of mothers also throws into sharper relief, at least in the cases of Fancy Day and Grace Melbury, the patriarchal power of the father, whose role it is to make, accept, or refuse the marital choice on behalf of his daughter. Mr. Day's attempt to prevent Fancy marrying Dick and Mr. Melbury's early desire to force Grace to marry Giles are only apparently opposites; in fact, they betray the same social power. In each case, too, the primary concern of the father is whether his daughter, educated beyond the level of her family and her peers, will justify the investment by making a socially advantageous marriage. In other words, the daughter is at once the object of and the vehicle for the social ambition of the father. But if the social ambition belongs to the father, the social mobility belongs to the daughter. A kind of freedom, it nevertheless threatens to leave her "as it were in mid-air between two storeys of society" (*W*, xxx, p. 214) until one or other of the class-positions is confirmed by the status of the husband. The exercise of such patriarchal power, if not always by a literal father, will prove tragic in some other of Hardy's texts, but in these interrelated novels, it is shown in the end to be futile. In *Under the Greenwood Tree*, the father's power to make the marital choice on behalf of his daughter is comically subverted – with, it must be said, only a token resistance – by the notably unsupernatural intervention of the wise woman Mrs. Endorfield. In *The Woodlanders*, the father's power is carefully foregrounded in Melbury's vacillations as he impels Grace in one direction and then another according variously to the dictates of his conscience, his ambition, or his information. Finally, he is left looking rather pathetic by Grace's decision to return to Fitzpiers, which he is unable to fit into the scheme of his own power: "I have been a little misled in this ... there has been some mistake – some arrangement ... which I didn't quite understand" (*W*, xlviii, p. 359). In both texts, then, the social power of the father is asserted even as his individual power is undermined through the structure of the narrative.

Under the Greenwood Tree, according to its author's 1912 Preface, deals with the story of the church musicians and their eclipse "lightly, even ... farcically and flippantly at times" (*UGT*, Preface, p. 5). Much the same could be said of its rather mild and low-key version of Hardy's central plot-motif, marital choice among class-differentiated suitors. Here, class differences are small, their determinations upon behavior insignificant, and their ultimate impact minimized; work and economic exploitation are largely absent; rivalries are minor, mistakes are rapidly retrieved, and tragedies averted. Narrative elements that will become significant in the other novels under discussion have not yet made their appearance: no man is financially ruined, no woman seduced and abandoned, and no one dies for love. Nevertheless, even in this lightly sketched version, it is the representation of class and gender relations that gives the novel much of its interest.

The text focuses in part upon a tension between community and individualism, tradition and modernity. It features a group of men – the Mellstock Quire – for whom the order of things, social as well as natural, lies in stasis, cycle, and repetition. Images of literal stasis (the picturesque, the statuesque, the silhouette) abound, and the novel's pastoral structure, focused on the cycle of the seasons, takes the narrative from the communal festivities of Christmas to those of Dick and Fancy's wedding. Against this background are set the two individual men whose role is to rupture the cyclical pattern and disrupt the stasis. Parson Maybold breaks the rhythm of the church festivals by substituting Fancy's "free" solo playing (*UGT*, IV, v, p. 167) of the organ for the communal performance of the Quire. Mr. Shiner has no respect for the traditions of the (literally cyclical and repetitive) dance:

> "All I meant was," said Dick, rather sorry that he had spoken correctly to a guest, "that 'tis in the dance; and a man has hardly any right to hack and mangle what was ordained by the regular dance-maker, who, I daresay, got his living by making 'em, and thought of nothing else all his life."
> "I don't like casting off: then very well: I cast off for no dance-maker that ever lived." (*UGT*, I, vii, p. 53)

Positioned between the group who want things to stay the same and the individuals who want to change them is Fancy Day, so that her choice among available suitors represents also a choice among attitudes to community and tradition. As Gatrell has pointed out,[2] the novel is full of expressions of suspicion and distrust toward women, voiced in a kind of choric fashion by the Mellstock men. From the moment when Fancy's boot disrupts the group by compelling their attention at once to its workmanship and its embodiment of femininity, neither the reader nor the members of the Quire are ever in doubt that the male group of the outset will yield to the heterosexual couple of the conclusion. Fancy's role, it seems to me, is to represent femaleness; it does not depend upon, or even require, any individualization of her. The reader is given virtually no direct representation of any desire, intention, or feeling of Fancy's; all must be inferred from the commentaries and interpretations of (male) others, and are usually generalized on the basis of gender. "[Women] be all alike in the groundwork: 'tis only in the flourishes there's a difference," advises Mr. Dewey (*UGT*, II, viii, p. 108). At the same time, though, Dick's doubts, wonderings, and general confusion are scrupulously reported to the reader: "This brought another meeting, and another, Fancy faintly showing by her bearing that it was a pleasure to her of some kind to see him there; but the sort of pleasure she derived ... he could not anyhow decide, although he meditated on her every little movement for hours after it was made" (*UGT*, II, i, p. 69).

As a result, thrown into relief against Dick's guileless incomprehension, Fancy often comes to seem a skillful manipulator, possessed of mysterious and unexplained knowledge about the ways of the world. In the conversation that leads to Dick's proposal, for instance, there is no level of commentary guiding the reader to know whether Fancy has consciously set out to elicit it, but the self-evidence of his naivety seems to impute worldly knowledge to her. This superior knowledge seems, too, more in the nature of womanly instinct than evidence of her much-vaunted education; the novel certainly allows her precious little of scholarship and intellectual activity. The narrative voice, then, is more or less aligned with the collective wisdom of the Mellstock Quire as Dick is initiated into the ways of women. As a result, the largely cynical generalizations about women receive a degree of narrative endorsement, as when Mr. Dewey's views are confirmed as "truth": "*In fact*, it is just possible that a few more blue dresses on the Longpuddle young men's account would have clarified Dick's brain entirely, and made him once more a free man" (*UGT*, IV, i, pp. 142–43; italics added).

Since there are no other young and marriageable women of any narrative significance in the text, Fancy is almost the exclusive focus of both erotic attention and gender generalizations, and her status as a kind of queen bee among the workers of Mellstock is brought out by the repeated references to beehives. In a sense, then, Fancy *is* Woman for the novel: if she is fickle, it is because women are fickle, and if the novel tells us Woman is fickle, it is because Fancy is fickle. Just as Tess Durbeyfield will later be "pure woman" precisely *because* she is impure, so Fancy Day is "perfect woman" (*UGT*, III, iv, p. 135) precisely by virtue of her imperfections; complete in her incompleteness, she is, for this text, the singular example of "united 'ooman" *(UGT*, I, vi, p. 44).

Fancy's symbolic choice between the old ways and the new comes to what is in a sense a predictable conclusion: a compromise. She does displace the Quire from the church, but she also adopts many of the old-fashioned customs, in order to have a wedding like her mother's. Her exposure to the ways of "persons of newer taste" (*UGT*, V, ii, p. 193) allows her to bring about some modest changes in manners and habits. This ending in compromise does not constitute an avoidance of resolution, though; it marks the novel's final recognition that the breaking of pattern and cycle by the intrusion of desire is in turn itself a pattern, a cycle. Only this, after all, enables the group to recognize from the moment of his first enraptured gaze that Dick Dewey is a lost man: "Distance belongs to it: slyness belongs to it: queerest things on earth belongs to it. There – 'tmay as well come early as late, s'far as I know. The sooner begun the sooner over; for come it will" (*UGT*, II, iii, p. 75).

Though pastoral and mythological allusions are still significant, *Far from the Madding Crowd* is a novel in which class and economic relations assume a much more prominent status. If not exactly predicated upon class, its central romance is certainly permeated by work, money, and considerations of social status. The fluctuations of Oak's fortunes, and indeed of Bathsheba's, are carefully detailed. Economic motivations are often powerful, as when Troy's final return to his wife is motivated as much by her ability to keep him as by the recrudescence of desire. Most importantly, the literal and metaphorical language of economic transaction – of debt, waste, begging, investment, gamble, and contract – here both doubles and displaces the language of emotional interaction: Bathsheba feels she owes Boldwood a "'debt, which can only be discharged in one way,'" for example, and his final proposal to her is improbably as "'A mere business compact'" (*FMC*, li, p. 368 and liii, p. 386). The sense that Bathsheba and Oak are right for each other is mediated through their development of what might be called the great virtues endorsed by the text: shared work and shared commitment to the importance of labor and money. In this last, they are distinguished from the fecklessness of almost all those around them. The detail of working life in the novel, considerable as it is, is also accompanied by the detail of work refused, wasted, or neglected. To some extent, the early Bathsheba and Oak share the same carelessness; she wishes she could afford to pay a man to do the work for her, and he dozes off to sleep and loses his sheep. They help to educate one another into responsible workers and landowners, with money-saving interventions as the currency of their romance. The twopence that Bathsheba will not pay at the turnpike and Oak's reputation as a "near" man, one who mends his own socks even when he can afford not to, predestine them for one another as surely as anything more romantic. The equilibrium of the end is doubly enabled: obviously, by their economic equivalence as Oak's application and thrift help him to climb back from wage-earning status to capital accumulation, but also by Bathsheba's final half-articulated proposal to Oak – a proposal which, to pick up one of the novel's dominant metaphors, she *owes* him.

The proximity of love relationships and economic relations (debt, dependency, possession) in the novel draws attention to its conception of gender relations as suffused by distributions and inequalities of power. For a novel which is certainly, on one level, among the great literary romances, *Far from the Madding Crowd* is also curiously, strikingly full of episodes of malice, both human and otherwise. Probably the most obvious and extreme instance comes in Troy's torturing of Boldwood by delaying the news of his marriage in a way that impels his rival to offer him higher and higher bribes. But there are other such moments, too, great and small: Bathsheba's sacking of Oak, his refusal in return to save her sheep until she begs, Troy's repudiation of Bathsheba over the coffin of Fanny Robin, the gargoyle's destruction of his dilettantish efforts at atonement, even the man at the workhouse's stoning of the dog that has assisted Fanny along the Casterbridge highway. Again, the novel's romance is repeatedly undercut by undertones of antagonism and even violence in its representation of erotic and love relationships: rowelled spurs, shears, swords, lashing reins, guns, mark the various stages of relationship. Troy's symbolic seduction of Bathsheba in the hollow amid the ferns takes the form of a sword-exercise, and its intensity has something faintly sado-masochistic in its exaggerated performances of cowering and swagger:

> She shuddered, "I have been within an inch of my life, and didn't know it!"
> "More precisely speaking you have been within half an inch of being pared alive two hundred and ninety-five times."
> "Cruel, cruel 'tis of you!"
> "You have been perfectly safe nevertheless. My sword never errs."
>
> (FMC, xxviii, p. 196)

Beside this figurative violence there also runs another, related strain of imagery. Though there is what might be called a narrative endorsement of Bathsheba in the novel's final scene of quiet marriage, it is also noticeable that the process of maturation which fits her to Oak is represented – often though her own speech or consciousness – as a humiliation, a taming, a conquering. Similarly, Boldwood is reduced from his initial haughty independence to a state of pitiful obsession and eventual incarceration, and Fanny Robin's suffering after her abandonment by Sergeant Troy is portrayed at a length and with a relish hard for the reader to enjoy. The world of desire and passion is here one of extremity and violence. That the novel is able to conclude with romance fulfilled is due largely to the displacement of sexual relationship, at least between Oak and Bathsheba, by economic interaction. It is less as male and female that they are finally united than as landowners, workers, and social equals. Their engagement is confirmed by the discussion of "the details of his forthcoming tenure of the other farm. They spoke very little of their mutual feelings" (FMC, lvi, p. 409).

There is a sense in which this is a surprising outcome; no first-time reader, I think, could predict from the novel's opening that particular turn of events. It begins rather awkwardly. Gabriel Oak is what might be called a class-type, representing and delimited by his social position: a faintly ridiculous rustic with his "ruddy mass" of a face, his "emphatically large" boots, and a watch that has only one working hand (FMC, i, pp. 7–8). Bathsheba, similarly, begins as a gender-type, an enactment of "[w]oman's prescriptive infirmity" (FMC, i, p. 10), complete with emblematic looking-glass. It seems appropriate that their earliest interactions are so disjointed and uncommunicative, each observing the other from carefully described vantage points as if they occupied distinct narrative spaces. As the novel progresses, however, something very different happens. The point is not that the evolution of the individual characters takes them further from stereotype, but rather that the very bases of the types are undermined. It is not a change in Bathsheba, but a different understanding of gender, that takes the novel from "[w]oman's prescriptive infirmity" to a situation in which Bathsheba is "so almighty womanish" that it abuts the mannish (*FMC*, xxx, pp. 209). Similarly, that Oak becomes gentleman enough for Bathsheba is not only due to his accumulation of capital, nor to any development that we know of in his dress or social habits, but also to a changed idea of the determining power of class. The exuberant ideological confidence of the novel's opening is chastened along with its characters in the course of the narrative.

In many ways, *The Woodlanders* draws upon the same range of narrative elements and allusions as these predecessors. It is a much more disturbing novel than either, though, in its gesture towards and final avoidance of the expected conclusion, its blurring of the roles of its initially clearly opposed hero and villain, and its unsettling generic ranging across social comedy, tragedy, and melodrama. There are two elements in particular, though, that create the sense of disturbance: the peculiarly unstable character of class and sexuality, and the prevalence of obsession. From the interaction of the two emerges something quite different in the handling of the central plot of marital choice.

As in the earlier texts, love and desire act as the medium of significant patterning of relationships and characters. At the same time, relationships among the central characters are often very *specifically* socio-economic. That is, relationships of class alliance and antagonism here take the form of relations of employer and employee, landlord and tenant, workmates and traders. For all the novel's allusions to Sophoclean tragedy, Norse mythology, and pastoral, *The Woodlanders* clearly does not represent "one of those sequestered spots outside the gates of the world" (*W*, i, p. 8). Rather, its society is grounded in economic interaction and sexual desire, often in complex interaction. It is a novel in which the language of "fate" and "destiny" is harnessed to something very much more like a materialist determinism:

> As with so many right hands born to manual labour, there was nothing in its fundamental shape to bear out the physiological conventionalism that gradations of birth show themselves primarily in the form of this member. Nothing but a cast of the die of Destiny had decided that the girl should handle the tool; and the fingers which clasped the heavy ash haft might have skilfully guided the pencil or swept the string, had they only been set to do it in good time. (*W*, ii, p. 10)

There is, then, nothing natural or inherent about class position. It does not betray itself in intrinsic physical traits – nothing about Grace shows Fitzpiers that she is not his social equal – though in time it *becomes* written upon the body, in Melbury's sore back as much as Marty's right hand. This idea contributes to the pervasive sense of class mobility in the novel: Felice the "lady of the manor" is an actress who married a wealthy manufacturer, Melbury is a self-made man, the professional Fitzpiers comes from an aristocratic family in decline, the coffin-stool in Marty's cottage reveals a formerly wealthy family background. In this disturbingly mobile social environment,[3] Grace is repeatedly described in economic terms, as a valuable gift, as yielding a return, as raw material or value added. She is, in a sense, an asset in transactions among men, who can cancel Melbury's debt to his wronged rival, or confer money and status on Giles, or balance money and social degradation for Fitzpiers. Most of all, she is Melbury's investment in the future and his profit from a lifetime's labor, and, like all capital, she must be carefully husbanded. Melbury's fixation on Grace's social position drives the plot, and there is real pathos in his prospective satisfaction that she might fulfill his obsessive social ambition by becoming too socially elevated to acknowledge him in public: "If you should ever meet me then, Grace, you can drive past me, looking the other way. I shouldn't expect you to speak to me, or wish such a thing – unless it happened to be in some lonely private place where 'twouldn't lower 'ee at all" (*W*, xxiii, p. 159).

Melbury is an obsessive in a novel of obsessives. At times – as with John South's inexplicable identification with the tree outside his window – it seems that irrationalism governs the novel. More particularly for my argument here, the combination of a high level of mobility and of obsessive single focus which runs through the novel's representation of social status is replicated in its version of sexuality. The plot is full of second marriages, infidelities, promises made and broken, actual or multiple attachments, and (at least as a possibility denied) divorce. It shows a society of what might be called erotic mobility, within which each sexual attraction exercises a power so compelling that it reduces character after character to symbolic somnambulism. As with class position, there is a sense that erotic choice is both arbitrary and determining; neither is fated, but each imposes its own fate. Once Marty's hands have been set to piecework, the chances of her acquiring artistic and musical accomplishments diminish to vanishing point. Similarly, once a sexual choice has been made, it cannot simply be ignored: Felice's murder at the hands of a rejected lover, Giles's death from typhoid and chivalry, Grace's departure with Fitzpiers after a narrow brush with the man-trap, all result from sexual commitments broken but not unmade.

Clearly, the novel's focus on the provisionality of class position and the restlessness of desire significantly transforms its fable of marital choice. The profoundly non-monogamous sexuality represented does not lend itself to any symbolically definitive commitment. It is fitting that Grace's choice of a suitor is in turn so restless and transitory, continually made and unmade until the novel's conclusion takes her out of the society of Little Hintock altogether. Grace acts as the appropriate focus of the novel's social and erotic choices precisely because she spends so much of it in a state of suspension, "between two storeys of society" (W, xxx, p. 215), "neither married nor single" (W, xl, p. 293), "a conjectural creature" (W, v, p. 39). Grace's vacillations and uncertainty signify the complexity of the novel's version of the plot of marital choice.

If the concluding couple of *The Woodlanders* frustrates expectations of rightness endorsed, there is one relationship of equality in the novel. Giles and Marty have the shared work, shared knowledge, and shared language that in *Far from the Madding Crowd* confer its rightness upon the Bathsheba–Oak marriage. In the erotically compulsive and socially restless world of *The Woodlanders*, though, their unchanging comradeship is sterile because it stands apart from the shifting obsessions of desire: "In all our outdoor days and years together, ma'am ... the one thing he never spoke of to me was love; nor I to him," says Marty (W, xliv, p. 327). Where difference is the erotic spur, their complementarity finally isolates them from their society and from each other.

In these three pastorally influenced novels of marital choice, then, class difference is as central to the generation of desire and its thwarting or fulfillment as gender difference. Indeed, it might even seem that, under the constraints imposed by nineteenth-century publishing conventions, experimentation with class position stands in for its sexual equivalent. It is important, though, that Hardy's versions of gender and class are never displacements of one another. Whether in the simplicity of Fancy's choice, the false starts that Bathsheba's financial independence allows her, or Grace's restive and half-made commitments, it is the interplay and contradiction between these two powerful social discourses that is the focus of narrative attention. In Hardy's fiction, the plot of romance – often seen as the plot of the private life – is profoundly social.

NOTES

1 Franco Moretti, *The Way of the World: The "Bildungsroman" in European Culture* (London: Verso, 1987), pp. 248–49, n. 33.
2 Simon Gatrell, "Introduction," in *UGT*, pp. xviii–xix.

3 See John Bayley, "A Social Comedy? On Re-reading *The Woodlanders*," in *Thomas Hardy Annual No. 5*, ed. Norman Page (London and Basingstoke: Macmillan, 1987), p. 17.

FURTHER READING

Bayley, John. *An Essay on Hardy.* Cambridge University Press, 1978.

Elbarbary, Samir. "The Male Bias of Language and Gender Hierarchy: Hardy's Bathsheba Everdene and His Vision of Feminine Reality Reconsidered." *Cahiers Victoriens et Edouardiens*, 41 (1995), 59–79.

Garson, Marjorie. *Hardy's Fables of Integrity: Woman, Body, Text.* Oxford: Clarendon Press, 1991.

Goode, John. "Hardy and Marxism." In *Critical Essays on Thomas Hardy: The Novels.* Ed. Dale Kramer with the assistance of Nancy Marck. Boston: G. K. Hall, 1990, pp. 21–38.

Green, Laura. " 'Strange [In]difference of Sex': Thomas Hardy, the Victorian Man of Letters, and the Temptations of Androgyny." *Victorian Studies*, 38 (1995), 523–49.

Higonnet, Margaret R., ed. *The Sense of Sex: Feminist Perspectives on Hardy.* Urbana: University of Illinois Press, 1993.

Ingham, Patricia. *Thomas Hardy.* Feminist Readings. Atlantic Highlands, N.J.: Humanities Press International; London: Harvester Wheatsheaf, 1990.

Jacobus, Mary. "Tree and Machine: *The Woodlanders*." In *Critical Approaches to the Fiction of Thomas Hardy.* Ed. Dale Kramer. London and Basingstoke: Macmillan, 1979, pp. 116–34.

Kramer, Dale. "Revisions and Vision: Thomas Hardy's *The Woodlanders*." *Bulletin of New York Public Library*, 75 (1971), pp. 195–230, 248–82.

Kramer, Dale, ed. *Critical Approaches to the Fiction of Thomas Hardy.* London and Basingstoke: Macmillan, 1979.

Levine, George. "Shaping Hardy's Art: Vision, Class, and Sex." In *The Columbia History of the British Novel.* Ed. John Richetti. New York: Columbia University Press, 1994, pp. 533–59.

Miller, J. Hillis. *Thomas Hardy: Distance and Desire.* Cambridge, Mass.: Harvard University Press, 1970.

Morgan, Rosemarie. *Women and Sexuality in the Novels of Thomas Hardy.* London: Routledge, 1988.

Morgan, William W. "Gender and Silence in Thomas Hardy's Texts." In *Gender and Discourse in Victorian Literature and Art.* Ed. Antony H. Harrison and Beverly Taylor. DeKalb: Northern Illinois University Press, 1992, pp. 161–84.

Poole, Adrian. " 'Men's Words' and Hardy's Women." *Essays in Criticism*, 31 (1981), 328–45.

Scarry, Elaine. "Work and the Body in Hardy and Other Nineteenth-Century Novelists." *Representations*, 1/3 (1983), 90–123.

Williams, Merryn, and Raymond Williams. "Hardy and Social Class." In *Thomas Hardy: The Writer and His Background.* Ed. Norman Page. London: Bell & Hyman, 1980, pp. 29–40.

Wittenberg, Judith Bryant. "Angles of Vision and Questions of Gender in *Far From the Madding Crowd*." *Centennial Review*, 30 (1986), 25–40.

Wotton, George. *Thomas Hardy: Towards a Materialist Criticism*. Dublin: Gill & Macmillan, 1985.

Wright, T. R. *Hardy and the Erotic*. London and Basingstoke: Macmillan, 1989.

9

LINDA M. SHIRES

The radical aesthetic of
Tess of the d'Urbervilles

Chapter 2 of *Tess of the d'Urbervilles* (1891) opens by describing Marlott, the village where Tess was born. But the passage goes beyond mere description by providing the reader with important aesthetic directives. After locating the village geographically in "the Vale of Blakemore or Blackmoor" and noting that tourists and landscape painters have usually avoided the valley, Hardy's narrator predicts that its beauty will attract future visitors. Yet he quickly chills the enthusiasm of such prospective viewers. After initially asserting that the fertile spot never succumbs to dried-up springs or brown fields, he now calls attention to the "droughts of summer" only to recite further obstacles: poor ways to travel, difficult roads, and consequent disappointments one might want to avoid. The narrator then reverses himself again by insisting that any traveler from the coast will inevitably be "delighted" by contrasts between the calcareous downs and lush cornlands (*T*, ii, p. 18).

It is easy to misread these oscillations in emphasis as something approaching equivocation. Yet, quite to the contrary, Hardy here conditions his readers by exposing them to a multitude of conflicting impressions. Offering different reasons for coming to the valley, different routes, and different kinds of walks, he introduces further variables by mentioning the pace of arrival, vertical/horizontal positionality, weather, time of year, and decisions about whether to come with a guide or alone. And, by including the two names used for the valley, Blakemore and Blackmoor, he suggests that place-names are socially constructed and that any meanings we ascribe to settings are as historically conditioned as our impressions of people or events.

Hardy's description of the valley is thus neither simply figural nor symbolic, but epistemological. It discourages the reader from making an easy analogy between the unspoiled valley and the purity of Tess, or from making the topography serve any understanding of future events. The description refuses to offer the guidance provided, for instance, by Jane

Austen's symbolic description of Pemberley, Mr. Darcy's country estate in *Pride and Prejudice*. This is not to deny that in many landscape descriptions Hardy establishes correspondences between the "soul" of a landscape and a human drama enacted by characters. But the drama enacted here is primarily that of coming to a new scene and it is a drama enacted by readers, rather than the nameless figures Hardy casts as tourists and painters.

Hardy here knowingly destroys a common literary convention, employed not only by Austen but by many other authors, novelists, and poets. Sir Walter Scott, George Eliot, Elizabeth Gaskell, William Wordsworth, S. T. Coleridge, and Percy Shelley offer symbolic landscapes in which each detail is endowed with emblematic significance by the perspective of a central narrator or strong poetic "I" who acts as the repository of sure, omniscient, and omnipresent wisdom. Here, instead, the narrator very much stresses every point of view as equally noteworthy and limited.

Prior critics of Hardy and of this novel have debated such issues as elements of narrative, imagery, philosophy, and the relationship of the author to his heroine (Bayley, DeLaura, Gregor, Howe, Lawrence, Lodge, Miller). Others have looked carefully at the novel and tragic form (Kramer). Some have read the novel sociologically (Williams, Goode, Wotton). Several critics have explored gender and class issues (Ingham, Boumelha, Brady, Morgan, Higonnet). A few have attended carefully to language use (Taylor) and jarring aspects of style (Zabel, Kincaid, Widdowson).

With a few important exceptions, such as Kincaid and Widdowson, critics who have studied Hardy's style, whether in passing or more fully, have read his novels pre-eminently through a realist, humanist lens. Their comments inevitably are cast in terms of a personal split they read either from Thomas Hardy the man into his work or from that work back onto the "nature" of the man. *Tess*, such critics say, acutely reflects such a division. The novel's intellectualism, marked by philosophical musings and cultural quotations, strikes them as being at odds with a high value placed on natural simplicity and purity.

Usually astute readers such as John Bayley and J. B. Bullen have thus offered explanations for a schizophrenic artistry. Some point to Hardy's class origin and subsequent rise; some explain this split as one of mental control and sad lapses. They name the two aspects of Hardy's creative personality: "consciousness and unconsciousness," "two voices," or "two views." Simon Gatrell's introduction to *Tess*, with more sophistication, offers a fantasy of two Thomas Hardys and rejects it in favor of a composite. His composite goes beyond a dialogue, struggle, or stand-off between two Thomas Hardys. One of the few novel critics to connect Hardy with Keats, Gatrell argues that Hardy could also "rest in uncertainties, mysteries, doubts, without any irritable reaching after fact and reason" ("Introduction," *T*, Oxford Classics Edition, p. xx.). Still, Gatrell returns to connect this "habit of mind" to "opposing insights of two Thomas Hardys." Hardy's narrative openness has still to be fully linked to the historical moment and the intellectual traditions informing it. Moreover, this capacity to rest in uncertainties must be viewed as more than a simple duality.[1] Rather, mental, emotional, philosophical, and ideological checks and balances are translated into a highly self-conscious interplay of narrative agents.

Only two critics, to my knowledge, explain the formal and ideological fractures of Hardy's texts in terms of the historical moment. Terry Eagleton and John Goode, moving beyond an older Marxist criticism, point persuasively to an historical break between experience and value and a subsequent change in the traditional handling of pastoral, a break which makes its way into Hardy's novels. In brief remarks on the *Dynasts*, Isobel Armstrong has supplemented such insights by connecting Hardy with the radical intellectual context of his time. Yet it is significant that no critic reads Hardy novels through self-consciously experimental Victorian poetry which drew heavily on that radical context.

With its emphasis on what we see, how we know and nominate, how we experience, how a thing can be viewed in different ways at the same time, and how something may affect us physically, mentally, and emotionally – the description of Marlott, with which I began, glosses Hardy's aesthetic undertaking in *Tess*. Hardy's aesthetic demands that readers grasp reality as objectively varied, changing, filtered by multiple and contradictory subjective impressions, and yet indubitably and solidly there when apart from human consciousness. The description of Marlott not only positions the reader geographically, then, for it also serves as an introductory directive on subject and method.

At every narrative level, as I will show, Hardy relies on multiplicity and incongruity. He adopts these strategies within a general structural framework of tragic and ironic ambiguity. In doing so, Hardy questions the very foundations of traditional representation and belief. He wants his reader to become conditioned into thinking simultaneously in terms that are multiple and even contradictory. *Tess* must be seen in relation to a larger nineteenth-century intellectual context provided by earlier writers who rely on similar aesthetic strategies put to radical ends. As I will show, writers as diverse as Carlyle, Browning, and Ruskin, as well as lesser-known figures such as William Johnson Fox, had stressed the alienated modern consciousness that Hardy so powerfully dramatizes in this novel.

In defining Hardy's aesthetic, it is well to remember his extremely important remarks about realism and vision, as well as his specific comments about *Tess*. Hardy is fundamentally anti-realistic. He does not practice a mimetic art which reproduces a likeness of the external world and draws that world into comprehension through an omniscient narrator we are asked to trust.[2] Nor does he present a teleological narrative based on the development of a character with clear cause-and-effect results. Though, as a pre-eminent story-teller, he does not abandon mimesis completely, Hardy undermines the bases of mimetic representation. For him, realism is a "student's style" (*LW*, p. 192).

Nowhere in Hardy's writings do we get a fully articulated aesthetic. Yet several statements of the late 1880s and early 1890s prove unusually helpful, especially when Hardy defines art as a deformation of reality: "Art is a disproportioning – (i.e., distorting, throwing out of proportion) – of realities, to show more clearly the features that matter in those realities, which, if merely copied or reported inventorially, might possibly be observed, but would more probably be overlooked. Hence 'realism' is not Art" (*LW*, p. 239). A notable example of such "disproportioning" in *Tess*, perhaps even a self-mocking of such distortions, is the scene where Mrs. Brooks of The Herons notices a red spot in the middle of her white ceiling, a spot which grows in size until it begins to drip blood (*T*, lvi, p. 369).

Hardy's imagination is primarily visual, as is attested by his painting-like set pieces and his many poetic effects. He told at least two of his biographers that mental pictures usually preceded the formulation of his ideas in language.[3] The word "impression," related to the notion of a mental picture, arises often in his writings, including a defense of the novel *Tess*. In his 1895 Preface to the Fifth and Later editions, Hardy claims that a novel is not an intellectual argument, but an "impression," that is, a general tone or effect imprinted on the mind, emotions, and eyes of the reader.

Hardy's interest in the peculiarities of perception led him to favor those nineteenth-century English painters who distorted reality in order to bring out specifics that might otherwise be overlooked. For instance, instead of merely reproducing a boat in a storm, Turner, whom Hardy much admired, painted what he felt as the essence of storm: wind, turbulent waves, spray. Hardy delights in "the tragical mysteries" Turner has plumbed and maintains that his prose seeks "the deeper reality underlying the scenic, the expression of what are sometimes called abstract imaginings" (*LW*, p. 192).

Such an "abstract imagining" even informs the title-page of *Tess*, which includes the phrase "a pure woman faithfully presented by Thomas Hardy." Most critics rightly argue that "pure," when modifying "woman," can carry multiple meanings, such as *essence of, chaste, wholly,* and *good.* Yet I prefer to focus on "faithfully presented." Since Hardy's presentation cannot be faithful in the sense of absolutely true or accurate, his use of the word is both ironic and sincere. How, then, and to whom, is the telling faithful? Gatrell suggests, in the fantasy he constructs of two Hardys, that Hardy remains faithful to his first, unconscious conception of an ideal Tess; countering such a view, Peter Widdowson holds that "faithfully presented" is only ironic. I would make a somewhat different case. Hardy's narrative mode challenges conventionally faithful presentation, but is faithful, instead, to an authorial aesthetic of incongruity. Hardy is thus ironic about faith, but also serious in offering a new kind of narrative fidelity.

Most reviewers of *Tess* in both its serial and book versions, however, failed to grasp Hardy's stylistic challenge to conventional narrative. They specifically blamed him for indecorous language, indecency, and irreligiosity. Attending specifically to style, one critic went so far as to complain that Hardy is "writing like a man who has been at a great feast of languages and stolen the scraps, or in plain English, of making experiments in a form of language which he does not seem clearly to understand." Hardy's intellectual poverty, he complains, leads inevitably to a coarseness and a want of good taste (Mowbray Morris in the *Quarterly Review,* quoted by Cox, p. 220).

Tess, however, relies on a self-conscious send-up of standard narrative conventions not only for its aesthetic effects, but also for its political and ethical effects, which should not be divorced from discussion of its artistic form. The general story and the plot, by which I mean the choice and organization of events and the temporal order into which they are arranged, were hardly unique in fiction at that time. A young girl's violation by one man and abandonment by another leads to tragic consequences for all. The temporal order of events is reassuringly sequential, yet linearity is doubly complicated. First, Hardy places the violation early, thus exploding the romance form by leaving space to treat a fallen life. Moreover, he fits the violation within a pattern of progressive loss for Tess, not gain.

Hardy also complicates linearity by introducing time schemes other than the strictly teleological. He thereby forces the question, repeatedly, of whether a seemingly isolated event is part of a larger pattern, or not. Gillian Beer has referred to a triple layering of plot in a Hardy novel: Predictive (agency usually of the character's making) as when Joan dresses Tess in white to go to Alec; Optative (seen through "if only" comments by the narrator and characters), as when the narrator says "if only" Tess's guardian Angel had been in the Chase protecting her; and the plot of Nature's Laws (blind interaction, randomness, determinism) seen in statements such as "Thus the thing began" (*T*, v, p. 45).[4] In addition to these temporal frames, Hardy draws on cosmic or cyclical time, family historical continuum of crime and punishment, cycles of retribution in a transgenerational class drama, and a patriarchal inevitability of results. For instance, the book is divided into "Phases." To be sure, the word can refer to periods of development in a linear pattern, as in Thomas Carlyle's use of it with regard to history. But "phases" can also refer to phases of the moon and thus to lunar/solar/tidal time. Tess's story is divided into sections that imply larger time schemes embodying her tale, but the word is multivalent and remains so.

Moreover, Tess's story is also placed in a history of repeated events, as part of a cycle, or, through analogy, as a regional myth. Crimes by the aristocratic d'Urbervilles, for example, may be related to Tess's barbaric murder of Alec, and, hence, run in the family. On the other hand, events can also be attributed to lasting class inequities and retribution cycles. The narrator wonders, for instance, if Tess has to be violated by a man superior in wealth, if not worth, because her aristocratic ancestors, the d'Urbervilles, "rollicking home from a fray," had dealt out the same fate to peasant girls (*T*, xi, p. 77). Angel reinforces the connection, depressing Tess, when he mentions the legend of the d'Urberville coach and the ancestor who committed a dreadful crime in it (xxxiii, p. 212). Tess's fate is also placed, by analogy and in disguised form, in the mythified historical tales of her district. Marlott's valley was formerly known as the Forest of White Hart, ever since a beautiful doe, spared by the King, was killed by one Thomas de la Lynd (ii, pp. 18–19). Tess's bitter phrase "Once victim, always victim: that's the law" (xlvii, p. 321) suggests the workings of a harsh inexorability, which overdetermines her own use of violence within a cycle of power struggles and revenge. As explanations of Tess's fate, however, such "laws" – whether human, institutional, or cosmic – remain partial, random, and incomplete. Uninterested in single answers, Hardy prefers to look at the many ways we (alternately and not uniformly) assign structures to motivations, actions, and fates.

Fascinated by the different meanings we assign to events, Hardy complicates their causal relation as much as their temporal arrangement. His handling of plot, therefore, goes against the grain of much nineteenth-century fiction. Other novelists writing of fallen women, say Elizabeth Gaskell, Charles Dickens, or George Eliot, might have linked violation to its traditional consequences of death or religious conversion. But Hardy is not content to dwell on the triad of fall, punishment, and redemption. Tess must be consistently misread, then abandoned, reduced to hard labor, humiliated into a return to her first victimizer, driven to murder, and forced to surrender herself, before she is allowed to be killed.

There is an aesthetic reason and a political reason for this overwriting of Tess's fate. As Hardy himself notes, he demolishes the "doll of English fiction" (*Letters* 1, p. 250; to H. W. Massingham) once and for all by not only rewriting the traditional heroine and her story, but also our relation to her. Violating traditional contracts with novel readers, he aggressively assaults an audience whose subtlety of understanding he repeatedly tests. Alec-like, he lures us into a fictional world to raise and violate our Angel-like desire for some monolithic essence of female purity. And he challenges our narrator-like sentimental and patriarchal wishfulness by showing that a violated woman can not "get over" her ordeals, as if she were just putting on new clothes.

Whereas in a classical tragedy, cause-and-effect explanations may elucidate a character's fate, Hardy makes sure that no one reason for Tess's fate can stand out among the many offered, because no one choice Tess might have made could have redirected her life. There is also no particular quality which she harbors that undoes her, unless it is, ironically, her sheer excellence as a human being. A series of relatively minor and logically unrelated events and facts are responsible for her fate, everything from her mother's not educating her properly about designs of some men, to the death of Prince, her family's horse, to Angel's not selecting her from the dancers at the start. Since each of these facts or events can similarly be attributed to multiple causes, a search for origins proves to be as doomed as Tess herself.

A look at one significant component of that set of events, the impalement of the horse Prince, which contributes to Tess's having to go to work for the d'Urbervilles, yields a host of causes. They include her father's drunkenness, which prevents him from taking the early morning journey to deliver the beehives, her mother's procrastination, which delays the trip, Tess's excessive sense of responsibility, Tess's allowing Abraham to sleep, Tess's own drowsiness and hence her obliviousness to the mail coach, the fact that her wagon light has gone out, the bad road conditions which slow her journey and possibly cause Prince to wander to the wrong side of the highway, the mail cart's speed, and, not least, the "blighted" star on which they live (*T*, iv, p. 35).

Moreover, in the single most important event of the novel, Alec's violation of Tess, Hardy undermines the notion of a narrative's central event. He indicates that something pivotal occurred, but clouds it in obscurity. We hear that in the Chase, on that night, Tess's "self" was altered irrevocably, for the narrator laments it as the point between "previous" and present selves (*T*, xi, p. 77). We know that she eventually bears Alec's child. But exactly what happened, how it happened, and why it happened are not easy to ascertain.

Like other very important moments in the novel, say Tess's confession to Angel, her murder of Alec, or her execution, the facts and details of the violation scene remains unnarrated. To be sure, Victorian propriety would necessitate coding or silence about sexual intercourse. Still, there is a distinct pattern here of key scenes omitted, a pattern for which Victorian propriety can not be the only reason. The night scene is marked by fog and confusion. When Alec returns, Tess is sound asleep. It remains unclear whether Alec rapes or seduces Tess. Whether Tess fights being raped or surrenders with half-willingness remains equally veiled, because, quite simply, the narrator does not tell us, nor does any character ever say.

Moreover, unless one is wedded to a realist series of explainable feelings and events in time or cardboard figures playing out predictable dramas, which Hardy is not, it is difficult to interpret Alec in this scene. Some readers resist a three-dimensional Alec. They despise him as a manipulating, power-hungry cad. Yet, Hardy repeats here what he is wont to do in other novels, for example with *commedia dell'arte*-inspired figures in *The Trumpet-Major* (1880). He draws on a known stereotype in outrageously obvious ways only to subvert that stereotype's very obviousness.

This scene is purposely ambiguous about Alec as well as Tess. It is unclear whether Alec's feelings of "genuine doubt" as to their location, his desire to "prolong companionship" with Tess, and whatever feeling compels him to violate her innocence are, on this night, in perpetual mixture or are developmental. That is, it is never revealed to us whether the agent, Alec, knows from the start that he will violate her or whether he stumbles into it as the occasion offers him a perfect opportunity. Likewise, it is unclear whether disregard for a lower-class woman, her possible confusion, the lust of a moment, or continuing passion makes him do it. Lust, passion, or taking advantage of the situation as it develops do not exculpate his deed, any more than dark intention. What he does has tragic consequences. Appropriately, the representation of this key event is marked by profound ambiguity concerning his feelings and motives and her responses.

Understanding the relation between Tess and Alec in the Chase is made even more problematic for readers by textual statements recorded both before and after the fact. For instance, when Alec feeds Tess strawberries, Tess accepts "whatever d'Urberville offered her" in a "half-pleased, half-reluctant state" (*T*, v, p. 44). The reader must weigh whether or not this half-pleasure is repeated later. An allusion such as that to "Lotis attempting to elude Priapus, and always failing" (*T*, x, p. 67), used of the dancers whom Tess watches, suggests Tess is not receptive and Alec is forceful. Then, how are we to interpret Tess's later explanation to Alec that she hates herself for her "weakness" and that her eyes were "dazed ... a little" (*T*, xii, p. 83). In what context do we judge the narrator's claim that Tess had been "made to break an accepted social law" (*T*, xiii, p. 91)? Critics of the novel often draw on these and other statements in order to extract coherence from a scene, which, as I've tried to show, resolutely resists any interpretation founded on logic, cause and effect, or precedents offered by tradition and stereotype.

Still, our interpretation of the rest of the book is much affected by the way in which we view Alec's violation of Tess. A 1996 e-mail debate among Victorianists on VICTORIA LIST reproduced in minuscule a range of responses by major critics of the last twenty-five years to the events in the Chase. Some critics seem to have implicitly agreed with Michael Millgate's 1971 contention that Hardy's ambiguous treatment of Tess's moments of crisis is to be applauded for a "restraint that is eloquent of artistic maturity" (*Career as a Novelist*, p. 280). In other words, Hardy's obfuscation about what happened is part of conscious artistic effect. Others decided that Alec's violation was a "rape," preceded and followed by harassment. William Morgan, who thinks so (according to his contribution to this e-mail discussion), thus shares the view expressed by Simon Gatrell in his and Juliet Grindle's recent Oxford Classics edition of the novel: "Alec d'Urberville, everyone agrees, is little more than a cardboard cut-out, two-dimensional rapist and bounder" ("Introduction," *T*, p. xxii). For his part, though, Keith Wilson, in another e-mail contribution, appears to agree with Ian Gregor's 1974 view that the encounter in the Chase is, ambiguously, both a seduction and a rape. But Wilson reads the ambiguity as thought-through, ethical, and political: it is a "deliberate attempt on Hardy's part to explode and expose stereotypical responses," including "easy moral categories."[5]

The critical debate about the Chase scene persistently raises issues of authorial self-consciousness and execution. Some critics believe that those who read ambiguity into the prose are aestheticizing a rape scene which Hardy expects his readers unequivocally to condemn. Others maintain that Hardy's ambiguity stems from his own confusion as a late-Victorian, who simply did not know the difference between rape and consensual sex. Still others, willing to credit him with a deliberate aesthetic and ideological agenda, believe that he knowingly blurred the scene in order to challenge the Victorian response to a fallen woman. My own sense is that aesthetic ambiguity and ethical re-vision are inextricably intertwined for Hardy; to argue for one over the other or without the other therefore encourages a misreading of the entire novel.

Hardy's text asks his readers to understand the relativity of their values and judgments. Does this mean that he is a relativist or that he is confused about rape and consensual sex? No. It means that he sees stereotypical values and judgments (whether against the woman: "blame the victim," against the man: the "seducer is a cad," or against the event: "oh dear, this is the end of her life") as being socially constructed, historically shaped, and often irrelevant to a particular situation or, more subtly, irrelevant to a discriminating readership. Self-satisfied members of Hardy's audience, the text repeatedly suggests, might wake up to some honest doubt and faith, instead of relying on untested opinions and clichés.

The scene at Sandbourne, where Tess lives as Alec's mistress in order to support her family, is another, if different, case in point. She is still a victim; she is still pure, even when she plays out the final scene of the patriarchal logic which has shaped her choices. Some readers blame Tess for killing Alec and some exonerate her. Hardy's interest goes beyond individual right and wrong. The system which has entrapped her into such grotesque choices deserves the blame as much as any individual may. Any system which perpetually victimizes women and men, by forcing them to assume reductive parts in a repetitive age-old drama, should itself be drained of blood and breath.

Hardy's treatment of his characters is also blatantly non-stereotypical. The character presented most stereotypically, Alec, assumes new identities as the book proceeds, to preacher, to industrial overseer, to victim. More-over, his posing with a pitch-fork as Satan is notably self-conscious and even self-mocking. On another level entirely, that of narrative treatment of character itself, Tess is both person and figure. Distinguished from others by her red ribbon at the May Day processional, Tess immediately assumes a distinctiveness for the reader. Yet as the book proceeds, she becomes less and less individualized: turned into a "figure in a landscape," she eventually disappears altogether, marked only as having once existed by the raising of a black flag. From a woman seen at close range – lips, eyes, dress – she becomes a type seen from afar in a field or on a horizon, herself now a mere metonymy of a person, represented by a grey serge cap, a red woolen scarf, buff-leather gloves.

Tess changes for the reader by shedding her historical and psychological identities (a past self leading to a future one), and by becoming, instead, parceled, metonymized, and finally a mere shape. The novel takes her from being a she, to a collection of aspects, to an it, and ultimately to a nothingness. Her personhood is restored for a brief moment, when she snatches happiness with Angel in the abandoned house before moving on to the sacrificial pillars of Stonehenge. But her recovered "fullness" is shortlived and itself compromised by her own idealization of Angel.

Hardy prevents his readers from regarding character as a unifying force or coherent reference point. He fractures his central characters through multiple point of view and multiple genres. Just as Marlott itself may be viewed from various locations and positions, so Tess is observed from perspectives that are not only variegated but are also conflicting. Tess is aristocratic by lineage, bourgeois by education, and a rural proletarian by birth. She speaks bilingually: dialect and standard English. The narrator deliberately makes her half-woman and half-girl. When we first meet her, Tess's face supposedly reflects different phases of her youth: "you could sometimes see her twelfth year in her cheeks or her ninth sparkling from her eyes; and even her fifth would flit over the curves of her mouth now and then" (*T*, ii, p. 21). Later, her fluctuating moods alter a face that is sometimes pink and flawless, yet pale and tragic at other times (xvi, p. 109). The narrator claims that she is forever severed from her childhood innocence by her experience in the Chase, yet counters his assertion whenever he continues to treat the adult Tess as a childlike innocent.

Though her suitors often perceive her monochromatically, Tess is never one thing. When Angel can no longer see her as the equally worshipful narrator does, he must stereotype her as soiled. Yet his earlier idealization of Tess as a nature goddess, which she disowned, was just as reductive. Despite the clarity his surname "Clare" evokes, Angel shows himself to be as limited in perception as Alec, who first narrowly admires her as a juicy morsel, a "crumby girl" (*T*, v, p. 46).

Unlike these two central suitors, the narrator does not waver in seeing Tess doubly. For example, even after she becomes a mother and assumes a more handsome womanliness, and even after her erotic attraction to Angel, she does not lose her virginal qualities for the narrator. But if the narrator's dual perspective undercuts the single-mindedness of Alec and Angel, it is not exempt from criticism. The presence of the implied author, known to the reader by the sum of all the text's points of view, reveals the narrator's point of view to be overly romantic and egocentric.

As Tess's third suitor and a mixture of the other two, the narrator combines Angel's spirituality and Alec's cynicism. Yet even though he exhibits an erotic sensuousness that resembles Alec's and often adopts the over-intellectualized pedantic and circumlocutionary style of Angel, this prime suitor is also mocked by an implied author who asks us to recognize that the narrator is as eager as these two male characters are to possess a femininity which remains unpossessed, dispossessed, unclaimed, and above all, unable to be possessed, because valued for the wrong reasons.

The Shakespearean epigraph Hardy affixes to the novel's title-page, "Poor wounded name! My bosom as a bed / Shall lodge thee," appears to refer to the novelist or the narrator, who offers his own breast to harbor his dispossessed heroine. While this feeling is certainly heartfelt, and while Tess represents something true and vulnerable, the overt literariness of the expression of desire here illustrates both the power and the limitations of art.

Writing may lodge Tess, but cannot contain her, for she and her powers are greater than the narrator's or the novelist's hold. This is not to make her into an idealized essence, object of a mythologizing process she herself resists. Rather, she exists outside as well as inside subjective impressions of her and hence she must necessarily elude whatever containers male viewers and tellers devise for her. In this sense, the novel knowingly mocks the novel tradition, as well as its own particular enterprise of representation.

Tess resists being held and appropriated. Even the narrator cannot narrate her sexuality; it is inaccessible even to him. Henry James's comment about the novel, "The pretence of sexuality is only equalled by the absence of it" (LW, pp. 259–60), seems fully justified in more ways than one. We get only traces of Tess's full sexuality: a breath, the color of her lips, energy. Her full sexuality is unobtainable by the narrator who, deeply invested in the story, gives evidence of being as physically attracted to Tess as Alec is, but like Angel falls back on a rhetoric of idealization. Hardy has created a narrator who oscillates between the extremes represented by Alec and Angel. The narrator's oscillations, however, are not those of the implied author, Hardy, who ironizes the incompleteness of the positions of Alec and Angel but also undermines his narrator. Through his handling of Tess and her three suitors, Hardy challenges the foundations of realist character-drawing and perspective.

In addition to his complex treatment of plot and character, Hardy invokes multiple genres which do not easily co-exist, but whose premises call each other into question. He sets up a hall of mirrors effect, what Millgate calls a "multiplicity of lightly invoked frames and patterns" (Career as a Novelist, p. 269) by juxtaposing or intermixing elements of classical tragedy, stage melodrama, realist novel, ballad, polemic, and comedy. Moreover, philosophic ideas in the novel do not cohere, as the conflicting and unresolved accounts of nature offered so poignantly attest. Romantic ideologies, upholding nature's "holy plan," clash with a Darwinian notion of nature's randomness and cruelty. Yet both are questioned by a view of cosmic forces indifferent, not just to woman and man, but to all species.

These different accounts of nature bring with them a host of jarring allusions: pagan deities and Christian angels, fallen and unfallen. Yet the landscape itself is always physical, sometimes posited as existing apart from the human mind and sometimes energized only by the human mind through the pathetic fallacy. It is hard to believe, as some critics assert, that Hardy is so fundamentally confused about philosophy, literature, and strands of evolutionary theory that he mixes up such views because he doesn't know better or even that Hardy's allusions are only local, intensifying the effects of one scene or chapter. Rather, the very muddle, suggesting randomness, challenges the unitary and anthropocentric aspirations of so many of our cultural systems. If none of the frames and patterns, allusions, and philosophies captures Tess, any more than her suitors do, they do work to make her and her story always richly layered and refracting.

Nowhere does Hardy subvert conventions more effectively, and more outrageously, than on the level of intertextual reference and lexical use. His allusions to other narratives are wrenched from their contexts, fragmented, and recombined. These include references, for instance, to Romantic and Victorian poetry, classical drama, philosophical tradition, the Bible, educational tracts, *Paradise Lost, Pilgrim's Progress*, paintings, American poetry. The narrator's intellectual glosses never cohere into a philosophy or even a logical argument and are often counterpointed or interrupted by his lyrical effusions, as sentiment and irony remain divorced.

Hardy's handling of language reproduces the narrative strategies of the book as a whole. Hardy's critics have repeatedly noted what seems his awkwardness with diction and syntax, his clumsiness and odd self-consciousness. He is notorious for an "awkwardness" which "challenges not just the decorums of a given genre but the decorums of the language."[6] As Taylor has shown convincingly, this poet-novelist and thinker very carefully studied the relationship of language past and present. Hardy views words as fossils – bearing traces of earlier ages and meanings. Rather than overvaluing them, however, he wants to brush off their dust and test them for their ability to guide or to tragically misdirect in the present.

Tess is even more concerned with representing, sometimes by gestures of language and sometimes through silence, that which altogether eludes meaning or interpretation either because unknowable or because impervious to knowing. In a text so profoundly concerned with names, spoken and written words, and meaning, language sometimes fails. The flag at the end of the text waves "silently" and the survivors are left "speechless." But language does not fail because of narrative deficiency; it fails by narrative design.

LINDA M. SHIRES

Hardy's subversion of language and use of silence, like his contortions of plot and intertextual mixing, help shatter the novel form as readers had previously known it in the nineteenth century. For Hardy resolutely refuses to placate his audience. The entire final chapter of *Tess* offends the average novel reader with its deliberately badly written prose. Hardy's decision to pair Angel and Liza Lu as progenitors of the species is designed to outrage. Hardy mocks the second-rate conceptualizer Angel Clare by providing him with a mini-Tess. But he also mocks the idealizing aspects of Angel in himself. Hardy kills Tess in order to free her from constructions put on her by society and by individuals – not to further idealize her, but to remove her.

The novel's ending is especially disturbing because Hardy deprives the reader of cathartic closure. Instead, his narrator aestheticizes Tess and those close to her. The ending of the novel troubles readers not only because Angel follows Tess's directive to marry her sister, but also because the implied author denies us an outlet for the deep emotional involvement we feel. The last chapter offers no catharsis as it rewrites the end of *Paradise Lost*. The shrunken, pale faces of Angel and Liza Lu, covertly compared to Adam and Eve and overtly compared to angels in a Giotto painting, signal a shrunken humanity in a closure markedly different from Milton's epic and from prior novels because of the heavy emphasis on aesthetization of the characters. In Milton's epic, at least, Adam and Eve have fallen but depart "hand in hand" holding a "paradise within." In *Tess*, the right Eve is dead, Adam joins hands with a lesser Eve, and there is no paradise within for these characters. Angel and Liza Lu appear as half-frozen, stylized artifacts, rather than living beings. They are unusual in comparison with other survivors of Victorian novels in that they are both more diminished in human terms and more elevated by analogy, but elevated into art rather than life. Hardy's narrator aestheticizes these figures because he has never had full access to any of them; his mode has been to conceptualize, describe, and idealize.

The narrator's diction also makes the ending particularly unsettling. As Taylor suggests, the phrase "President of the Immortals," for instance, undermines the whole notion of deity and immortality. The artifice of the phrase "President of the Immortals" conjoins words and ideas that do not go together: a political term such as "President" of an Athenian Council with a traditional term for the gods, blessed ones, which in Hardy's translation becomes "Immortals." Moreover, the sentence self-consciously announces its own mixed status: "Justice" is in quotes; "in Aeschylean phrase" draws attention to the intertext, and, when justice is counterposed to "sport" (*T*, lix, p. 384), Aeschylean tragedy is awkwardly blended with

Gloucester's nihilism in *King Lear* (Act iv, Scene i, lines 36–37) (Taylor, *Hardy's Literary Language*, pp. 78–79).

The paragraph that invokes the dead d'Urberville knights and dames and ends with a biblical and Miltonic reference to Angel and Liza Lu as Adam and Eve leaving Eden, hand in hand, conjoins pagan and Christian, political and religious, gaming and ethics, aristocratic and middle classes, Norman and Gothic architecture, and the speechless living and the muted dead. Such savage sporting with Tess and such a profusion of references at the close is an odd strategy for a male author who loves his heroine for her simple purity. Yet educating his readers by defamiliarization is the primary goal of a novelist who would have us treat women differently, alter linguistic conventions, and reform the institutions that misshape women as much as language.

Tess of the d'Urbervilles is not only the richest novel that Hardy ever wrote, it is also the culmination of a long series of Victorian texts which identify, enact, and condemn the alienated condition of modernity. The undermining of a reader's expectations is already common in the Victorian novel form. Yet Hardy goes further with irony and surprise than even his favorite novelist, the equally subversive William Makepeace Thackeray. Doubleness, multiplicity, and irony are key aspects of a strain of Victorian aesthetics and artistic practice working at the limits of conservative doxa from the 1830s until the end of the century. It is through this intellectual formation that Hardy's work can best be understood.

Strands of this intellectual formation would include William Johnson Fox's reading of Jeremy Bentham in conjunction with his remarks on poetry in the *Monthly Repository*, Robert Browning's poetic strategies and philosophy of art, John Ruskin's theories of art and the social, especially his comments on the Gothic "grotesque," and Thomas Carlyle's pronouncements about his era's self-consciousness and the alienated modern mind.[7]

It is useful to keep in mind the Victorian poetic tradition. Techniques upon which Hardy draws in all his work, including irony, dialogism, multiple perspective, imbalance, and fractured characters, flourished in that genre from the 1830s on. Hardy, who started and ended his literary career as a poet, would presumably have been well-read in prior and contemporary achievements. In particular, the Benthamite aesthetic of the 1830s, articulated by Fox, is germane as a context for Hardy's literary practice.

Fox believed that texts should take up current issues and that they should analyze "modern" states of mind – projecting and exploring different associative processes as they are formed in different time schemes and environments. Fox would support Hardy's sense of time as a layering of pasts and presents and he would support Hardy's understanding of character as constructed by socialized mental processes. To analyze "modern" states of mind, though, means more to Fox than "showing" consciousness or "telling" about it.

The aesthetic put forward by Fox features dramatic projection, dialogic representations, and a large role for the reader. Fox isolated drama as the central art-form because it explores conflict and relationships in complex ways that place demands on viewers and listeners. The dramatic element proved useful to poets, as well, who wished to get away from the purely subjective, made popular by Romantic lyrics. Poems like Browning's "Pippa Passes," referred to in *Tess* (xxxvii, p. 248), and the dramatic monologue show how mental events can be externalized and objectified through dramatic projection and presentation. This is what Fox urged.

As Isobel Armstrong has recently argued, Victorian double poems foreground two very different and contradictory readings at the same time, by offering frames of reference which comment on each other ("Introduction," *Victorian Poetry*). The gap between the frames of references produces ironic effect which causes the reader to question and probe motives and meanings of the lyric voice, while remaining enthralled by its power. The generic extension of this kind of poem was the long dramatic sequence or series, from Browning's *The Ring and the Book* to Christina Rossetti's *Monna Innominata*, itself a response to Barrett Browning's *Sonnets from the Portuguese*, to George Meredith's *Modern Love*, to Thomas Hardy's *Poems of 1912–13* and *The Dynasts*. Thomas Hardy, I am arguing, takes into fiction this dialogic, ironic strategy of expression, critique, irony, self-consciousness, and reader responsibility. And he does so on every level of the narrative construct.

This radical aesthetic does not need to be tracked in Hardy's reading or even traced back to one or two thinkers, for it formed the fabric of an entire way of thinking through the conversation of Victorian intellectuals. In particular Carlyle's "Signs of the Times" (1829) and *Sartor Resartus* (1831) and Ruskin's account of the Gothic "grotesque" in *The Stones of Venice* (1851–53) influenced intellectuals in many disciplines. Years before Karl Marx produced his theories about the ill-effects of capital, both Carlyle and Ruskin perceived that they were part of a new historical situation which was altering the relations of society. Mechanization, especially, was changing the relationship of the laborer to her work, and was producing an effect of alienation, a divorce of experience and value.

The aesthetics of alienated consciousness is most directly addressed by Ruskin. He believed that enslaved and oppressed modern consciousness can only embody itself through distortion, not wholeness. The art which best enacts such distortion, in his view, is the grotesque, a form of the gothic imagination which Ruskin noted had been already embodied in the dramatic monologues of Browning. Ruskin suggested that the art-forms of his era attempted to *be* the form in which modern consciousness sees, experiences, and desires. Thus the text is not only unstable and fractured but unable to be unified in conventional ways, and thus unable to be read without hard labor. In this context, it is possible to see Hardy as a proto-modernist in his last three novels especially.

Texts in this tradition were expected to participate in ideological critique and transform the consciousness of readers. I would claim such effects for Hardy's text, just as I would claim the general intellectual influence of this tradition on him, whether indirect or direct. Texts in this tradition both reproduce the myths through which the nineteenth century operated and imagined itself (how it sees the past, how it views the fallen woman, how it defines love, how it rationalizes industrialism) and critique them at the same time. This is, I believe, the substance of Hardy's literary project not only in *Tess* but in all his novels, to greater or lesser degrees. What has often been dismissed as awkward, clumsy, or perverse in Hardy's work may well be a rather accurate enacting of the Benthamite aesthetic and the Ruskinian grotesque.

Tess enacts the confusions and divisions of modern consciousness, the "ache of modernism" (*T*, xix, p. 129), by reproducing its illogic and its divorce between experience and value. The novel assaults the reader with materials both shocking and subversive. In offering no final explanations or a satisfying resolution, Hardy defiles narrative community by exploding conventions which cement the bond between audience and teller to show them as being unfit for the times. He shatters narrative form to make his readers simultaneously love Tess and experience fragmentation. That breakage, aesthetic, ideological, and social, would eventually issue forth a different aesthetic for fiction. *Tess of the d'Urbervilles*, however, takes the Victorian novel to its limits without turning it into a didactic diatribe, a satiric parody, or a series of lyric moments. This is its achievement and its power.

NOTES

1 Michael Millgate writes of multiplicity, but still finds unity rather than fragmentation in Hardy's aesthetic effects. See *Thomas Hardy: His Career as a Novelist* (New York: Random House, 1971), part v, ch. 1.

2 On realism, see George Levine, *The Realistic Imagination: English Fiction from Frankenstein to Lady Chatterley* (University of Chicago Press, 1981), and Catherine Belsey, *Critical Practice* (New York: Routledge, originally Methuen, 1980). I was not able to take advantage of Margaret R. Higonnet's reading of

Tess, as our essays went to press at the same time. However, for a reading similar to my own, with regard to issues of realism, see her "Introduction," *Tess of the D'Urbervilles*, ed. and notes by Tim Dolin (New York: Penguin, 1998).

3 See Ernest Brennecke, Jr., *The Life of Thomas Hardy*, pp. 113–14, and Clive Holland, *Thomas Hardy, O.M.*, p. 60, both quoted by J. B. Bullen, *Thomas Hardy: The Expressive Eye* (Oxford: Clarendon Press, 1986), p. 2.

4 Gillian Beer, *Darwin's Plots: Evolutionary Narrative in Darwin, George Eliot and Nineteenth-Century Fiction* (1983; New York: Ark, 1985), p. 240.

5 Particularly useful comments in this discussion were made by Richard Nemesvari and Keith Wilson, both on 5 April 1996. It is Wilson's comment that is quoted in the text. The listowner of the VICTORIA e-mail List is Patrick Leary (Indiana University). The archives of the List, which can be consulted for the entirety of the discussion, can be located at LISTSERV@LISTSERV.INDIANA.EDU. Richard Nemesvari, in personal correspondence, 6 April 1996, singled out Millgate and Gregor as representative voices in past critical debates concerning whether it is more correct to term Alec's conduct toward Tess rape or seduction, or a combination of both.

6 Dennis Taylor, *Hardy's Literary Language and Victorian Philology* (Oxford: Clarendon Press, 1993), p. 7.

7 I am indebted to Isobel Armstrong, *Victorian Poetry: Poetry, Poetics, and Politics* (New York: Routledge, 1993), chapters 4 and 11 for material on Fox, the Benthamite tradition, and the connection to Ruskin. By way of example, see William Johnson Fox, *Monthly Repository*, n.s. (1832), 1–4, 189–201, and "Coleridge and Poetry," *Westminster Review*, 12 (1830), 11; also see the debate on drama conducted in the *Monthly Repository*, e.g., in William Bridges Adams's "Coriolanus No Aristocrat," *Monthly Repository*, n.s. 8 (1827), 33–48. The main study of this journal is F. E. Mineka, *The Dissidence of Dissent: The Monthly Repository 1806–1838* (Chapel Hill: University of North Carolina Press, 1944). Readers might also refer to F. R. Leavis, *Mill on Bentham and Coleridge* (London: Chatto & Windus, 1950).

FURTHER READING

Bayley, John. *An Essay on Hardy*. New York: Cambridge University Press, 1988.

Boumelha, Penny. *Thomas Hardy and Women: Sexual Ideology and Narrative Form*. Brighton, Sussex: Harvester Press, 1982.

Brady, Kristin. "Textual Hysteria: Hardy's Narrator on Women." In *The Sense of Sex: Feminist Perspectives On Hardy*. Ed. Margaret R. Higonnet. Urbana: University of Illinois Press, 1993, pp. 87–106.

De Laura, David J. "'The Ache of Modernism' in Hardy's Later Novels." *ELH*, 34 (1967), 380–99.

Eagleton, Terry. *Criticism and Ideology*. 1976; London: Verso, 1978.

Goode, John. *Thomas Hardy: The Offensive Truth*. London: Blackwell, 1988.

Gregor, Ian. *The Great Web: The Form of Hardy's Major Fiction*. London: Faber & Faber, 1974.

Higonnet, Margaret R. "A Woman's Story: Tess and the Problem of Voice." In *The Sense of Sex: Feminist Perspectives On Hardy*. Ed. Margaret R. Higonnet. Urbana: University of Illinois Press, 1993, pp. 14–31.

Howe, Irving. *Thomas Hardy.* London and Basingstoke: Macmillan, 1967 (1966).

Ingham, Patricia. "Provisional Narratives: Hardy's Final Trilogy." In *Alternative Hardy.* Ed. Lance St. John Butler. London and Basingstoke: Macmillan,1989, pp. 49–73.

Thomas Hardy. Feminist Readings. Atlantic Highlands, N.J.: Humanities Press International; London: Harvester Wheatsheaf, 1990.

Kincaid, James R. "Coherent Readers, Incoherent Texts," *Critical Inquiry,* 3 (1977), 781–802.

"Hardy's Absences." In *Critical Approaches to the Fiction of Thomas Hardy.* Ed. Dale Kramer. London and Basingstoke: Macmillan, 1979, pp. 202–14.

Kramer, Dale. *Tess of the d'Urbervilles.* Cambridge University Press, 1991.

Thomas Hardy: The Forms of Tragedy. Detroit: Wayne State University Press, 1975.

Kramer, Dale, ed. *Critical Essays on Thomas Hardy: The Novels.* Boston: G. K. Hall, 1990.

Laird, J. T. *The Shaping of "Tess of the d'Urbervilles."* Oxford: Clarendon Press, 1975.

Lawrence, D. H. *Study of Thomas Hardy and Other Essays.* Ed. Bruce Steele. The Cambridge Edition of the Works of D. H. Lawrence. Cambridge University Press, 1985, pp. 7–155. [Originally published in *Phoenix: The Posthumous Papers of D. H. Lawrence.* Ed. Edward D. McDonald. London: William Heinemann, 1936, pp. 398–516.]

Lecercle, Jean Jacques. "The Violence of Style in *Tess of the d'Urbervilles.*" In *Alternative Hardy,* as above, pp. 1–25.

Lock, Charles. *Thomas Hardy.* Bristol: Bristol Classical Press, 1992.

Lodge, David. "Tess, Nature, and the Voices of Hardy." In *The Language of Fiction: Essays in Criticism and Verbal Analysis of the English Novel.* London: Routledge; New York: Columbia University Press, 1966, pp. 164–88.

Miller, J. Hillis. *Thomas Hardy: Distance and Desire.* Cambridge, Mass.: Harvard University Press, 1970.

Morgan, Rosemarie. *Women and Sexuality in the Novels of Thomas Hardy.* New York and London: Routledge, 1988.

Silverman, Kaja. "History, Figuration and Female Subjectivity in *Tess of the d'Urbervilles.*" *Novel,* 18 (1984), 5–28.

Widdowson, Peter. *Hardy in History: A Study in Literary Sociology.* New York: Routledge, 1989.

" 'Moments of Vision': Postmodernising *Tess of the d'Urbervilles*; or, *Tess of the d'Urbervilles* Faithfully Presented by Peter Widdowson." In *New Perspectives on Thomas Hardy.* Ed. Charles P. C. Pettit. London and Basingstoke: Macmillan, 1994.

Williams, Raymond. *The English Novel from Dickens to Lawrence.* 1970; St. Albans: Paladin, 1974.

Wotton, George. *Thomas Hardy: Towards a Materialist Criticism.* Dublin: Gill and Macmillan, 1985.

Wright, Terence. *The Critics Debate: Tess of the d'Urbervilles.* New York: Macmillan, 1987.

Zabel, Morton Dauwen. "Hardy in Defence of His Art: The Aesthetic of Incongruity." *The Southern Review,* 6/1 (1940), 125–49.

10

DALE KRAMER

Hardy and readers: *Jude the Obscure*

Jude the Obscure is an account of the doomed existence of the protagonist named in the title, from the moment he is first inspired by a rural schoolmaster to think of a university education as the highest possible attainment, to his dying alone, while hearing celebratory shouts and organ notes in the distance from Remembrance Day at Christminster University, a place which has given not the slightest heed to his ambitions. Between these two moments are twenty years of self-directed study, and defeats in sex and love inflicted on him by two women, one sensual and pragmatic, the other intellectual and intensely seeking.

The intellectual woman, Sue Bridehead, is Jude's cousin. In effect she is the novel's co-protagonist although not named in the title; she is arguably Hardy's most challenging character to understand. Jude's mother and Sue's father were siblings, and had experienced disastrous marriages, the basis for one of the novel's minor themes, that some people are poor candidates for marriage. On top of what is taken to be a family curse is the reprehensible and constricting nature of marriage itself as Jude and Sue perceive it. The times and their own personalities conspire to thwart their best intentions and hopes. Well-meaning, intermittently sensitive to the other's needs while usually insistent upon the inherent justice of his and her own needs, the couple interact with a rawness of ego that includes lacerating self-condemnation. The novel's characterizing tone is bitterness, seemingly unmediated because the narrator shares the characters' sense of outrage that society censures both their unconventional sexual relations and their idealism.

This bare outline of plot and some of the novel's characteristics, inadequate though it is to canvass the novel's rich diversity, may provide some reasons for its impact on readers. An impact that had a resounding counter impact on Hardy. For the novel did not occur in a vacuum but in a certain time in its author's career and in cultural/literary history.

The reception of *Jude the Obscure* upon its publication as a book in

November 1895 (post-dated 1896) shaped a dilemma for Hardy that the similar reception of *Tess* four years earlier had prepared him for. *Tess* had been severely criticized for the moral attitude conveyed in the subtitle "A Pure Woman," added by Hardy after reading final proofs. Many people otherwise well-disposed to Hardy were taken aback by the sardonic slighting of convention premised in that subtitle, and Hardy's disingenuous response that he felt everyone would share his view of Tess's moral character only roiled the controversy. The controversy helped sales, but did not dissuade such admirers, and outright critics, from misgivings about Hardy's increasingly outspoken criticism of conventions that destroy people unable or unwilling to forswear their particular aspirations in order not to offend community values. *Jude* was even more controversial.

Hardy had from the beginning of his career enjoyed approval and admiration from discerning readers and reviewers; but he had always dealt with subjects that other readers and reviewers strongly reacted to. Notorious examples of the reviews that offended or deeply hurt Hardy are the 1871 *Spectator* review of *Desperate Remedies* that suggests its anonymous author has a "low curiosity about the detail of crime" (Cox, p. 3), R. H. Hutton's review of *The Woodlanders* in the *Spectator* that called for Hardy to "give us a little less 'abstract humanism' and a little more of human piety" (Cox, p. 145), and Mowbray Morris's sarcastic and condescending review of *Tess* in *Quarterly Review*. (Morris was editor of *Macmillan's Magazine* during the serial appearance of *The Woodlanders*, but he had declined to publish *Tess*.) Morris's review (which was published anonymously) said, among other slurs, that *Tess* is "a coarse and disagreeable story [told] in a coarse and disagreeable manner, which is not rendered less so by his affectation of expounding a great moral law, or by the ridiculous character of some of the scenes into which this affectation plunges the reader" (Cox, p. 219). It was in relation to this review that Hardy commented that "[a] man must be a fool to deliberately stand up to be shot at" (*LW*, p. 259); and it is quite likely that biographers (such as Millgate, *Biography*, p. 329) are correct that Hardy dedicated himself to *Jude* with the idea that this would be his last novel, and with every intention of having his full say in defiance of the convention-ridden reviewers who refused his fictional characters the kind of sympathy and tolerance that in most cases they would have granted their personal acquaintances. It is true that he began the story assuring his publisher, the Harper firm, that it would not offend even a most fastidious maiden, and that when his manuscript seemed to be approaching dangerous areas he offered the publishers the option of backing out of their contract; but even his initial title – "The Simpletons / Part First / Hearts Insurgent / A Dreamer" – hints at elements whose likely development would challenge his expressed assurance that it would be "in every respect suitable for a family magazine" (quoted in Purdy, p. 89). One suspects that Hardy knew perfectly well from this early point the essential direction the story would take. In any event, Harper chose Hardy's second option, that he bowdlerize the story for serial publication in *Harper's Magazine* by removing potentially offensive material, and restore the cuts for the book publication.

As a consequence of this censorship, the first readers of *Jude* faced materials significantly milder and less realistic than were in the version Hardy initially intended, and that did appear in the book version. Nineteenth-century periodical readers were thought too straight-laced to be able to stomach a full display of pain and frustration lived by ambitious but fallible members of the lower classes, whereas the book-buying public were assumed to have the discrimination and moral fiber necessary to judge fairly the consequences of economic and social inequalities. That one audience may have been composed more largely of church and chapel members, of families fairly recently achieving the status of reading the better periodicals for intellectual and secular guidance, and that the other audience may have included primarily families and individuals with a tradition of buying books and subscribing to lending libraries, such as the aristocratic and gentry classes, may explain in part the distinctions that authors and publishers were trying to meet and profit from, although the differences among the various reading publics in the nineteenth century are still not well enough understood to justify simple explanations.[1] *Jude* was not the first novel Hardy had modified to gain serial publication. Hardy had confronted numerous times previously in his career editors' anxieties about sexual complications, in particular, and at this stage of his career could quickly (and cynically) expurgate his manuscripts for serials and arrange to restore his first intentions in the book versions. Among other works, the manuscript versions of *The Return of the Native*, *The Mayor of Casterbridge*, and *Tess* were changed for serial publication in ways similar to the manuscript version of *Jude*. The large framework of the novels remained in the bowdlerized serial versions, but he paid little regard to fundamental consistency or plausibility. Conditions crucial to the "true" novel – the manuscript and the book versions – were crudely and even ludicrously altered for the serials, the sole intention being the pragmatic one of providing the transitions needed to link the remaining sections of the novel, those that did not require "watering down" to avoid offending periodical readers.

For example, the serialized *Harper's Magazine* version of *Jude*, when compared to the manuscript, drastically diminished the particulars in the pig-killing scene, evidently because American readers had recently been offended by reports of cruelty to animals on Western ranches. But more telling of the repressive force of periodical distribution are the changes in Jude's and Sue's sexual lives. In the serial version Arabella does not seduce Jude, and consequently she cannot fake pregnancy to induce him to marry her; instead, she refers to another suitor to spur Jude's jealousy. After they go away together, Jude and Sue do not cohabit, but live in separate houses. Never having sexual relations, they do not have children of their own, but adopt one child (who is hanged by Father Time).[2] Citing just these few variations suggests how different is the serial version produced by Hardy and his publishers with their collaborative eye on their first principal audience.[3]

The revisions that have attracted the most attention in recent years occurred after the serial, and are related to the object that Arabella throws at Jude to draw his attention to her, away from his idealizing fantasies, an action that initiates their relationship. It was probably in reaction to reviews of the first book edition that attacked the novel's coarse language,[4] with frequent reference to this scene, that for a 1903 re-issue of an inexpensive edition of *Jude* Hardy changed some references to the piece of pig that Arabella throws, although it remains a pizzle (*Letters* 2, p. 93), or penis, named in the novel as "the characteristic part of a barrow-pig" (*J*, 1, vi, p. 35). For example, Arabella in the first edition says that "If I had thrown anything at all, it shouldn't have been such an indecent thing as that!"; in 1903 this became "If I had thrown anything at all, it shouldn't have been *that!*" (*J*, 1, vi, p. 35); and Hardy removes from the text reference to the origin of the "lump of offal": "the bladder, from which [Arabella] had obviously just cut it off." This mild reduction of explicitness is interesting mostly because its direction is the opposite of the revisions Hardy made in 1893–94 for many of his other novels (and later in 1911–12), which added material to clarify, and usually to make more explicit, their sexual aspects.[5] Several revisions for *Jude* made between 1896 and 1912 are more functional than these involving a pig's penis, for example changes giving Sue a more "normal" sexual passion for Jude, clarifying that her feeling for Phillotson is one of "aversion" not just of "loathing," and indicating that Phillotson still has a sexual desire for Sue encouraging him to their late reconciliation even though he denies it. All of Hardy's changes, however, are valuable for an understanding of his manner of composition, both the changes made after writing the manuscript – i.e., those made for the serial version – and the changes made for the first book version following serial publication. These last are not always a return to the manuscript readings: in some cases material is shifted from one place to another in the narrative; in some cases material removed for the serial is not restored to the book version in spite of directions in the manuscript; and there are many incidental "improvements."[6] All of these revisions, both the late and the early ones in the novel's textual history, would be of great value for studies of characters and situations, and constitute one of the compelling reasons for a complete printed edition of Hardy's novels that would include all the variant and rejected readings.[7] Hardy's frequent acquiescence to moral and aesthetic conservatism may to twentieth- and twenty-first-century eyes seem opportunistic, and scornful of his readers. It is a subject we can hope will be interrogated by current and future scholars. But they will need to take into account his nearly-as-frequent refusal to make requested changes – one instance being his decision to sell *The Return of the Native* elsewhere after Leslie Stephen, editor of the *Cornhill Magazine*, expressed anxiety that it would prove "'dangerous' for a family magazine" (quoted by Millgate, *Biography*, p. 188).

These bibliographical details and sketch of the reception by editors and reviewers of Hardy's fiction present only partially the intersection of an author and his life and times, and of contexts combining marketplace and social-cultural considerations. *Jude* presents more complexities as a cultural marker than the other "great" Hardy novels in some degree because of the accident of its appearing just as the traditional Victorian novel form was being revised. *Jude* was not the first nineteenth-century British novel to appear in a single volume – among others, George Moore's *A Mummer's Wife* (1885) and Rider Haggard's *She* (1886) appeared earlier – but it was the only one of Hardy's novels first published in one volume in Britain; and its success and notoriety helped to abbreviate the already declining authority of the lending libraries (Mudie's; W. H. Smith) and their moralistic restrictions on subject matter and treatment, which were based on their ability to control what was published in the three-volume format.[8] Traditional Victorian values were being questioned on many fronts. To borrow a phrase, Hardy was "read" by *Jude* as much as *Jude* is a reading by Hardy of his times.

Jude is – like most novels – a combination of personal interests or obsessions and contemporary ideas and events. The novel's direct approach to issues sensitive for both Hardy and his society helps account for the public furor it created and for the popular success it gained. This novel gets as close to Hardy's raw rage at the rigidity of British social expectations and religious conventionalities as anything he'd written since "The Poor Man and the Lady." In view of *Jude*'s being written soon after the great critical and commercial success of *Tess* and its culminating the series of novels that had steadily increased Hardy's stature in the literary and social worlds, one might well ask what called forth the intensity and particularity of its anger that make this novel the most challenging for readers to enjoy as a piece of literature. Even a hundred years after its first appearance it has still the freshness of affront and the rawness of despair.

Jude the Obscure is an unmistakably contemporary novel in concentration on central questions of the late nineteenth century: the difficulties of being a working woman (and of being simply an independent woman), the strain of professional ambition in an increasingly striated society, the loss of religious faith in a conventional society, the revision of class-based university ambitions. It has not lost its currency a century later. With the current spread of fundamentalist and cult religions and the common necessity that families have two wage-earners it could be said that some of the issues are mirror images of today's.

Each of Hardy's novels in its own way fuses with its times, as in *Ethelberta*'s projection of shifting social strata and of the amorphousness of "class" and as in *Mayor*'s domestication of heroic myth at a time of rising political participation by the masses. The connections of *Jude* to current dilemmas are both numerous and interlocking. If not precisely interchangeable they are comparably evocative. Evidences in the manuscript indicate that the part of the early plot dealing with Phillotson and Christminster – i.e., with the class and financial difficulties facing working-class men who wish a university education – was inserted into a narrative that stressed Sue's presence in Christminster as the motivation for Jude's ambition; an accompanying concern, with the status of young women in the employment and marriage markets, suggests gender does not invert social critique but intensifies it.

From the complexity and contradictions in each of these matters, it seems clear that Hardy was more concerned to explore them than to develop unilateral positions, undermining the assumption of many readers, both nineteenth- and twentieth-century, that *Jude* is predominately a didactic, polemical novel. A fundamental gauge of the importance of writing is its representation of what its author took to be reality, and the response to *Jude* may depend considerably on one's sense of the specific historical time underlying Hardy's portrayal. But that the novel has retained its power to agitate its readers attests the pervasiveness of its themes – what attracts readers is not restricted to a single era. These various points can be illustrated by addressing one of the novel's themes underlaid by temporal concerns, Sue's relation to her society. In the 1912 Preface Hardy noted that reviewers in Germany had associated Sue with women of the feminist movement – "bachelor" girls; and a lively critical dispute since then has not settled whether Hardy intends the time to be the 1860s or the 1890s, and whether the issue is with awareness of economic restrictions on women's work or with analogies with the New Woman "movement." Gail Cunningham has argued for the 1890s, pointing to rejection of "stifling social conventions," a "franker approach to sexuality," interest in "vast new areas of female psychology and behaviour," "alternatives to marriage, including divorce and free love," a drive toward formal education, and other topics that appeared in the works of such writers as Sarah Grand and George Egerton (Mary Chavelita Dunne). "Sue Bridehead ... has ... the distinctly contemporary features of the New Woman": Hardy goes so far as to adapt phrases and concepts from one of George Egerton's short stories to describe her. Robert Gittings makes the claim that instead of "representing 'the New Woman'" of the 1890s, Sue more significantly evokes "The Girl of the Period" of the 1860s. Gittings argues that a New Woman would probably have had political interests (specifically socialism), have been engaged "in opening the professions to women," and have had at least some post-secondary education. In contrast to any of that, Sue's defining association seems closer to the operators of *The Englishwoman's Journal*, which "aired, for practically the first time, the independent views of women" and to the works of John Stuart Mill. Gittings argues also that Sue's loss of faith and "the idea she finds as a substitute for it," the Positive Philosophy of Auguste Comte, are of the 1860s. "[Sue] condemns Oxford and its orthodox religious beliefs as 'a place full of fetichists' [in] the language of Comte, or rather of the Harriet Martineau translation [of the 1850s]. For Comte believed that mankind passed through religion in its early history, to arrive, via metaphysics, at scientific or 'positive' philosophy, which was the 'religion' of the future ... By 1890, Positivism in England was virtually dead ... No new intellectual woman in the 1890s would have been a positivist."[9]

It is not necessary here to work out these conflicting perspectives, and one related historical issue may be worth noting – the novel's posture toward divorce. Much of the desperation of Sue's resistance to marriage with Jude comes from her sense of the "irrevocableness" of the tie, whereas within the plot both of the primary married couples – Sue and Phillotson, Jude and Arabella – are able to secure divorces with neither trouble nor undue delay (*J*, v, vi, p. 269), based on the wives' adultery, a principal justification under the Matrimonial Causes Act of 1857, the first significant modification of British marriage law. The characters' opening ignorance but dawning awareness of the possibility of divorce would seem characteristic of the initial period of available secular divorces in the 1860s (as in *The Woodlanders*); but this position could be countered by the observation that the supposed ease of divorce represents a legal condition which Hardy was implying simply had not by the 1890s become commonly known in rural counties or permeated the consciousness of the convention-shaped working class. Probably most readers feel that the tone of impassioned contemporary involvement surely requires the setting to be at the time of its writing, the 1890s (when some New Woman novelists were criticizing society's continuing disapproval of divorce); but similar logic applied to the characters' state of knowledge would lead to the deduction that Hardy was drawing on the confusion naturally prevalent shortly after the centuries-old restrictions on divorce had been eased by the 1857 Act. (A revision in 1878 expanded the 1857 law, but in a slight way, involving separate maintenance rather than divorce.)

Of course, a reasonable way to read the situation is that Hardy did not intend to invoke a single definable time, preferring instead a productive ambiguity of contexts that would abate the seeming didacticism that his bluntness elsewhere fostered. If we accept that the novel's two possible times are the 1860s (when Hardy was a young man in London) and the 1890s (when Hardy was moving through a restless stage in his marriage), we can link a psychological involvement with the historical, it is true; but more importantly we can see that substantive issues are not defined by a single time and place.

To this point my aim has been to summarize the novel's contemporary reception and some of the ways that the novel's versions confirm a complex of cultural construction and authorial disposition (which of course includes an author's individual relation to his or her culture). The remainder of this essay explores formal aspects of these forces interacting within *Jude* itself – what one might call formal dimensions of cultural creation. Information about the production and reception of a literary work, although seemingly of a secondary nature, can lead directly to closer awareness of the artistry.

The political and social and religious formations provoked by the personal and societal pressures on Hardy develop within the range of the relationship between Jude and Sue, which in turn interrogates standards Hardy implies dominate society. The paramount hermeneutic conundrum that the varied reception of *Jude* forces upon the reader is whether the novel is "about" Jude, or Sue. A. Alvarez thinks that "the entire novel is simply the image of Jude magnified and subtly lit from different angles until he and his shadows occupy the whole Wessex landscape"; J. I. M. Stewart puts the case for Sue with equal dogmatism: "Viewed as centred upon Jude Fawley, *Jude the Obscure* is a fatigued and awkward and really rather dismal performance. Viewed as centred upon what the impressed but scandalized Edmund Gosse called Sue's *vita sexualis*, there can be no doubt that *Jude the Obscure* stands among the most impressively exploratory and intuitive of modern English novels."[10]

Tracing the division of reader allegiances could follow many paths; here I want to concentrate on the quite different methods Hardy uses in presenting the two protagonists. The difference is simple and powerful. The narrator presents Jude from the inside, as it were, whereas readers and critics must grasp Sue almost entirely from external evidence – what she says and does, and what people report about her. The usual assertion that the narrative is never presented as from Sue's perspective is mistaken, but internal glimpses certainly are infrequent. Readers, like Jude, have to trust to empathy. Consequently, Jude is understandable even if one doesn't admire what one sees; with Sue, the reader must intuit the narrator's (and Hardy's) intentions. The result is that even though the novel is most clearly readable as the impassioned speculation on the career of its male protagonist, who deserves sympathy for the frustration and pain caused him by personal and intellectual dilemmas, for most readers the core of their reactions to the novel lies within the conflicting values and feelings of Sue.

Jude's virtues can be stated, no less than his weaknesses; and both fall within well-understood boundaries.[11] He insists on sticking with the principles he comes to after hard effort, rigorous thought, and frustration; the strain of his effort to live honestly and to advance himself causes him frequently to accept, usually with disastrous consequences, either strong drink or sex, or both. Readers can hold different judgments of Jude's life – for example, contempt for his weakness or deep sympathy for his suffering – but they customarily base their judgments on similar criteria. Jude is far from a simple character, but nonetheless one whose scope can be measured by established frames of reference. He can reasonably be evaluated as a tragic figure, and can with plausibility be rejected because his portrayal is too bleak and pessimistic (Arthur Mizener)[12] or defended because his narrative satisfies Aristotelian principles (as Hardy himself says in his 1912 postscript to the novel's preface).

Sue escapes this kind of systemic analysis. Certainly, enough readers have applied one system or another to Sue, and have felt content that they have "placed" her. But the multiplicity of perspectives, nearly all of which if they are to lead to a satisfactory explication must ignore important supporting "evidences" of others, demonstrates the necessarily tenuousness of global or inclusive readings of Sue. The history of the reading of *Jude the Obscure* depends to a major degree upon the readiness of the audience to see what is there combined with an insistence to see what they wish to see. This principle is true for most canonical works, of course; and in *Jude* it affects

Jude as well as Sue; but the materials surrounding Sue are, simply, more complex and rich, and finally irreconcilable. It is not a question of incoherence, or of forcing an interpretation: it is rather a sign of Hardy's genius (whether deliberate and conscious, or not) to create in Sue a character that cannot be restrained to explication. Sue's range of extreme decisions deflects attempted comprehensive analysis. As Hardy put it in the midst of the furor at the novel's publication, "Sue is a type of woman which has always had an attraction for me – but the difficulty of drawing the type has kept me from attempting it till now" (*Letters* 2, p. 99).

Most obviously there is the matter of Sue's sexual nature, scarcely less so is the matter of her exploitation of this nature, and of the totemic relationship of sexuality to her society.[13] In no other aspect of the novel than this does the focus of the present essay on Hardy's readers have greater pertinence. Certainly professional readers, and probably no less so general readers, shape their reactions to, and analyses of, Sue according to their essential reading strategies. In recent years feminist assumptions underlie many strategies. Among the plethora of recent readings, a particularly interesting approach is by Kathleen Blake, who suggests that Sue's feminist method is to remain a virgin, which will permit her to evade the pain and sufferings attendant upon her gender.[14] A reading based on gender that has gained a good deal of recent attention was first made by Edmund Gosse, Hardy's friend and reviewer, who implies, somewhat obscurely, that Sue's shrinking from sex and marriage is motivated by lesbianism: "She is a poor, maimed 'degenerate,' ignorant of herself and of the perversion of her instincts" (Cox, p. 269). Hardy's response, in a letter to Gosse – "The abnormalism consists in disproportion: not in inversion, her sexual instinct being healthy so far as it goes, but unusually weak & fastidious" (*Letters* 2, p. 99) – does not erase Gosse's explanation of Sue's behavior. With present-day awareness of the psychological anguish caused by suppression of homosexual feelings, this potential aspect of Sue's situation will reward a more coherently addressed scrutiny than any I have seen yet.

As theories of gender and methods of interpretation have grown more complex, Sue has become ever more of a cultural marker, a "test" of the hermeneutic adequacy of theory and of a given era's manner of adopting literature for its needs. One must not overstate the matter: critics remain individuals using their abilities, or even genius, as well as they can, but logically, they also benefit from current thinking, and are part of the culture they study. To mention only a few of those who have read Sue with acuity: D. H. Lawrence and Marjorie Garson employ paradigms or analytical systems into which they "fit" Sue;[15] others, like Robert Heilman (see note 11), don't lay out a paradigm but have strong expectations (in Heilman's case, that ambiguous females are unstable and unsettling) that amount to paradigms. A paradoxical twist is that critics who by the nature of their work need to have pre-existing frameworks confront a fictional matrix whose author eschewed strict consistency, "fairness," and exhaustive coverage of background or motivation. The confrontation becomes a history of reception that has made critical reading of *Jude* a commentary on the (shifting) contemporary. In most cases the result is positive – an enriching of our understanding of *Jude* (or of Hardy) even when we disagree with the specific reading. In some cases contemporary market forces overwhelm or usurp Hardy's fiction, as in Michael Winterbottom's 1996 film *Jude*. The star-system mandated that a major box-office draw play Sue, with a less-famous actor playing Arabella, even though each actor seems better suited for the other's role (at least as *I* read Hardy!). That movie presents a Sue who not only is buxom (a quality Hardy attributes to Arabella [*J*, I, vi, p. 36 – "prominent bosom"], whereas he often describes Sue as "slight" [e.g., III, i, p. 136] or "slim" [III, iii, p. 150], climaxed by reference to "the small, tight, apple-like convexities of her bodice, so different from Arabella's amplitudes" [III, ix, p. 195]), but who is a swaggering young woman who shows her rebelliousness from convention not by quoting Mill but by smoking and drinking beer in a Christminster pub, the only female in company with Jude and his stonemason mates. As further evidence of the felt need to make Sue appealing to an audience most of whom will not have read the novel, it is not the cinematic Sue who says all the things that impel Father Time to murder-suicide. Jude gets to say about half of them, in a sensitive and meditative nocturnal chat with Father Time that in addition to turning blame from Sue makes for an attractive late-twentieth-century moment of father–son bonding.

The interplay between Hardy and his audience can further be traced in a structural maneuver through which Hardy promotes subliminally reader diagnosis of the protagonists' struggle. Diagnosis is more effective if rational analysis and deduction are paralleled on a non-conscious plane that, while not *ir*rational, arouses initiative and insight: the combination enhances the power and authority of the text. This common procedure of narrative (seen, for example, in *The Mayor of Casterbridge* when Henchard's sudden verge from his intention to destroy Farfrae brings the reader into intuitive reassessment of Henchard's character) occurs in *Jude*. The protagonists' "progress" is toward devastation, as their experiences strip them of their will to survive. Initially, they are opposed by the material enmity of class and income, and by universal forces of "the way things are." Being givens of existence, these conditions do not destroy Sue and

Jude; but they weaken them through their continual opposition and leave them open to destruction by whatever is the *unique* opposing force in their lives – which, it turns out, is revealed halfway through the plot. The novel is divided in almost equal parts, the first part of which emphasizes the dominant role of social and philosophical and religious agencies in preventing Jude and Sue from gaining happiness (either with each other or with such others as Arabella), the second half of which concentrates on the forces internal to Sue that constitute a fatal barrier to her and Jude's happiness.

This division does not make the novel discordant; instead, it contributes immensely to the power and sense of rawness with which the novel concludes. Strong social and political emphases in the early part continue to color the atmosphere and contribute to the definition of the nature of the appeal that Sue has for Jude, namely the idealizing function of abstraction and high ideals. Through his manipulation of the tone of rhetoric, of the level of tension, Hardy (or his narrator) provides guidelines to the reader's appropriate reaction. This is a structural dimension to Hardy's artistry, that parallels the set of oppositions he sketched out in his letter to Gosse already quoted – "the book is all contrasts – or was meant to be in its original conception ... e.g., Sue & her heathen gods set against Jude's reading the Greek Test[amen]t; Christminster academical, Chr in the slums; Jude the saint, Jude the sinner; Sue the Pagan, Sue the saint; marriage, no marriage; &c. &c." (*Letters* 2, p. 99).

The most efficient way to demonstrate the two-part division is to concentrate on the relatively short expanse in the plot where this major shift in the novel's mode of presentation takes place. It culminates the plot events leading from the frustration of Jude's academic ambitions, his marital relationship with Arabella, and the complex movement to and fro that his and Sue's relations have as she seems simultaneously to be enticing him and treating him like a colleague rather than a potential lover, and as he yearns for her in a way that prevents his telling her that he already has a wife. In a sense, the novel resembles a comedy to this point,[16] as Arabella's healthy sexiness and Sue's witty command of ideas would seem to protect both of them from significant harm, particularly from anyone so seemingly aimless and morally scrupulous as Jude.

Jude the Obscure is Hardy's fullest analysis of the relationship between the individual struggling in the context of both universal and temporal forces that work in tandem to restrict happiness and freedom. The universal force is represented in passages of unfocused despair, as when – in the early part of Jude's career – the narrator says that much suffering could have been avoided had someone come along to give comfort and sound advice at the time Jude realizes there is no system of transmutation between languages. The narrator's wisdom is summed up, "But nobody did come, because nobody does" (*J*, I, iv, p. 27). The more vibrantly felt and articulated enmity to individuals, however, is from social and religious conventions. Jude observes the lack of logic in the convention that forces people to marry because of a temporary lapse from sexual chastity (*J*, I, ix, pp. 60–61 – just after he finds out that Arabella is not pregnant); and the rules of class that cause the head of Biblioll College to recommend that Jude has the best chance of happiness if he were to stay in his own position rather than aspire to higher education (*J*, II, vi, p. 120) represent the unreflective exercise of prejudice.

In the first part of the novel the emphasis is on Jude's ambition, hopes, and perpetual disillusionment and frustration. He is portrayed as a kind of Everyman, whose weaknesses – drink, ambition, sexual energy – are seen as either natural in themselves or as inevitable, if temporary, consolations for the frustration of an aspect of his representativeness (as when his application for advice to enter Christminster is peremptorily turned aside because of his class status). He is an individual also, of course, even in the early part of the novel, but it is as Everyman that he is equal to the frustrations his society forces upon him. After his representativeness is well established, that which is *personal* or idiosyncratic in his life (which is conveyed primarily in the personality and behavior of Sue) becomes insupportable and painful progressively, as hopes for social advance lessen and the recourse to human consolation becomes more central to Jude's life and mind.

What is perhaps the first mark of this shift can be thought of as ironic and incongruous, in the passage in which, shortly after Sue marries Phillotson, Jude is described as not wishing to think of Phillotson as part of any propagation that Sue will participate in. Jude is referred to as a dreamer in wishing that Sue could create children all by herself (i.e., sans sex). "And then he again uneasily saw, as he had latterly seen with more and more frequency, the scorn of nature for man's finer emotions, and her lack of interest in his aspirations" (*J*, III, viii, p. 184). Despite the drily satiric tone in projecting Jude's rejection of reality (at least until cloning became an option), it *is* an expression of the kind of idealization of Sue that shortly becomes intense and thereafter is made a motif.

That idealization appears in more traditional form a few pages later in Jude's elevated thoughts about Sue, inspired by his self-chastisement at having had sex with Arabella instead of keeping an appointment with Sue on their way to visit together their Aunt Drusilla. Jude's language is heightened during Sue's and his meeting the next day: "like a good angel";

"heartily ashamed of his earthliness in spending the hours he had spent in Arabella's company"; "rude and immoral." He thinks of Sue as "so ethereal a creature that her spirit could be seen trembling through her limbs" and as "one who, to him, was so uncarnate as to seem at times impossible as a human wife to any average man" (*J*, III, ix, pp. 194, 195). Previously to this point, Sue has not been thus characterized as beyond ordinary possibility of sex.

Sue is also different here than before her marriage, in a direct sense: she is "all nerves" (*J*, III, ix, p. 195) from anxiety for Jude because he hadn't met her the night before as promised. Although her conversation with Jude is tentative and tremulous in this their first meeting after her marriage, she does not want to talk about Arabella. It is clear that, were Sue to know of Jude's sleeping with Arabella, she would be resentful (as she is when she does learn, later, that during this trip to see their ill aunt he *had* slept with Arabella). Previously – despite her having set a date to marry Phillotson immediately in response to learning that Jude already had a wife – there is not the same degree of startled, intense, unreasoning, self-centered, and perverse righteousness.

Sue disguises her repulsion from Phillotson only for a short duration. In her first frank and self-revealing conversation with Jude after her marriage to Phillotson, during their subsequent trip to Marygreen for their aunt's funeral, she refers to her "physical objection," "a fastidiousness," and "pruderies" in relation to her marriage with Phillotson (*J*, IV, ii, p. 221). Her lament about Phillotson and marital sex commences the novel's increasingly desperate tone of paranoia and doomedness. But it is not until the day she returns from Aunt Drusilla's funeral and the passionate "farewell" kiss with Jude – that had *not* been the kiss of cousins (*J*, IV, iii, p. 227) – that she flees from the marital embrace and goes to the closet under the stairs to sleep (*J*, IV, iii, p. 231). The timing implies clearly that it's love for Jude that makes her shrink decisively from Phillotson, that despite the narrator's description of her as "the ethereal, fine-nerved, sensitive girl, quite unfitted by temperament and instinct to fulfil the conditions of the matrimonial relation with Phillotson, possibly with scarce any man" (*J*, IV, iii, p. 229), she would not have shrunk from sex with Jude with the same intensity and revulsion.

Up to this midpoint of the novel, in fact, the mode of presentation of the narration has been Jude's coming to terms with social rigidities – the need to marry a pregnant girl-friend; the difficulty of a working-class man getting into Oxbridge; impediments to divorce. About this last "rigidity": given the ease with which both Sue and Jude are divorced later on, that he/ they do not consider the option of his divorcing Arabella so that he and Sue can marry seems at least as much a function of narrative necessity as it is a deviation from New Woman mind-set. They both behave – presuming the truth of it – as if a marriage oath of perpetual bond is genuinely a determining social/religious necessity. Interestingly, there is no indication that Sue is ignorant of sex (she knows she's frustrating the Christminster undergraduate), and she seems at least moderately warm toward Jude. Rationally, then, Hardy's management of structure carries the implicit message that had Jude and Sue pursued the possibility of a Jude–Arabella divorce and a marriage *before* Sue is repulsed by sex with Phillotson, they would have had a "normal" marriage, especially since Jude wants Sue's presence more than he wants her sexually.

Of course, this previous paragraph postulates a different novel than the one Hardy set out to write. My point is that Hardy manipulates structure, and the mode of presentation, in such a way as to make more striking and horrifying the destruction wrought by Sue's shrinking from Phillotson. It is his very success at this that helps account for the painful impact of the novel, and of the sense of excess that causes readers like Arthur Mizener to query whether *Jude the Obscure* has the distance and objectivity they expect in tragedy. It is remarkable how different are the tones of the novel previous to, and following, Sue's marriage. The emphasis shifts almost entirely from the damage caused by social convention and philosophical unconventionality to damage caused nearly purely on psychological grounds. The shift of attention to Sue's sexuality and then the ensuing intensification of that attention broadens and deepens the novel's impact, because the psychological level enhances the sense of unfairness and irrationality of suffering caused by society and philosophy.

The change in emphasis is cumulative. It gains momentum from the narratorial interjection about Sue's thought which suggests there is material in this novel for a study of Sue from the inside, despite most critics' assumption that there *is* no internal projection of Sue. When Sue tells Jude she did not elope with him with the idea of becoming lovers, he resists, but submits: "He could never resist her when she pleaded (as she well knew)" (*J*, IV, v, p. 253). This section (IV, v [*J*, pp. 248–57]) is central in any exploration of Sue's personality regarding sex and her chances for a traditional life. She refuses Jude's natural assumption that her leaving Phillotson means she is willing to have a full relationship with Jude; then she becomes distressed and frantic when she discovers Jude has had marital relations with Arabella in the same hotel she takes a room in when she refuses to stay in the Temperance Hotel with Jude. Jude puts it directly: "You concede nothing to me and I have to concede everything to you" (*J*, IV, v, p. 255); and she wants, evidently, flattery of her ethereality (*J*, IV, v, p. 257). The series of chapters I have been discussing marks the end of the novel's placing the basis for unhappiness in the established system of things, of conventions, and the beginning of placing it resoundingly within personality. Jude tells Sue that "A Nemesis attends the woman who plays the game of elusiveness too often" (*J*, v, i, pp. 272–73), so that she gains the contempt of her old admirers. This definitive turn is highlighted by the just-disclosed revelation that divorce is easy to obtain, which simply obliterates the oppressiveness of social dicta, and by the appearance in the next chapter of Arabella, in supposed need, which precipitates Sue's sexual surrender (or, Jude's sexual conquest). The surrender/conquest leads to a family, further oppression by society, and the collapse of Sue's fragile sense of self – all contributing to the novel's power – and to its history of attack and defense by generations of readers.

Whether the readers of this essay agree that Hardy has manipulated readers in the way I've sketched will depend on their own preconceptions that they bring to the essay, and to the novel. Readers of Hardy's own time responded less obviously to the structure of the plot and more viscerally and vehemently to the portions of the novel that point up the differences between life as they expected it to be lived and life as Hardy saw it taking place among unconventional women and men of his time. Of course many (perhaps the majority) of his contemporary readers admired Hardy for his forthrightness; but he listened to those who objected to his portrayal of life, and, with his distaste for controversy enhanced by a similar reader reaction to the book version of *The Well-Beloved* in 1897, moved with relief to the next phrase of his career, poetry.

NOTES

1 Useful studies of Victorian audiences and publishers include John A. Sutherland, *Victorian Novelists and Publishers* (London: Athlone Press; University of Chicago Press, 1976), and N. N. Feltes, *Modes of Production of Victorian Novels* (University of Chicago Press, 1986).

2 Discussions of the manuscript and the serial: Robert Slack, "The Text of *Jude the Obscure*," *Nineteenth-Century Fiction*, 11 (1957), 261–75; John Paterson, "The Genesis of *Jude the Obscure*," *Studies in Philology*, 57 (1960), 87–98; and Patricia Ingham, "The Evolution of *Jude the Obscure*," *Review of English Studies*, 27 (1976), 27–37, 159–69. See also Dennis Taylor's textual note in his Penguin edition of *Jude* (1998).

3 For an extended discussion of the relationship of the aesthetic quality of the serial version and the reactions of its readers and reviewers, see Linda K. Hughes and Michael Lund, *The Victorian Serial* (Charlottesville: University Press of Virginia, 1991), pp. 229–43.

4 The best-known denunciatory reviews are by Margaret Oliphant, who included *Jude* amongst such other "anti-marriage" novels as Grant Allen's *The Woman*

Who Did (1895) (*Blackwood's Magazine*, 159 [January 1896], 135–49; partially rpt. in Cox, pp. 256–62), and Jeannette Gilder, *New York World*, 8 December 1895, p. 33.

5 A brief but detailed discussion of this pattern of increased directness in sexual references is in Simon Gatrell, *Hardy the Creator: A Textual Biography* (Oxford: Clarendon Press, 1988), pp. 157–64.

6 A sampling of variant passages from several of the versions of the novel are in the notes for the World's Classics Edition (*J*, ed. Patricia Ingham [1985], pp. 433–51 *passim*).

7 The closest to such an edition of *Jude* is unpublished: Robert Slack's dissertation at the University of Pittsburgh (1953); dissertation editions of other novels and stories are in the libraries of various universities. Only two editions of novels have been published: *The Woodlanders*, ed. Dale Kramer (1981), *Tess of the d'Urbervilles*, ed. Juliet Grindle and Simon Gatrell (1983), and one of uncollected stories, *The Excluded and Collaborative Stories*, ed. Pamela Dalziel (1992), all three published by Clarendon Press.

8 Guinevere L. Griest, *Mudie's Circulating Library and the Victorian Novel* (Bloomington: Indiana University Press, 1970) contains much valuable information on Mudie's methods and downfall, and on contemporary social background.

9 Gail Cunningham, *The New Woman and the Victorian Novel* (London and Basingstoke: Macmillan, 1978), pp. 17, 81, 82, 104–06; Robert Gittings, *Young Thomas Hardy* (London: Heinemann, 1975), pp. 94–95. Cunningham gives a different definition of "Girl of the Period" (pp. 8–9), based on Eliza Lynn Linton's essay of that title (*Saturday Review*, 14 March 1868), than Gittings does; and he offers refutations of some of Gittings's arguments. William Greenslade, in *Degeneration, Culture and the Novel, 1880–1940* (Cambridge University Press, 1994) stresses Sue's "nerves" as characteristic of the 1890s New Woman (pp. 174–76).

10 A. Alvarez, "Afterword," *Jude the Obscure* (New York: New American Library, 1961), p. 413; J. I. M. Stewart, *Thomas Hardy: A Critical Biography* (London: Longman, 1971), p. 188. Gosse wrote two reviews, one for the *St. James's Gazette*, the other for *Cosmopolis* (see Cox, pp. 268–69, for his comments on Sue's "*vita sexualis*").

11 The best definition of this quality in Jude is Kate Millett, *Sexual Politics* (Garden City, N.Y.: Doubleday, 1970), p. 131. Robert Heilman thoroughly sketches the opposite quality in Sue, her ambiguity and self-contradictoriness: "Hardy's Sue Bridehead," *Nineteenth-Century Fiction*, 20 (1966); rpt. as "Sue Bridehead: A Brilliant Portrait," in *The Workings of Fiction: Essays by Robert Bechtold Heilman* (Columbia: University of Missouri Press, 1991), p. 267.

12 Arthur Mizener, "*Jude the Obscure* as a Tragedy," *Southern Review*, 6/1 (1940), 193–213; rev. as "The Novel of Doctrine in the Nineteenth Century: Hardy's *Jude the Obscure*," *The Sense of Life in the Modern Novel* (Boston: Houghton Mifflin, 1964), pp. 55–77.

13 A common approach to Sue's attitude toward sex is as a reading by Hardy of Victorian conventions defining female purity("placing women on a pedestal") and of consequences of prudery. Worth reading for their bearing on *Jude* are Lloyd Fernando's discussions, however brief, in *"New Women" in the Late*

Victorian Novel (University Park: Pennsylvania State University Press, 1977) of such topics as the liberal, even revolutionary, ideas of Victorian sexual theorists Karl Pearson ("The Woman's Question" [1885]) and G. R. Drysdale (*The Elements of Social Science, or Physical, Sexual, and Natural Religion* [1854; rpt. thirty-five times by 1905]) (Fernando, *"New Women,"* pp. 14–19); one of the aspirations of the "New Woman" movement, a sexless society in which love would be wholly spiritual and mental (pp. 23–24); and the "unacknowledged neuroses caused by new life styles" (pp. 24–25).

14 Kathleen Blake, "Sue Bridehead: A Woman of the Feminist Movement," in *Love and the Woman Question in Victorian Literature: The Art of Self-Postponement* (Brighton, Sussex: Harvester Press, 1983), pp. 146–67.

15 D. H. Lawrence, in *Study of Thomas Hardy and Other Essays*, ed. Bruce Steele. The Cambridge Edition of the Works of D. H. Lawrence (Cambridge University Press, 1985), pp. 7–155 [originally published in *Phoenix: The Posthumous Papers of D. H. Lawrence*, ed. Edward D. McDonald (London: William Heinemann, 1936), pp. 398–516]; Marjorie Garson, *Hardy's Fables of Integrity: Woman, Body, Text* (Oxford: Clarendon Press, 1991).

16 Some of the novel's qualities as comedy have been addressed by Millgate, in *Thomas Hardy: His Career as a Novelist* (London: The Bodley Head, 1971), pp. 326–27; and Ronald P. Draper, "Hardy's Comic Tragedy: *Jude the Obscure*," in *Critical Essays on Thomas Hardy: The Novels*, ed. Dale Kramer with the assistance of Nancy Marck (Boston: G. K. Hall, 1990), pp. 243–54.

FURTHER READING

Ardis, Ann L. *New Women, New Novels: Feminism and Early Modernism.* New Brunswick, N.J., and London: Rutgers University Press, 1990.

Boumelha, Penny. *Thomas Hardy and Women.* Madison: University of Wisconsin Press, 1982.

Daleski, H. M. *"Jude the Obscure*: The Defective Real," in *Thomas Hardy and Paradoxes of Love.* Columbia and London: University of Missouri Press, 1997, pp. 180-205.

Fisher, Joe. *The Hidden Hardy.* London and Basingstoke: Macmillan, 1992.

Gallivan, Patricia. "Science and Art in *Jude the Obscure.*" In *The Novels of Thomas Hardy.* Ed. Anne Smith. London: Vision, 1979, pp. 126-44.

Goode, John. *Thomas Hardy: The Offensive Truth.* Oxford: Blackwell, 1988.

Ingham, Patricia. *"Jude the Obscure,"* in *The Language of Gender and Class: Transformation in the Victorian Novel.* London and New York: Routledge, 1996, pp. 160-82.

Jacobus, Sue. "Sue the Obscure." *Essays in Criticism*, 25 (1975), 304-28.

Knoepflmacher, U. C. "The End of Compromise: *Jude the Obscure* and *The Way of All Flesh,*" in *Laughter & Despair: Readings in Ten Novels of the Victorian Era.* Berkeley and Los Angeles: University of California Press, 1971, pp. 202-39.

Kucich, John. "Moral Authority in Hardy's Late Novels: The Gendering of Art." In *The Power of Lies: Transgression in Victorian Fiction.* Ithaca: Cornell University Press, 1994, pp. 199-238.

Ledger, Sally. *The New Woman: Fiction and Feminism at the "Fin de siècle."* Manchester University Press, 1997.

Lodge, David. "*Jude the Obscure*: Pessimism and Fictional Form." In *Critical Approaches to the Fiction of Thomas Hardy*. Ed. Dale Kramer. London and Basingstoke: Macmillan, 1979, pp. 193-201.

McDonald, Peter D. *British Literary Culture and Publishing Practice 1880-1914*. Cambridge University Press, 1997.

Maynard, John. "Hardy's *Jude*: Disassembling Sexuality and Religion." In *Victorian Discourses on Sexuality and Religion*. Cambridge University Press, 1993, pp. 271-98, 372-75.

Pyle, Forest. "Demands of History: Narrative Crisis in *Jude the Obscure*." *New Literary History*, 26 (1995), 359-78.

Saldívar, Ramón. "*Jude the Obscure*: Reading and the Spirit of the Law." *ELH*, 50 (1983), 607-25.

Schweik, Robert. "The 'Modernity' of Hardy's *Jude the Obscure*." In *A Spacious Vision: Essays on Hardy*. Ed. Phillip V. Mallett and Ronald P. Draper. Newmill, Cornwall: Patten Press, 1994, pp. 49-63.

Widdowson, Peter. *Hardy in History: A Study in Literary Sociology*. London: Routledge, 1989.

II

DENNIS TAYLOR

Hardy as a nineteenth-century poet

In the Victorian period, poetry was still the high genre of literature. Speaking of his early twenties, Hardy said: "A sense of the truth of poetry, of its supreme place in literature, had awakened itself in me" (*LW*, p. 415). "Poetry," he said in 1912, "is the heart of literature" (*PW*, p. 246). As Hardy (born in 1840) began to write in the 1860s, the era of Tennyson, Browning, and Arnold was slowly changing into the era of Swinburne, Hopkins, and Hardy. This formulation would surprise contemporary Victorians, since Hopkins and Hardy's poetries were not well known until the twentieth century. Even in the twentieth century, while Hopkins became celebrated by the new critics, Hardy remained a controversial case as a poet, partly because of his fame as a novelist, partly because of certain characteristics of his verse that were less amenable than Hopkins's to the analytic methods of the new criticism. Yet now Hardy is seen as a primary source in the founding of a major stream of modern English poetry, as charted for example by Donald Davie.[1] Only in the last half of the twentieth century has Hardy's major stature as a poet come to be assumed.

Hardy early had a driving ambition to join the company of famous poets. "His dream had been that he would make his living as a poet."[2] The first seeds of Hardy's ambition were perhaps planted by his mother, Jemima, a woman ambitious for her son, whose gifts to him at eight years of age were "Dryden's Virgil, Johnson's *Rasselas*, and *Paul and Virginia*" (*LW*, p. 21). Other accounts claim that her favorite work was Dante's *Commedia*, that she admired Byron, and that she preferred Scott's *Marmion* to his prose works (Millgate, *Biography*, p. 39), a judgment later echoed by Hardy. Jemima's mother, Hardy's grandmother, had the kind of culture not uncommon in the English countryside: "She knew the writings of Addison, Steele, and others of the *Spectator* group, almost by heart, was familiar with Richardson and Fielding, and, of course, with such standard works as *Paradise Lost* and *The Pilgrim's Progress*" (*LW*, p. 11). Hardy's ancestral background was, thus, literature and poverty, since after her husband's death, his grandmother and her daughter had experienced severe hardship. "Jemima saw during girlhood and young womanhood some very stressful experiences of which she could never speak in her maturer years without pain, though she appears to have mollified her troubles by reading every book she could lay hands on" (*LW*, p. 12). "Like her mother, too, she read omnivorously" (*LW*, p. 19). She also loved music and piano, and married a man who came from a long line of church and country-dance fiddle players. Church hymns and ballads filled the air in Hardy's young life. Hardy's father also came from a background of ancestral poverty; the terrifying tales of his mother, Mary Head, would provide Hardy with the harsh setting of *Jude the Obscure* (*LW*, p. 453).

With his mother's encouragement, Hardy at age twelve "was started on the old Eton grammar and readings in Eutropius and Caesar" (*LW*, p. 27). At fourteen, he copied out Charles Swain's poem, "The Old Cottage Clock," on the back of the door of the family clock, and signed it with his own name (Purdy, p. 325). Hardy's schooling was limited – he would leave school at age sixteen – but his experience as a self-motivated student would provide many details of his description of Jude. Hardy would rise at four a.m., and eventually get through "several books of the *Aeneid*, some Horace and Ovid, etc.... . He also took up Greek ... getting on with some books of the *Iliad*" (*LW*, p. 32). The need to work, and the love of classical learning and literature, was the fundamental tension of Hardy's young years. The ambiguity of his position, and his literary ambitions, were encouraged by his friendship with the Moule family and their associations with Cambridge, an association which glorified classical learning – so much so that one vocational possibility Hardy considered was becoming an Oxbridge-trained minister. The turn toward poetry in particular was also encouraged by the local example of William Barnes, a polymath school-teacher, famous for his Dorset poems, which Hardy early admired for their skill and regionalism and use of dialect.[3]

A key moment of Hardy's early twenties was when Horace Moule in 1862 gave him a copy of *The Golden Treasury*. Moule himself had the potential to be "a distinguished English poet" (in Hardy's words [Millgate, *Biography*, p. 67]) and so was a role model for Hardy. In the last year of his life, Hardy's wife noted: "Speaking about ambition T. said today that he had done all that he meant to do, but he did not know whether it had been worth doing. His only ambition, so far as he could remember, was to have some poem or poems in a good anthology like the *Golden Treasury*. The model he had set before him was 'Drink to me only,' by Ben Jonson" (*LW*, p. 478). Hardy began a serious study of *The Golden Treasury*, and made markings (either at the time of the gift or a little later) against various short

Renaissance poems, especially sonnets by Shakespeare; also Spenser's "Prothalamion," Milton's "Lycidas," and various poems by Gray, Collins, Burns, Wordsworth, Shelley, and others. Next to Herrick's "Gather ye rosebuds," Hardy wrote: "my grandf[athe]rs song." One of the *Golden Treasury* poems had a particularly important effect on him: "Lodge's poem to Rosaline was one of the first two or three which awakened in me a true, or mature, consciousness of what poetry consists in – after a Dark Age of five or six years which followed that vague sense, in childhood, of the charms of verses that most young people experience" (*Letters* 1, p. 122). Moule's gift eventually inspired Hardy to proceed to an even more systematic study of poetic language. In this year, Hardy began a notebook, which he entitled *Studies, Specimens &c.*, a semi-scientific linguistic notation of words and phrases taken from the *Golden Treasury* poets and others. The *Studies, Specimens &c.* notebook included specimens of Swinburne, Shakespeare's *Richard II* and other plays, the Bible (mostly the prophets), Scott (especially *Marmion* and *The Lady of the Lake*), Tennyson's *In Memoriam*, Spenser (especially the *Epithalamion*), Shelley's *The Revolt of Islam*, Byron (mostly *Childe Harold*), and also of course Lodge's "Rosaline." Hardy's notes on "Rosaline" are typical of his study of "specimens":

> twines (of hair) / sapphires set in snow / blushing cloud … selfsame … her lips are like two *budded* roses whom *ranks* of lilies *neighbour nigh* / *centres* of delight / orbs / feed perfection = keep perfect what is already so / with orient pearl, with sapphire blue with marble white, with ruby red her body every way is fed yet soft in touch & sweet in view / nymphs … bemoan … brand … apt to entice / imprisoned (abstractions in material forms) / moulds = makes / muse not.[4]

This is one of hundreds of such entries in the notebook which illustrates what Horace Moule called Hardy's "minute way of looking at style."[5] The "Dark age of five or six years" which Hardy describes above as preceding his reading of "Rosaline" corresponds to the period separating his early poem "Domicilium" (1857–60) from the period (1865–69) when he compiled the *Studies, Specimens &c.* notebook and began his mature poetic career. Other authors excerpted and studied in the notebook are Wordsworth, Barnes, Ingelow, Burns, Dante (translated by John Carlyle), Coleridge, Milton, Shelley, and others. Hardy also began buying (and marking up) books which he signed and dated in the 1860s, specifically 1863–66. These included: Coleridge (signed 1865), Dryden (signed 1865), Milton (copies signed 1865 and 1866), Shakespeare (signed 1863), Shelley (signed 1866), Spenser (signed 1865), Thomson (signed 1865), W. Dodd's

The Beauties of Shakespeare (signed 1865), Walker's *Rhyming Dictionary* (signed 1865), Nuttall's *Pronouncing Dictionary* (signed 1865), and Henry Reed's *Introduction to English Literature* (signed 1865). In order to build his vocabulary, he underlined most extensively in his Milton, Thomson, Shelley, Shakespeare (especially in Dodd's *Beauties*), and *Golden Treasury*, and added many rhyming words to his Walker.[6] In 1868 Hardy made a special note that he was reading Browning, and also Whitman (*LW*, pp. 59, 61).

The 1860s, when Hardy began studying and writing poetry, was an important decade for Victorian poetry. Important developments were taking place in sonnets, ballads, hymns, classical imitations, romance imitations.[7] Hardy would compose more than 150 poems in some form of hymnal stanza. "The Impercipient" from his first volume (*CPW*, I, p. 87) typically takes the hymn form, in Emily Dickinson fashion, and adapts it to a consciousness which can no longer believe in the old religion. Other, more exotic forms were coming into the foreground in the 1860s. Swinburne's use of French romance forms like the rondeau heralded the great revival of romance forms to come, a revival in which we shall see Hardy participate. Even more influential on Hardy was the fact that the 1860s witnessed the greatest revival of imitation of classical meters since the late sixteenth century. A most important influence on Hardy was again that of Swinburne, whose *Poems and Ballads* burst on the scene in 1866, with its radical developments in prosody, language, and philosophy. Swinburne's *Atalanta in Calydon* appeared the year before. Swinburne's effect on Hardy was like Hemingway's effect on young American fiction writers. Swinburne became Hardy's earliest poetic idol, both for metrical skill and for those ideas which helped deconvert Hardy from his Anglicanism. Later, Hardy wrote of this time of discovering Swinburne:

> O that far morning of a summer day
> When, down a terraced street whose pavements lay
> Glassing the sunshine into my bent eyes,
> I walked and read with a quick glad surprise
> New words, in classic guise.   (*CPW*, II, p. 31)

Hardy would become one of the most learned of poets. In 1866–67, he read only books of poetry, believing "that, as in verse was concentrated the essence of all imaginative and emotional literature, to read verse and nothing else was the shortest way to the fountain-head of such." He "never ceased to regret that the author of ... *Marmion* – should later have declined on prose fiction" (*LW*, p. 51). He began a lifelong career of notetaking, some of these early notes represented in the early entries of his *Literary*

Notes, and also in the so-called "'1867' notebook" whose first twenty entries may date from the 1860s: some of these are from Swinburne and Shakespeare.[8] Later Hardy advised a young poet: "The only practical advice I can give ... is to begin with *imitative* poetry" (*PN*, p. 272). Another notebook, entitled "Poetical Matter," which includes copies of earlier notes, contains the following note: "*Lyrical Meth[od]* Find a situ[atio]n from exp[erien]ce. Turn to Ly[ri]cs for a form of express[io]n that has been used for a quite diff[eren]t situ[atio]n. Use it (same sit[uatio]n from experience may be sung in sev[era]l forms)" (quoted in Millgate, *Biography*, p. 89). The "Lycs" in this note is a reference to *The Golden Treasury* whose spiral cover title reads: *Golden Treasury of Songs and Lyrics*. Hardy continued to love anthologies, and would say: "I myself have been led to read poets by seeing specimens in these anthologies" (*Letters* 4, p. 256; see the list discussed in Taylor, *Hardy's Metres*, p. 212). But for every stanza form Hardy borrowed, he invented almost four. Indeed, his later poetry shows increasingly complex and inventive stanza forms.

About 1860, Hardy "began writing verses" (*LW*, p. 37). He began with conventional Wordsworthian blank verse in "Domicilium" (*CPW*, III, pp. 279–80) in 1860 (begun 1857), tried a ballad fragment *c.* 1863–67 (Millgate, *Biography*, p. 89), then proceeded to write sonnets, the earliest being perhaps "Discouragement" (*CPW*, III, p. 155) (begun 1863), a poem which combines the literariness of Hardy with the bitterness bred in him by his harsh ancestral background. Over half of the poems by Hardy dated before 1872 are sonnets. In total he would write thirty-eight sonnets that have been preserved, beginning mostly with Shakespearean sonnets in the 1860s, and moving toward Petrarchan and then Wordsworthian forms later. In 1863, he considered "that he might combine literature with architecture by becoming an art-critic for the press – particularly in the province of architectural art." He quickly gave up this notion, and aimed to become a practicing poet: "by 1865 he had begun to write verses, and by 1866 to send his productions to magazines ... these were rejected by editors" (*LW*, p. 49). In 1865 "he perceived ... that he could not live by poetry ... So he formed the idea of combining poetry and the Church ... This fell through ... [because] he could hardly take the step with honour while holding the views that on examination he found himself to hold" (*LW*, pp. 52–53). In 1867 "he had formed an idea of writing plays in blank verse" (*LW*, p. 55), thus moving perhaps from Shakespearean sonnets to Shakespearean drama. But he continued with the short poem. One of his early attempts is a quatrain entitled "Epitaph by Labourers" written in the back of his copy of Milton (see Taylor, "Hardy's ... Copy of Milton," pp. 50–60). After "Discouragement," he experimented with song stanzas, in the 1865 poem,

"Amabel" (*CPW*, I, pp. 8–9), reflecting his father's spirit; then he wrote a poem in Renaissance septet stanzas, "The Unplanted Primrose" (*CPW*, III, pp. 280–81) (begun 1865), reflecting the high learning of *The Golden Treasury*; then he turned back to his hometown influence in the ballad narrative of "The Bride-Night Fire" in 1866 (*CPW*, I, pp. 93–98); then in the same year he veered toward his classical training in "Postponement" (*CPW*, I, p. 12) loosely reflecting a sapphic structure that he employs more exactly in the early undated "The Temporary the All" (*CPW*, I, pp. 7–8). The year 1866 continued to be his *annus mirabilis* as a young poet, as he began a sonnet series, "She to Him" (*CPW*, I, pp. 18–20), in imitation of traditional sonnet sequences, but especially of Meredith's *Modern Love* and its sixteen-line "sonnets" published in 1862 that narrate the death of love from the husband's point of view. Hardy, however, would adopt the woman's point of view. Hardy's four sonnets are "part of a much larger number which perished" (*LW*, p. 55).

Most of the poetic forms Hardy uses before 1900 are conservative forms – sonnets, song measures or stanzas with only one or two different line lengths, and ballad or hymnal quatrains. Such quatrains quickly became an early preferred form, in several poems of 1866–1869, and are also extended into sestets and octaves. In 1866, Hardy also wrote a modified terza rima ("To a Bridegroom" [*CPW*, III, pp. 281–82]) and some elegiac stanzas ("Her Dilemma" [*CPW*, I, pp. 16–17]). Except for his first poem, the Wordsworthian imitation in "Domicilium," he almost always opted for rhyming stanza forms. Inspired by his recent reading in Spenser and *Childe Harold*, Hardy "began turning the Book of Ecclesiastes into Spenserian stanzas, but finding the original unmatchable abandoned the task" (*LW*, p. 49). His nineteenth-century poems would come to include triplets, quintets, heroic couplets, and ghazal stanzas. Several of his poems imitated specific examples, "The Sergeant's Song" mimicking the form of an old song, "Richard of Taunton Dean," "Sine Prole" mimicking the Latin form of Adam of St. Victor's "On the Martyrdom of St. Catherine," "The Church-Builder" mimicking Jean Ingelow's "A Sea Song," "The Harbour Bridge" mimicking Prior's version of the Eighty-Eighth psalm, "In a Wood" mimicking Burns's "Phillis the Fair" (marked by Hardy in his 1863 edition), and so on. Mimicry and variation of traditional verse forms were constants in Hardy's career.

These converging influences, the world of Dorset and the world of learning, the harsh stoicism of his mother and the exhilaration of partici-pating in a literary universe, climax early in two poems, "The Ruined Maid" of 1866 and "Neutral Tones" of 1867.

"The Ruined Maid" (*CPW*, I, pp. 197–98) is a tour de force of dialect and comedy, which captures Hardy's own divide between home and London:

> – "I wish I had feathers, a fine sweeping gown,
> And a delicate face, and could strut about Town!" –
> "My dear – a raw country girl, such as you be,
> Cannot quite expect that. You ain't ruined," said she.

The mingling of standard and dialect language in earlier stanzas is a mode Hardy will follow in several poems. "I would not preserve dialect in its entirety," Hardy said, "but I would extract from each dialect those words that have no equivalent in standard English and then use them; they would be most valuable, and our language would be greatly enriched thereby."[9]

"Neutral Tones" is a miracle of achievement for this self-manufacturing poet. Indeed, the poem perplexes studies of Hardy's "development," in that such an accomplished poem occurs so early.

> We stood by a pond that winter day,
> And the sun was white, as though chidden of God,
> And a few leaves lay on the starving sod;
>   – They had fallen from an ash, and were gray.
>
> Your eyes on me were as eyes that rove
> Over tedious riddles of years ago;
> And some words played between us to and fro
>   On which lost the more by our love.
>
> The smile on your mouth was the deadest thing
> Alive enough to have strength to die;
> And a grin of bitterness swept thereby
>   Like an ominous bird a-wing . . .
>
> Since then, keen lessons that love deceives,
> And wrings with wrong, have shaped to me
> Your face, and the God-curst sun, and a tree,
>   And a pond edged with grayish leaves.   (CPW, I, p. 13)

Hardy is a poet of continuous syntheses: here, the power of the Dorset landscape, the tragedy of love, the loosely sapphic structure of the stanza, and the loss of a center to meaning itself, in the words that play uselessly now between the lovers. The retrospective backward look, a common motif in Hardy, gives no illumination except for repetition, a repetition gone old and etched in the mind, but still painful.[10] Wordsworth's spot of time has become a frozen photographic frame. Hardy will become expert in creating visual images for those patterns that impose themselves but are only seen belatedly, too late; here the imagery is implicit in the evolution of the opening stanza's images into the leaf-edged-pond grayly illuminated by a God-curst sun. The poem leaves us with those great Hardyesque questions which he helps make so central to the late-Victorian period: what is the ultimate source of deception, what lessons can be learned, what is the meaning of human life in a universe which has lost its moorings? When he finally collected his early poems into his first volume of 1898, *Wessex Poems*, Hardy included his drawing of a broken key (*CPW*, I, p. 86). In 1896, when he abandoned the novel and moved back to poetry, Hardy will say that he wished "to cry out in a passionate poem that (for instance) the Supreme Mover or Movers, the Prime Force or Forces, must be either limited in power, unknowing, or cruel" (*LW*, p. 302); but earlier this principle is already operating. Another poem of 1866, "Hap," answers a major question, with a statement strangely problematic in the way it anthropomorphizes sheer chance:

> But not so. How arrives it joy lies slain,
> And why unblooms the best hope ever sown?
> – Crass Casualty obstructs the sun and rain,
> And dicing Time for gladness casts a moan . . .
> These purblind Doomsters had as readily strown
> Blisses about my pilgrimage as pain.   (*CPW*, I, p. 10)

The poem, in standard sonnet format, points up the peculiar historical challenge facing Hardy, how to write poetry in a universe where "[e]vents did not rhyme" (*J*, I, ii, p. 13). Similarly, "Her Dilemma" (*CPW*, I, pp. 16–17) defines Hardy's ground for rejecting "a world . . . / Where Nature such dilemmas could devise," a complaint which will occasion Jude's loss of faith when his religion tells him he cannot love a married woman.

Thus, in 1866, the most productive year of his beginning career as a poet, Hardy showed himself capable of wide mastery in sonnets, ballads, and classical imitations. Many of these poems were later published and grouped mainly in two places, the first part of *Wessex Poems* and the section entitled "More Love Lyrics" in the 1909 volume, *Time's Laughing-stocks*. In publishing his poetry in volume form later, Hardy would continue to come across early poems which he would publish in twentieth-century volumes. These poems are almost always postscripted in some way to indicate their early dates.

For now, however, Hardy continued his architectural work, but he hoped, almost against hope, that he would be able to earn his living as a poet. Soon, however, the sober facts dictated that if he was to make a vocation out of literature, he would need to turn to something more commercial, the novel. And so in 1867, the year of "Neutral Tones," he began "The Poor Man and the Lady," a novel full of a young man's "socialistic" passions, with the subtitle "A Story with no plot; Containing some original verses" (*LW*, p. 58); but he was unable to publish it. So again tempering his passion and ambition, he turned to a romantic mystery novel, *Desperate Remedies* (published 1871), a novel full of references to the *Golden Treasury* and also to other poems by Coleridge, Moore, Scott, Tennyson, Browning, Rossetti, and Whitman. With the 1872 publication of his next novel, *Under the Greenwood Tree*, which exploited the audience for regional fiction of a place later (in *Far from the Madding Crowd*) to be named "Wessex," Hardy began to turn from architecture to literature as his vocation, a vocation financially based on the novel. Success enabled him to marry in 1874; with *Far from the Madding Crowd* in the same year, his reputation was established; and thus began the amazing nineteenth-century career of a Dorset native whose novels would rank among the greatest in the English language.

Oddly, however, Hardy continued to regard himself as first, if not last, a poet; and he continued to maintain his poetic ambitions through the novel-writing years, 1870–96. In 1874 his attitude was that "he did not care much for a reputation as a novelist in lieu of being able to follow the pursuit of poetry – now for ever hindered, as it seemed" (*LW*, p. 102). Before 1870, he had written many poems, of which at least thirty have been preserved. From 1870 until 1896, when he stopped writing novels, he wrote about fifty poems which have been preserved. Often in the novels he would incorporate impressions and fragments of poems, as well as continue the novelistic tradition of using poetic excerpts as epigraphs. In the late 1870s and early 1880s he tried a group of longer ballad narratives, some trying out the Napoleonic themes which he would later develop into *The Dynasts*. His earliest note forecasting *The Dynasts* was written in 1875 (*LW*, p. 110). In some of these poems, Hardy explores a Barnesian idiom but adapted to his own sharper satire, as in "Valenciennes," begun in 1878:

> I never hear the zummer hums
> O' bees; and don' know when the cuckoo comes;
> But night and day I hear the bombs
> We threw at Valencieën ...   (*CPW*, I, p. 26)

The greatest of these mid-novel balladic narratives is "The Dance at the Phoenix" (*CPW*, I, pp. 57–62), finished about 1878 (the year Hardy was finishing *The Return of the Native*), which uses a ballad stanza form to capture those dance rhythms to which Hardy would return often again in his poetic career:[11]

That night the throbbing "Soldier's Joy,"
The measured tread and sway
Of "Fancy-Lad" and "Maiden Coy,"
Reached Jenny as she lay
Beside her spouse; till springtide blood
Seemed scouring through her like a flood
That whisked the years away.　　　(lines 57–63)

In 1880, Hardy makes a note: "It is somewhat strange that at the end of November he makes a note of an intention to resume poetry as soon as possible" (*LW*, p. 150). At a moment's notice, he can carry through on this intention. In the year he published *The Mayor of Casterbridge* (1886) William Barnes died, and Hardy wrote a fine elegy, "The Last Signal" (*CPW*, II, pp. 212–13), making the flash of light from a coffin seen across a field analogous to a flash of realization:

Then, amid the shadow of that livid sad east,
Where the light was least, and a gate stood wide,
Something flashed the fire of the sun that was facing it,
Like a brief blaze on that side.

Barnes would have been pleased by Hardy's use of the Welsh cynghanedd in this poem: "Yellowly the sun sloped low down to westward," and so forth. Indeed, what Hardy said of Barnes in 1908 reflects a notion of the learned poet that characterized Hardy himself: "Barnes ... really belonged to the literary school of such poets as Tennyson, Gray, and Collins, rather that to that of the old unpremeditating singers in dialect. Primarily spontaneous, he was academic closely after" (*PW*, pp. 79–80). The academic side of Hardy can be seen in the fact that he kept complicated "verse skeletons" of metrical forms: "These verse skeletons were mostly blank ... but they were occasionally made up of 'nonsense verses' – such as, he said, were written when he was a boy by students of Latin prosody with the aid of a 'Gradus'" (*LW*, p. 324). Again, in 1890, the year before the serialization of *Tess of the d'Urbervilles*, Hardy wrote "Thoughts of Phena," a wonderful forecasting of Philip Larkin's great poem, "Lines on a Young Lady's Photograph Album." Hardy etches the presence of what is absent, a spectral presence outlined in the mind and on the page:

Thus I do but the phantom retain
Of the maiden of yore
As my relic; yet haply the best of her – fined in my brain
It may be the more
That no line of her writing have I,
Nor a thread of her hair,

No mark of her late time as dame in her dwelling, whereby
    I may picture her there.   (*CPW*, I, p. 82)

The past remains a powerful resource for Hardy, for the past contains his early loves, and also his early ambition, to be a great poet. The poem is a breakthrough poem (*pace* "Neutral Tones") in its new sense of the complex visual and aural possibilities of the stanza, possibilities exploited to the full in the later poem "The Figure in the Scene" (*CPW*, II, pp. 216–17). An earlier narrative poem, "The Alarm" (*CPW*, I, pp. 46–51), had been Hardy's first experiment with an unusual complex stanza form, but it is wrought to a consummate effect in "Thoughts of Phena."

The 1890s is the greatest decade of Hardy's novelistic creativity, with the publication of *Tess of the d'Urbervilles* in 1892 and *Jude the Obscure* in 1895. This decade is also the transition decade for Hardy as he moves toward the realization of his early dream, to become a full-time poet. Thus, on the one hand, his novelistic art approaches its greatest height, as he publishes essays on the art of the novel in 1890 ("Candour in English Fiction") and 1891 ("The Science of Fiction"). Yet in 1890, he records: "While thinking of resuming the 'viewless wings of poesy' before dawn this morning, new horizons seemed to open, and worrying pettinesses to disappear" (*LW*, p. 241). And in 1892 he again is planning to write poems: "Lyric Ecstasy inspired by music to have precedence" (*LW*, p. 255). In 1895, he writes a consummate lyric dance poem, "Reminiscences of a Dancing Man," bringing together his love of the ballad and music, into a form which personalizes the kind of ballad narration we saw in "The Dance at the Phoenix":

> Who now recalls those crowded rooms
>   Of old yclept "The Argyle,"
> Where to the deep Drum-polka's booms
>   We hopped in standard style?
> Whither have danced those damsels now!
> Is Death the partner who doth moue
>   Their wormy chaps and bare?
> Do their spectres spin like sparks within
> The smoky halls of the Prince of Sin
>   To a thunderous Jullien air?   (*CPW*, I, p. 267)

The poem also employs an ancient stanza form, similar to that used by Gray in "Ode on a Distant Prospect of Eton College."

In 1896, Hardy announces, at least to himself: "Perhaps I can express more fully in verse ideas and emotions which run counter to the inert crystallized opinion" (*LW*, p. 302). The oddity of this statement is not that the great novelist is expressing a preference for poetry, but that his preference has been consistently evident all along. The critical storms provoked by *Jude*, Hardy said, "turned out ultimately to be the best thing that could have happened; for they well-nigh compelled him, in his own judgment at any rate ... to abandon at once a form of literary art he had long intended to abandon at some indefinite time, and resume openly that form of it which had always been more instinctive with him, and which he had just been able to keep alive from his early years, half in secrecy, under the pressure of magazine-writing" (*LW*, p. 309).

Hardy's return to poetry in the middle 1890s repeated some of the characteristics of his first turn to poetry in the 1860s: he starts underlining lists of words again (see Taylor, *Hardy's Literary Language*, pp. 391–92). One reason later critics had difficulty relating Hardy to their contemporary issues was that he continued to develop themes which had been current in the 1860s. Several poems of the new poetical era are inspired by Hardy's trip to Italy in 1887, resulting most spectacularly in "Shelley's Skylark" (*CPW*, I, p. 133). One of the results of his Italian trip, in which Hardy pilgrimmed to spots associated with Keats, Shelley, Byron, and the Brownings, was the poem "Rome: The Vatican: Sala delle Muse" (*CPW*, I, p. 136), which reconfirmed his commitment to "form" and "tune" as the expressions of his primary muse. And he adds:

> But my love goes further – to Story, and Dance, and Hymn.

A most important Hardy poem, probably of the early 1890s, was "Nature's Questioning" (*CPW*, I, p. 86), an example of a poem which brings together two key aspects of Hardy's art, the personal meditation and the philosophical discourse, each consistent with the other. As the poem discourses about a world of incompletion and interruption, so also it proceeds to its own interruption and incompletion at the end. Hardy will continue to develop this theme of the interrupted meditation over the course of his poetic career. "Nature's Questioning" will also inaugurate a series of "philosophical poems" (that group beginning with "The Mother Mourns") which appear in his second volume of poetry, *Poems of the Past and the Present*, published in 1901.

At the end of the century, and at its turn, Hardy's poetic career is in full tilt. Between 1890 and 1901, Hardy wrote about 130 poems, most of them after 1895. The century ends with key Hardy poems of 1899: "On an Invitation to the United States," "Drummer Hodge," "The Souls of the Slain," and "The Darkling Thrush" (*CPW*, II, pp. 142, 122, 124, 187). The subjection of Hardy's mind to a larger world is rendered comically in the

1899 poem "An August Midnight," where Hardy sits besieged by insects at his desk:

> – My guests besmear my new-penned line,
> Or bang at the lamp and fall supine.
> "God's humblest, they!" I muse. Yet why?
> They know Earth-secrets that know not I. (*CPW*, I, p. 184)

Hardy's famous objectivity, a humility combined with craft, is clear here. Hardy's poetry takes place within a larger world, and is interrupted by that world. We can almost see the besmearing of the printer's ink on the page. At the same time, Hardy keeps developing his craft. He had been reading Gleeson White's 1887 anthology, *Ballades and Rondeaus ... Villanelles, etc.*, a gift from Florence Henniker in early 1893 (*Letters* 2, pp. 24, 227). In 1899 Hardy composed several imitations of these romance forms: "Birds at Winter Nightfall," "The Puzzled Game-Birds," "'How great my grief,'" "The Coquette and After," "Winter in Durnover Field," "The Caged Thrush Freed and Home Again," "At a Hasty Wedding." I mention these minor (but interesting) poems because they show how Hardy's learning and practice continue; he continues to research the technical possibilities of versification, even as he is composing major statements about human life. In 1900 Hardy conducts research on Latin hymnal versification which will result eventually in "Genitrix Laesa" (*CPW*, III, pp. 88–89) and "Sine Prole" (*CPW*, III, pp. 30–31) (*LW*, p. 329). Also in 1899, Hardy writes a series of poems on the Boer war, which significantly develop the war insights only played with in the Napoleonic poems of the novel-writing years. The chief achievement of these is "Drummer Hodge," which combines the occasional with the universal in a way that forecasts the century of Kafka and Beckett:

> Yet portion of that unknown plain
>   Will Hodge for ever be;
> His homely Northern breast and brain
>   Grow to some Southern tree,
> And strange-eyed constellations reign
>   His stars eternally.   (*CPW*, I, p. 122)

The fact that the poem alludes to Gray's "Elegy" illustrates how Hardy continues to combine the tradition of the poet's poet, with modern themes.

The other great poems which Hardy wrote at the end of the century can be made to stand for key aspects of Hardy achievements. One is the achievement of a unique poetic language that incorporates the historical insights into vocabulary associated with the *Oxford English Dictionary*

(*OED*). "On an Invitation to the United States" pointedly distinguishes Hardy's history-soaked language from that of the land of Whitman:

I

My ardours for emprize nigh lost
Since Life has bared its bones to me,
I shrink to seek a modern coast
Whose riper times have yet to be;
Where the new regions claim them free
From that long drip of human tears
Which peoples old in tragedy
Have left upon the centuried years.

II

For, wonning in these ancient lands,
Enchased and lettered as a tomb,
And scored with prints of perished hands,
And chronicled with dates of doom,
Though my own Being bear no bloom
I trace the lives such scenes enshrine,
Give past exemplars present room,
And their experience count as mine.   (*CPW*, I, pp. 142–43)

Hardy's poetry engages the English language at its deepest, most variegated levels, as he explores how the deep strata of different vocabularies "play" (as in "Neutral Tones") through the reflections of modern minds. He is signally the poet of the *OED*, and the era of new philological insight into the history of English. In the 1860s, Hardy had read in his copy of Reed's *Introduction to English Literature*:

> Language is liable to undergo perpetual changes; any person may observe, in even a short space of years, new forms of expression coming into use, old ones growing obsolete. Time brings along with it new modes of life, of thought, and action. Opinions and feelings often grow old-fashioned – fall behind the times, as the phrase is; and, as these are things that enter so largely into the composition of books, it needs must be that they, too, grow old-fashioned, obsolete, obscure.[12]

So impressed by such insight, Hardy had said of his early life:

> Having every instinct of a scholar he might have ended his life as a Don of whom it could be said that
>
> > He settled *Hoti's* business,
> > Properly based *Oun*.   (*LW*, p. 38)

Instead of becoming a philologist, however, Hardy incorporated philology in his poems. Hardy tried to dramatize the principle of linguistic historical change in the intimacies of his language. Hardy's poem "A Sign-Seeker," which may have been one of his first poems written as he prepared to resume poetry full time in the 1890s, shows how the linguistic and philosophical questions connect:

> But that I fain would wot of shuns my sense –
> Those sights of which old prophets tell,
> Those signs the general word so well
> As vouchsafed their unheed, denied my long suspense.
>
> (*CPW*, I, p. 66)

Though the general run of mankind presumes to know prophetic signs, those signs are imbedded in an obsolescing language of "unheed," too late for Hardy, who cannot see what he "fain would wot of."

"The Souls of the Slain" is Hardy's most impressively orchestrated meditative poem of the nineteenth-century: a great war poem (associated with the Boer war) in which a massive meditation about ghosts of the dead is rooted in the speaker's personal experience in a darkening setting:

> The thick lids of Night closed upon me
> Alone at the Bill
> Of the Isle by the Race –
> Many-caverned, bald, wrinkled of face –
> And with darkness and silence the spirit was on me
> To brood and be still.   (*CPW*, I, p. 124)

The poem is attentive to changes in the setting as the speaker broods, and his awakening at the end of the poem is skillfully accommodated to the dispersing of the ghosts. In 1869, Hardy had retreated to Weymouth: "Being – like Swinburne – a swimmer, he would lie a long time on his back on the surface of the waves, rising and falling with the tide in the warmth of the morning sun" (*LW*, p. 65). By the time he wrote "The Souls of the Slain," he can incorporate the experience of a wave-led reverie in the structure of the verse, a structure Hardy had experimented with in the earlier "Friends Beyond" (*CPW*, I, pp. 78–79) and "Nature's Questioning." One of Hardy's most interesting developments is his creation of what he calls "onomatopoeic" meter, namely a metrical form that captures the way the mind is influenced by the rhythms of the outside world, like wave rhythms here, dance rhythms (as in "Reminiscences of a Dancing Man"), and musical rhythms as in "Lines to a Movement in Mozart's E-Flat Symphony" (begun in 1898) where the complex stanza imitates the rhythms of the symphony (as well as waves):

> Show me again the day
> When from the sandy bay
> We looked together upon the pestered sea! –
> Yea, to such surging, swaying, sighing, swelling, shrinking,
> Love lures life on.
>
> (*CPW*, II, p. 195)

In his 1864 edition of Pope, Hardy marked Pope's verse paragraph containing the classic statement, "The sound must seem an Echo to the sense"; and in his poem Hardy proceeds to create his own version. An even more inventive use of this principle of "Lines to" an external rhythm is the imitation of the movement of light in the 1897 poem, "A Cathedral Façade at Midnight":

> The lunar look skimmed scantly toe, breast, arm,
> Then edged on slowly, slightly,
> To shoulder, hand, face; till each austere form
> Was blanched its whole length brightly
> Of prophet, king, queen, cardinal in state,
> That dead men's tools had striven to simulate;
> And the stiff images stood irradiate. (*CPW*, III, p. 9)

A little later, Hardy will manage an even more complex visual and aural "onomatopoeia" of flickering light in "A Commonplace Day" (*CPW*, I, pp. 148–49), published in the 1901 volume. Hardy is also capable of the consummate use of simpler effects. For example, his mastery of the quatrain produces finely finished results by the end of the century:

> I look into my glass,
> And view my wasting skin,
> And say, "Would God it came to pass
> My heart had shrunk as thin!" ...
>
> The dust of the lark that Shelley heard,
> And made immortal through times to be; –
> Though it only lived like another bird,
> And knew not its immortality. ...
>
> I saw a dead man's finer part
> Shining within each faithful heart
> Of those bereft. Then said I: "This must be
> His immortality." ...
>
> Wintertime nighs;
> But my bereavement-pain
> It cannot bring again:
> Twice no one dies.[13]

In "A Broken Appointment," written in 1893 or shortly thereafter, Hardy crafted a relic of the Petrarchan sonnet sestet, within a two-beat refrain, which also suggests the "onomatopoeia" of the rhythm of the clock which interrupts the speaker's reasoning. The poem draws on the theme of "She to Him I," but does something very inventive with part of the sonnet structure. The Donne-like self-mocking irony of the rhetoric is punctuated by the strokes of the clock:

> You did not come,
> And marching Time drew on, and wore me numb. –
> Yet less for loss of your dear presence there
> Than that I thus found lacking in your make
> That high compassion which can overbear
> Reluctance for pure lovingkindness' sake
> Grieved I, when, as the hope-hour stroked its sum,
> You did not come.   (*CPW*, I, p. 172)

The haunting refrain carries through *Jude the Obscure*, where Jude complains periodically about Sue: "She did not come ... why should she not come? ... But she did not come ... She did not come." We can see Hardy poetically express in a distilled form this central emotion of the novel.

"The Darkling Thrush," which Hardy said was written "on the Century's End" (*LW*, p. 330), climaxes a century which began with romantic bird poems, Keats's "Ode to a Nightingale," Shelley's "To a Skylark," and Wordsworth's various bird poems, and continued with other such poems through the century. Here Hardy recapitulates the tradition of the romantic bird who sings its diminished note within the void of the century's exhaustion:

> At once a voice arose among
>   The bleak twigs overhead
> In a full-hearted evensong
>   Of joy illimited;
> An aged thrush, frail, gaunt, and small,
>   In blast-beruffled plume,
> Had chosen thus to fling his soul
>   Upon the growing gloom.   (*CPW*, I, p. 188)

Hardy's career as a nineteenth-century lyric poet, who also wrote novels, climaxes with the canonical "The Darkling Thrush" which announces itself as the last nineteenth-century revision of the great tradition.

By 1895, the year in which *Jude the Obscure* was published, Hardy had embarked on the transition to the recovery of his original vocation. When he turns sixty in 1900, Hardy is ready to assume a role next to Swinburne, Browning, and Tennyson. In the offing lie nearly three decades of poetry, including the epic drama, *The Dynasts* (1903–08), the great elegiac series "Poems of 1912–13," the collection *Moments of Vision* (1917), and other central poetic works of the twentieth century. Hardy was now ready to become a twentieth-century poet, though his poetry continued to be built on the paradox that new poetry was an exhumation of the past. His distinctive modernism is discussed in this volume by John Paul Riquelme.

   The Dynasts falls outside the nineteenth century but is the culmination of Hardy's long pondering of its theme along with his poetic ambition since childhood. He conceived of *The Dynasts* as the culminating epic poem of the nineteenth century, in the line of Spenser, Milton, and Wordsworth, with some of the post-Romantic disillusion of the Victorian epic like Tennyson's *Idylls of the King* and perhaps Browning's *The Ring and the Book*. *The Dynasts* is the climax of Hardy's sense of himself as a poet on the classical model taught him by Horace Moule. The epic's full title is: *The Dynasts, An Epic-Drama of the War with Napoleon, in Three Parts, Nineteen Acts, and One Hundred and Thirty Scenes, the Time Covered by the Action being about Ten Years* (i.e., between Napoleon's threatened invasion of 1805 and Waterloo). The "epic-drama" is thus also a huge history chronicle play, climaxing a tradition from Shakespeare to Swinburne and Tennyson and lesser figures like Robert Buchanan and Henry Taylor. Into the epic Hardy pours all of his poetic resources in order to render the different strata of European society. The prose he had perfected in the novels he now uses for the scenes of the common people, for natural speech rhythms and country dialect. The blank verse which he had abandoned since "Domicilium" he now develops and uses (along with prose) for the speeches of English statesmen, aristocrats, and officers. And the metrical forms which he has been researching for half a century he uses (along with blank verse) for the speeches of the Chorus of Spirits, who develop Hardy's imagery of the Immanent Will, a kind of cosmic artist who "*works unconsciously, as heretofore, / Eternal artistries in Circumstance / ... patterns, wrought by rapt aesthetic rote*" (Part First, Fore Scene, lines 2–4; *CPW*, IV, p. 14), a little like Hardy himself who said he had been driven to poetry by "unreasoning ... *tendency*" (*LW*, p. 415). The Spirits are "the best human intelligence of their time in a sort of quintessential form" (*Letters* 3, p. 117); thus, in 1911, in his preface to the Wessex Edition of his works, Hardy noted "how much more concise and quintessential expression becomes when given in rhythmic form than when shaped in the language of prose" (*PW*, p. 48). In *The Dynasts*, Hardy expands his lyric version of the riddle of consciousness into a vast cosmic principle which blindly governs the manifold workings of the universe. To convey this vision, over forty different metrical forms are used in the epic, including interestingly "blank verse sonnets" (see Taylor, *Hardy's Metres*, p. 258), and also stanzas of nine or more lines, thus preparing the way for the long complex stanzas that Hardy will perfect in the twentieth century. The different linguistic registers of statesmen, common people, and Spirits also enabled Hardy to exploit all the ranges of his diction, from archaism to current speech. The "Spirit of the Years" says that Pitt's words

> *Will spread with aging, lodge, and crystallize,*
> *And stand embedded in the English tongue*
> *Till it grow thin, outworn, and cease to be.*
>   (Part First, v, v, lines 80–82; *CPW*, iv, p. 142)

These words might stand as Hardy's own epitaph, recording his lifelong ambition and his persistent sense of human limitation.

   Hardy wrote poetry for nearly sixty years, his earliest known poem finished in 1860 and his last dated in early 1928. Twenty-five of these years of course were mostly devoted to novel-writing, though as we have seen he kept his hand in as a poet. His full-time poetic career lasted longer than that of any other Victorian, indeed any other English poet. He composed over a thousand poems. He wrote poems in more metrical forms than any other major English poet, indeed perhaps than any other poet. He invented over 600 stanza forms. A glossary of his metrical borrowings serves as a comprehensive guide to the English metrical tradition (see "Metrical Appendix," in Taylor, *Hardy's Metres*, pp. 207–66). He participated in the great Victorian theoretical clarification of the nature of accentual-syllabic verse. I have argued elsewhere that Hardy was perhaps the first major English poet in the tradition of Sidney to know a theory of meter adequate to the complexity of his own versification. His 1899 statement on the "cunning irregularity" of his meters (*LW*, p. 323) alludes to this theory. Interestingly, he claimed that his experiments with poetic language then influenced his prose: "It is, of course, simply a carrying into prose the knowledge I have acquired in poetry – that inexact rhymes and rhythms now and then are far more pleasing than corrections" (*LW*, p. 108). His poetic career, from 1860 to 1928, encompassed the mid- and late-Victorian periods, the Edwardian and Georgian periods, the war and post-war period, and the 1920s. He straddled the great transition from traditional versification to free verse. While he always maintained accentual-syllabic stanza forms, he moved toward poems composed in unique and complex stanzas increasingly conscious of their own visibility in the manner of the free verse poem. (The visually complex "Thoughts of Phena" looks forward to these later poems.) If Hardy had not been so prominent as a novelist, his stature as a poet would have come clear earlier. Hardy continued to define himself as primarily a poet. In 1904 he said that in poetry he found "the condensed expression that it affords so much more consonant to my natural way of thinking & feeling" (*Letters* 3, p. 133). In 1915 he told a critic "to treat my verse ... as my *essential* writings, & my prose as my *accidental*" (*Letters* 5, p. 94). Objecting to a critic's widely shared claim that "Hardy is a realistic novelist who ... has a grim determination to go down to posterity wearing the laurels of a poet," he noted what we have been tracing in this essay, the consistency of his vocation of poetry: "At the risk of ruining all my worldly prospects I dabbled in it ... was forced out of it ... It came back upon me" (*LW*, p. 415).

NOTES

1 Donald Davie, *Thomas Hardy and British Poetry* (New York: Oxford University Press, 1972). On Hardy's controversial reputation as a poet, see Dennis Taylor, *Hardy's Metres and Victorian Prosody* (Oxford: Clarendon Press, 1988), pp. 199–202.
2 J. M. Murry, *Katherine Mansfield and Other Literary Portraits* (London: Nevill, 1949), p. 229.
3 In 1859, Hardy was given Longfellow's *Poetical Works* as a birthday present. As a boy, he was also "much interested" in the poems of W. J. Mickle; see *Letters* 6, p. 266.
4 Hardy, *"Studies, Specimens &c." Notebook*, ed. Pamela Dalziel and Michael Millgate (Oxford: Clarendon Press, 1994), pp. 9–11.
5 See Dennis Taylor, *Hardy's Literary Language and Victorian Philology* (Oxford: Clarendon Press, 1993), p. 48.
6 For an account of Hardy's early notations in the books he owned, see Dennis Taylor, "Hardy's Missing Poem and His Copy of Milton," *Thomas Hardy Journal*, 6/1 (1990), 50–60; also *Hardy's Literary Language*, pp. 390–91.
7 See Taylor, *Hardy's Metres*, pp. 49 ff., for details.
8 See Lennart Björk, *The Literary Notebooks of Thomas Hardy* (London and Basingstoke: Macmillan, 1985).
9 "'Hodge' As I Know Him. A Talk with Mr. Thomas Hardy," *The Pall Mall Gazette*, 2 January 1892; quoted in Laurence Lerner and John Holmstrom, *Thomas Hardy and His Readers* (New York: Barnes & Noble, 1968), p. 156.
10 The "germ" of "Neutral Tones" is fully developed in the later "Wessex Heights," perhaps written as early as 1896 though I suspect not till after the turn of the century: "I cannot go to the great grey Plain; there's a figure against the moon, / Nobody sees it but I, and it makes my breast beat out of tune" (*CPW*, II, p. 25).
11 Edmund Gosse suggests this dating in "Mr. Hardy's Lyrical Poems," written after consulting with Hardy (*Edinburgh Review*, 207 [1918], rpt. in Cox, pp. 444–63).
12 Henry Reed, "Introduction," *English Literature from Chaucer to Tennyson* (1857; London: J. F. Shaw, 1865), p. 109.

13 "'I look into my glass'" (*CPW*, I, p. 106); "Shelley's Skylark" (I, p. 133); "His Immortality" (I, p. 180); "In Tenebris I" (I, p. 206).

FURTHER READING

Bailey, J. O. *The Poetry of Thomas Hardy: A Handbook and Commentary*. Chapel Hill: University of North Carolina Press, 1970.

Bayley, John. *An Essay on Hardy*. Cambridge University Press, 1978.

Davie, Donald. *Purity of Diction in English Verse*. London: Chatto & Windus, 1952.

Elliott, Ralph. *Thomas Hardy's English*. Oxford: Blackwell, 1984.

Guerard, Albert. "The Illusion of Simplicity: The Poetry of Thomas Hardy." In *Thomas Hardy*. Norfolk, Conn.: New Directions, 1964.

Hardy, Thomas. *Complete Poems: Variorum Edition*. Ed. James Gibson. London and Basingstoke: Macmillan, 1979.

The Original Manuscripts and Papers. Wakefield, Yorkshire: EP Microform Ltd., 1975.

Selected Poems. Ed. Tim Armstrong. London: Longman, 1993.

Hynes, Samuel. *The Pattern of Hardy's Poetry*. Chapel Hill: University of North Carolina Press, 1961.

Larkin, Philip. *Required Writing: Miscellaneous Pieces, 1955–1982*. London: Faber & Faber, 1983.

Lock, Charles. "'The Darkling Thrush' and the Habit of Singing." *Essays in Criticism*, 36 (1986), 120–41.

Paulin, Tom. *Thomas Hardy: The Poetry of Perception*. London and Basingstoke: Macmillan, 1975.

Perkins, David. "Hardy and the Poetry of Isolation." *ELH*, 26 (1959), 253–70.

Pinion, F. B. *A Commentary on the Poems of Thomas Hardy*. London and Basingstoke: Macmillan, 1976.

Southern Review, 6/1 (Summer, 1940). "Thomas Hardy Centennial Issue."

Taylor, Dennis. "Hardy and Drayton: A Contribution to Pastoral and Georgic Traditions." In *The Literature of Place*. Ed. Norman Page and Peter Preston. London and Basingstoke: Macmillan, 1993.

Hardy and Wordsworth." *Victorian Poetry*, 24 (1986), 441–54.

"Hardy Inscribed." In A *Spacious Vision: Essays on Hardy*. Ed. Phillip V. Mallett and Ronald P. Draper. Newmill, Cornwall: Patten Press, 1994.

"Hardy's Copy of Tennyson's *In Memoriam*." *Thomas Hardy Journal*, 13 (February 1997), 43–63.

"Thomas Hardy and Thomas Gray: The Poet's Currency." *ELH*, 65 (1998), 451–77.

Wright, Walter F. *The Shaping of "The Dynasts."* Lincoln: University of Nebraska Press, 1967.

12

JOHN PAUL RIQUELME

The modernity of Thomas Hardy's poetry

Hardy among the modernists

As with literary Romanticisms, a variety of literary modernisms can be described, and no description of modernism as a singular, determinate movement will gain universal assent.[1] Among the varieties of poetic modernism, Thomas Hardy's is distinctive because of its class-inflected, skeptical, self-implicating tendencies. The modernity of Hardy's poetry reveals itself in highly ambiguous language, in a resistance to conventional attitudes and hierarchies involving nature and society, in the transforming of lyric traditions, and in an insistence by means of negativity on the possibility of achieving a defiant, permanently revolutionary freedom to choose and to refuse. It is worth admitting at the outset, however, that any depiction of Hardy's modernism is of necessity a selective affair. There is evidence of Hardy's modernity in poems that span the entire period of his career as a publishing poet from 1898 through 1928. Considering that Hardy's collected poetry consists of more than nine hundred texts, not including *The Dynasts*, a variety of patterns and tendencies can be identified. Primary to my reading of his modernity are poems that reflect on nature and on Romantic attitudes, war poetry, elegies, and poems that use negative language prominently.

Out of Hardy's poems emerge new options for the elegy and for lyric poetry, options that make it possible for later writers to pursue alternatives to other influential poetic modernisms, especially those associated with Yeats and Eliot. All three poets challenge the singular character of the self. But Hardy's style is neither abstract nor fragmented in the manner of Eliot, who uses ambiguous pronoun references, multiple literary allusions, and a group speech based on liturgical language, among other techniques, to disrupt the continuity and spontaneity of the individual voice. Hardy projects at times an anti-self comparable in some ways to the anti-self in Yeats, but he does so in a less mellifluous style. Yeats and Eliot respond in one way to the crass, secularized character of modern culture by turning to the spiritual, that is, by directing attention in some of their poetry to visionary or Christian truths. Hardy also protests against the abusive, destructive, self-destructive tendencies of his society, but his response tends to focus on a recognizably human world of personal relations, work, and death.

Hardy against the Romantics

Hardy's transformations of poetic traditions result in arresting elegies that are in salient ways both anti-elegiac and unconsoling and in lyrics that present the voice falling silent or that prominently include figures of speech that go against the grain of conventional lyric utterance. The unconsoling elegies and the lyrics in which voices are joined to silence and stillness emerge from a common impulse, to resist the tendency of elegies to provide comfort in situations of loss and the tendency of lyrics to present a voice in song or to humanize the world in a self-regarding, self-validating way. "No answerer I," says the speaker of one of Hardy's early poems, "Nature's Questioning," toward the end of a sequence of figurative crossings-over that typifies Hardy's modern imagination. Decades later the speaker in the poem that closes Hardy's final volume still "resolves to say no more." Hardy's speakers in these poems adopt a position of principled silence.

In "Nature's Questioning," published in *Wessex Poems and Other Verses* (1898), Hardy's first volume, the ambiguous use of language and the implications of Hardy's figures of speech, especially figures involving voice, face, and negation, distinguish Hardy from his precursors and connect him to younger writers, including Yeats and Eliot. The title phrase, "Nature's Questioning," is an amphiboly, an instance of language in which the meaning of the individual words is clear but the meaning of their combination is not. Hardy's title can mean both the questioning of nature by someone or something and the questioning that nature itself does of someone or something. This is an example of the genitive, or possessive, use of language in which subject and object are reversible.[2]

The poem opens with the speaker looking at nature and nature looking back in an instance of personification that suggests reversible relations. That is, nature is presented as if it possessed a human consciousness like the speaker's. Each observes the other, and the possibility of communication is implied, as it often is in personification:

> When I look forth at dawning, pool,
>   Field, flock, and lonely tree,
>   All seem to gaze at me
> Like chastened children sitting silent in a school. (*CPW*, I, p. 86)

In the word "dawning," we encounter another example of irresolvably ambiguous language. The speaker may be looking forth at the pool and other aspects of the scene at dawn. Or the dawn may be an aspect of scene that the speaker has in view. The speaker looks at dawn in both the temporal and, grammatically speaking, objective senses; it is *when* he looks and part of *what* he looks at. The double meaning causes no insurmountable complication to understanding the poem, except that "dawn" is figurative, not just literal language, particularly since it occurs in the form of a gerund, "dawning." The verbal noun communicates a process, not only a time and a scene. When something dawns on us, we become aware of a new situation or idea. While something is dawning on the speaker, what the speaker becomes aware of is the "dawning," or coming into awareness, of the aspects of scene being observed. At the moment of dawn, the speaker looks at the dawn scene during his own dawning that is also the observing of something dawning on what he observes. When pressed in this way for implications, the convoluted play and looping back of the language are as complex and puzzling as the often more extravagant linguistic effects of later modernist writers. By anticipating and participating in a modernist direction, Hardy's early poetry marks the dawn of modernism.

Despite nature's personification and its apparent connection to the speaker, the poem's details do not reinforce the suggestion that nature has been humanized as a thinking being. Instead, nature and the speaker are presented, respectively, as stifled or speechless. This qualifying of personification's usual implication revises and challenges a central element in Romantic poetry in a manner that is typical of Hardy and of modernist poetry in general. The five stanzas in the poem's middle that focus on nature's "chastened children" present them as human but worn down, not at dawn but at the end of a long day with "faces dulled" by a teacher who has "cowed them." The verb *cow* in this context clearly means *intimidate*, but Hardy would have known that some readers would register the homonymous noun *cow*, with its reference to a farm animal. Rather than a lapse in judgment, the incongruity is Hardy's joke about personification's humanizing aspect. There are no jokes in Wordsworth's use of this poetic trope. Hardy's humor causes a dislocation, since the bovine implication turns the humanized "flock" back into something less than human.

The lesson that humanized nature learns through education is not to be more aware but to be "cowed." In that state, the only speech that "stirs," described as "lippings mere," emerges as questions about the children's origin and end. The emphasis on faces and voices that are moribund raises for the reader the question of how fully the natural world mirrors the human and in what ways. The evident suggestion is that this implicit questioning of nature points to a debilitation in nature that is the truth about humanity as well. Rather than recognizing itself in a lively, joyous, humanized nature, humanity is invited to see itself reflected in nature as "worn," "forlorn," and "dying." Further, the force that has shaped nature is presented in nature's questions as itself less than fully human; it is imbecile and "impotent," an "Automaton" that is "Unconscious." In an obvious reference to the "embers" that guarantee the continuity between child and man in the ninth stanza of Wordsworth's "Immortality Ode," the children suggest that they may be "live remains" but of something "dying downwards," not likely to survive. With "brain and eye" gone, they are closer to being "remains" in the sense of a corpse than they are to being "live."

The place of the human speaker appears in the seventh, and final, stanza. The poem raises questions about nature implicitly, but this "I" is not in dialogue with nature. He neither questions nature directly nor responds to nature's questioning with his own validating voice, a voice that, could it answer, might confirm the similarity between humanity and nature in positive terms. Instead, a step further toward dying downward than the children, the speaker is "No answerer I." By choosing not to answer back or by being unable to do so, the "I" cuts itself off or is cut off from the possibility of continued speaking as a sign of life and thought on both sides of a dialogue. The children speak, perhaps to him, but he does not address them as Wordsworth addresses the child in the "Immortality Ode."

The silence of not answering finds its stilly echo in elements of nature, "the winds, and rains," and humanized natural "glooms and pains" that are, in another instance of ambiguous phrasing, "still the same." Like the speaker, they have not been changed by the questioning. They are, like the "I" who does not answer, "still" or quiet; that is, they are "the same" as "I" as well as "still the same." "Still" suggests not life and human consciousness, but death as well as quiet, especially in a poem that closes by presenting "Life and Death" as close neighbors. The implications here resemble those of the opening of Eliot's "The Love Song of J. Alfred Prufrock," in which "you and I" are presented as going "like a patient etherised upon a table," or else, because of the irresolvably ambiguous phrasing, the "evening is spread out against the sky" like such an unconscious figure. In both poems, the border between the human and the natural has been crossed to suggest not that either one gains by the crossing over but that both are less, not more, conscious and lively than we might have thought. Self and nature are "etherised" or dulled. There is also a quality in Hardy's poem that resembles Samuel Beckett's work, with its emphasis on silence and the loss of parts and faculties. As in the ambiguous title of Beckett's "Stirrings Still," what stirs in "Nature's Questioning" is all but still.

The modernist challenge to a Wordsworthian Romanticism emphasizing consolation is typical of Hardy's early poems. For instance, "In a Eweleaze near Weatherbury" (*Wessex Poems*) reverses the "Immortality Ode" by including no consolation for the changes that time has brought. Instead, it brings irony strongly to bear on time's passage by using a hymn stanza to present the lack of consolation. The poem also mixes styles by using both dialect and educated language; the mixture of high and low anticipates the mixture of styles in later poets. In Hardy, however, the low style creates the impression not of a mask worn by a refined speaker but of the speaker's lower-class origins. In an uncanny touch that replicates the crossovers of "Nature's Questioning," Hardy illustrates the poem in an amphibolic way with a drawing of a landscape made up of fields, flocks, and trees over which is superimposed a pair of glasses. This is more than incongruous, since it is impossible to say whether the glasses are those of the viewer who looks at nature or those of nature looking back at us. In the drawing and the poem, the fit between the human and the natural is less than close, comfortable, or determinate.

The poem following "Nature's Questioning" in *Wessex Poems*, "The Impercipient," also illustrates Hardy's modernity in its use of the negative, in this case not "No" but the prefix "im-," to present a diminution of consciousness. The word *impercipient*, which means lacking perception, implies the loss of a faculty that makes us human. What the speaker as "a gazer" cannot perceive in the fourth stanza is the sound that an "inland company" thinks it hears, that of a "'glorious distant sea'" (*CPW*, I, p. 88). The gazer hears instead only the wind in the trees. The poem specifically rejects the consolation that Wordsworth's speaker experiences in the ninth stanza of the "Immortality Ode." In that stanza, though "inland far," the speaker has "sight" of an "immortal sea" and can "hear the mighty waters rolling evermore." That sight and that sound are ones that, because they are unavailable, can provide no comfort and no consolation to Thomas Hardy's impercipient poetic speakers.

The radically ambiguous effects, refusal of consolation, and negativity persist in ways that respond to Romantic poets besides Wordsworth. "During Wind and Rain," published in *Moments of Vision and Miscellaneous Verses* (1917), owes a clear debt to Shelley's "Ode to the West Wind." Harold Bloom even calls Hardy's poem "a grandchild" of Shelley's.[3] In saying that, however, Bloom claims not just that wind, rain, leaves, and storm are important in both poems but that Hardy is a late-Romantic poet who follows Shelley thematically and not just chronologically. That is not the case. Shelley's poem is formally elegant, with long lines of verse arranged into five numbered parts that combine the Shakespearean sonnet with an English version of terza rima in imitation of Dante. Hardy's poem is a ballad, a popular form as far from Dante and Shakespearean sonnets as Hardy is from Shelley. The difference is apparent in the poems' contrasting diction. In Shelley, "the leaves dead / Are driven like ghosts from an enchanter fleeing." In Hardy, "the sick leaves reel down in throngs!" (*CPW*, II, p. 239). "Reel" suggests going round in a whirling motion, but, in the context of singing and the playing of music referred to earlier in the same stanza, "reel" can also call to mind the Scottish dance. In this poem, which concerns change and death, the dance is a *danse macabre* or dance of death in which all participate. Shelley's poem projects instead a cyclical process that renews life, as the closing optimistically asserts: "O Wind, / If Winter comes, can Spring be far behind?"

Shelley's closing apostrophe to the wind differs from Hardy's use of apostrophe. Both apostrophe and personification can suggest that a human speaker and humanized nature are mutually supportive. Hardy regularly avoids that suggestion. Shelley's poem begins and ends with an apostrophic invocation to the wind, addressed as "O wild West Wind" in the first line. Several times in the poem, at the end of a line Shelley's speaker invokes the wind as "O thou" or enjoins it to listen with "oh, hear!" Hardy mimics but transforms Shelley's use of apostrophe at line-ends in two of his stanzas by closing the ballad-like refrain at the sixth line with the "O" of an apparent apostrophe: "the years O!" (lines 6, 20). But this "O" is the sound of the voice sighing, a sign of loss rather than an indication of full-throated lyric address. Hardy does not begin and end his poem in a Shelleyan way with apostrophes to an aspect of nature that appears to stand for the imagination. Instead, he literalizes the wind by making it part of the natural context in which the poem's events and his presentation of those events occur. T. S. Eliot does something similar in "Rhapsody on a Windy Night," published in *Prufrock and Other Observations* (1917) the same year as *Moments of Vision*.

This literalizing of Romantic figures, like the use of *cow* in "Nature's Questioning," creates a revisionary distance between the later poem and the earlier Romantic one. Hardy's "O" at the end of a line rhymes internally with "Ah, no" from earlier in the line and expresses a response to "the years." That is, instead of addressing "the years" as human by saying "O Years," Hardy links "O" internally with "no" and with time's passage. In the alternative versions of the refrain, "the years O" becomes "the years, the years" (lines 13, 27) in a repetition that explains what "O" means.

Rather than inspiring a prophetic response, which Shelley requests of the wind, the years, along with the wind and the rain, define the context, time, and the weather, in which life proceeds to its inevitable end.

At the end of Shelley's poem, the speaker asks that the wind carry a trumpeting prophecy through his lips to an "unawakened earth," presumably in order to wake it up. The west wind and the poet's breath would fuse in poetic singing. In this projected mutuality of voice, Shelley has sung to and for the wind, which he asks now to sing through him. There is singing in "During Wind and Rain," at the beginning, but it is singing by "He, she, all of them" (line 2), apparently real people in a domestic scene, not by a poet intent on prophecy. The domestication of song works in tandem with the literalizing of wind. At the end of Hardy's poem, instead of the promise of prophetic song, we hear that "Down their carved names the rain-drop ploughs" (line 28). The scene has become a cemetery in the rain, with drops running down the names of those who once sang. The rain has become a tear that responds to the fact that those who lie in the earth cannot be awakened.

The tear of rain indicates more than lamentation about a loss, for it is figuratively engaged in the agricultural work of ploughing, which is related to carving as an act of marking a surface through human labor. Unlike Shelley, Hardy focuses in his poem's ending not on imaginative wind and prophetic singing but on the human labor of carving, ploughing, and, by extension, writing as work that remembers what once was but has now passed. The response to Shelley involves centrally a corrective gesture in which the "O" of apostrophe is negated, opposed, and written over by the "Ah, no" repeated in all four stanzas in the lines of refrain. Instead of emphasizing a wind that is always there to inspire poetic singing, Hardy stresses time's passage and the changes that compose human history. Rather than imitating the Romantic precursors to whom he responds, Hardy expresses distinctive attitudes. The poetic future that "During Wind and Rain" anticipates and enables includes Seamus Heaney's "Digging," in which the poet chooses to dig with his pen. For Heaney, as for Hardy, writing resembles working with the earth or with stone, not Shelley's prophetic, wind-inspired trumpeting.

War poems and other self-reflective doublings

Hardy shares with later modernist poets an experience that their nineteenth-century precursors never had, that of modern warfare, with its attendant social and psychological effects. But Hardy's concern with matters of war begins during the nineteenth century in his lifelong interest in the Napoleonic conflicts. The primary literary result of this interest is *The Dynasts*, subtitled "An Epic-Drama of the war with Napoleon, in three parts, nineteen acts, & one hundred & thirty scenes, the time covered by the action being about ten years." The three parts appeared in 1903, 1906, and 1908. In an important, though brief, commentary on this immense work, Isobel Armstrong asserts that *The Dynasts* is both the culmination of a politically resistant nineteenth-century poetic tradition and a new beginning for poetry as modernist experimentation.[4] The work's multiple perspectives and styles and its combining of heroic and democratic forms justify Armstrong's claims for its originality and significance. Hardy's double, antithetical vision of Wellington and Napoleon as versions of each other provides an emphatic, historically focused instance of the tensions and contradictions evident as well in his shorter poems written in response to contemporary wars.

Hardy responded to modern war in two groups of short poems. The first, written about and during the Boer War (1899–1902), appear as eleven "War Poems" in *Poems of the Past and the Present* (1901), Hardy's second volume of poetry. The best-known of these is "Drummer Hodge," a poem that exhibits Hardy's withering irony about the pretensions of Imperial Britain in its colonial excursions as they affect the lower classes. The class-inflected character of Hardy's modernism is evident in this anti-jingoistic poem. Hodge, whose name evokes British agricultural laborers, provides an example of how England is able to carry its imperial burden only at great cost to its uneducated, laboring class. Instead of helping successfully to transform the non-British world into Britain's own image, Hodge becomes fertilizer for foreign plants. Not Britannia but "strange-eyed constellations" (*CPW*, I, p. 122) rule Hodge's stars. Stylistically, the poem is distinctive because Hardy extends his tendency to mix styles by including phrases of Afrikaans dialect. The infiltration of this strange language, as in the word *kopje-crest*, meaning hillcrest, into a poem about a simple British soldier, enacts in the style a reversal of British expectations. Another poem in this group, "Song of the Soldiers' Wives and Sweethearts" (*CPW*, I, pp. 128–29), is an early example of Hardy's adopting a female voice. As does Yeats in his Crazy Jane poems, he chooses a persona so distant from himself that it amounts to what Yeats called an anti-self.

The later group of seventeen war poems, written shortly before or during WWI, appears as "Poems of War and Patriotism" in *Moments of Vision and Miscellaneous Verses* (1917). The widely admired "In Time of 'The Breaking of Nations'" (*CPW*, II, pp. 295–96) is less about war than it is about all that is not war. In this regard, the most memorable of these poems evoke opposites that are mutually defining. "In Time" includes numerous references that in another text could suggest violence and war primarily, but here they do so only indirectly as if by echo. Because of the diction, the perspective is resolutely double. We hear of "harrowing" (as in the harrowing of hell at the last judgment), "stalking," "smoke," "flame," and death. The harrowing is predicated not of the world's end but of the earth during ploughing. The stalking refers not to the deadly activity of soldiers or even hunters but to the cultivating of soil. The smoke is that of a grassfire "without flame." And the death refers figuratively to the unlikely disappearance of a story that will outlast tales of war. Rather than writing about war, Hardy has set about righting our sense of war's importance by transferring its vocabulary to another, preferable context.

The first poem in the sequence, "'Men Who March Away'" (*CPW*, II, pp. 289–90), also includes a doubled perspective, that of the soldiers who sing and that of the silent, doubting observer whom they address. But the poem's effect is to suggest that the double perspective is actually that of the soldiers, who are ambivalent and doubtful about their own endeavor. Hardy cunningly communicates the poem's ambivalence by means of rhymes. The two most frequent rhyme words, "away" and "us," used in the first stanza, are taken up later in the poem. Those who are marching "away" are heard emphatically to say "Nay" at the opening of two lines (lines 15, 20). These nay-sayers who present themselves as so positive about their own enterprise emphasize their solidarity by saying "us" repeatedly. "Us" comes back, however, as part of the "m*us*ing eye" (line 9; italics added here and below) of the observer who is their apparent opposite but actually part of themselves. It returns when they assert in words linked by rhyme to each other and to "us" that they are the "j*us*t" because of whom "braggarts m*us*t" "bite the d*us*t." Rather than distinguishing "us" from them, who are the skeptics and the enemy, "us" creates a connection to the musers and to those who bite the dust, who may well be "us."

Doubling and self-reflection begin early in Hardy's poetry-writing independently of his war poems in texts such as "Wessex Heights," written in the 1890s but published in *Satires of Circumstance, Lyrics and Reveries* (1914). The emphasis in "Wessex Heights" on the speaker's present self in uneasy relation to a past self is replicated by the parenthetical date (1896) forming part of the title of a poem published in a volume almost twenty years later. The poem's self-observing element is embodied stylistically in radically ambiguous phrasing that prevents us from separating into two distinct parts something simultaneously doubled and singular:

> Down there I seem to be false to myself, my simple self that was,
> And is not now, and I see him watching, wondering what crass cause
> Can have merged him into such a strange continuator as this,
> Who yet has something in common with himself, my chrysalis.
>
> (*CPW*, II, p. 26)

The speaker appears at first to see himself as in the past false to the self he is now, but the phrasing suggests that he was also being false to himself then, in an act of self-betrayal that is internally divisive. The "I" sees "him watching," that is, engaging in a related activity of looking, apparently looking at the "I" who is his continuator. The reciprocal activity is like the gazing of the speaker at nature and nature's gazing back at the speaker in "Nature's Questioning." Both the "I" and his previous self are "wondering" in a mutually reflective way. Mutuality and persistence, as well as the difference, between him and me emerge in the pronoun references when third person and first person are set in apposition as "himself" and "my chrysalis." The questions raised by this language concerning the continuity or discontinuity between the poet and his earlier self challenge the assertions of continuity in the poet's life found in Wordsworth's poetry, as in the lines from "My Heart Leaps Up" that form the epigraph for the "Immortality Ode."

A related crossing-over or self-regarding doubling occurs in the last of the "Poems of War and Patriotism," "'I Looked Up From My Writing.'" This poem of observation and self-observation expresses skepticism about the speaker's own writing because of the possibility, as in "Wessex Heights," that he has been false to himself. The later poem again involves looking at something that looks back in a way that enables a recognition:

> I looked up from my writing,
>   And gave a start to see,
> As if rapt in my inditing,
>   The moon's full gaze on me.   (*CPW*, II, p. 305)

By means of a pun, itself a form of doubling, the phrase "rapt in my inditing" links the writer and the moon while setting the two in violent opposition. Both are "rapt" or deeply engrossed in the poet's "inditing," or writing, but the Indo-European root that gives rise to "rapt" means "to seize," and it stands behind various words with violent implications, such as *rapacious*. The violent element is confirmed when we hear "indicting" as a pun on "inditing." The writer may be indicting something in his writing, but the moon is definitely looking at the poet in an accusatory way, as if indicting him for a crime. In doing that, the personified moon proceeds as if reading a poem, first "scanning" the landscape in search of a man who has "put his life-light out," that is, committed suicide, because his son has been slain in war.

To scan means to look out over something, such as a scene, but also to analyze the metrical pattern of verse. The moon's scanning leads her "to look / Into the blinkered mind" of someone who would write anything in a world in which children are slain and parents commit suicide. "Look into" suggests a physical act of perception, but it also means "investigate," as one would a crime. What she investigates is the crime of being "blinkered," or blinded. In an undoing of personification's usual implications, the moon presents itself as different from the human, since what she sees is that this particular human being cannot see; he is impercipient. The blinded mind of the poet, like the blinded bird in Hardy's contemporaneous poem of that title, is dead in life. The moon's "temper," her mood or her anger, has, by the final stanza, "overwrought" him. *Wrought*, the past participle of *work*, is related to the word *wright*, someone who makes, such as a playwright or, by extension, a poet. He has become overwrought, or anxious, because of the moon's looks, but she has also overwritten him. The poet ceases to speak under the pressure of having been written over, when he realizes he must "shun her view," not look at her and not be looked at by her, because she thinks he "should," either ought to or will, "drown him too" (line 24). To be "rapt in his inditing" now means that the poet is wrapped in his own writing, like a corpse in a winding-sheet of his own creating, a winding sheet that is his own indictment.

Anti-elegiac elegies

The refusal in "'I Looked Up From My Writing'" to hide from the possibility of his own complicity in the violent, unjust process of war finds its counterpart in the sometimes withering honesty and refusal of easy consolation in Hardy's elegies. Those elegies, or poems of mourning in response to a loss, are regularly anti-elegiac. They swerve as clearly as do the war poems from identifying anything as an unalloyed basis for celebration or satisfaction. They recognize that loss is irreversible. Rather than compensating for the loss or finding satisfaction in what remains behind or in the act of writing, Hardy's modern elegies express the dimensions of the loss in surprising, unconventional ways. As in "During Wind and Rain," those who have departed cannot be called back, but they can be recalled in an act of poetic work that, like ploughing their names with tears, honors them by reinscribing the carved names on headstones or recognizing the ambivalent meaning of flowers growing on a grave. In the process of writing his many powerfully moving elegies, Hardy rewrites the elegiac tradition by shunning one of its frequent features, the suggestion that the dead survive in some form, especially as speaking subjects or as spirits inhabiting a landscape. There can even be a grimly jocular element in the elegies, comparable to Eliot's humor about death in "Sweeney Among the Nightingales," where the birds defecate on Agamemnon's shroud, as presumably they will on Sweeney's.

Hardy's most widely admired elegies are the twenty-one poems comprising "Poems of 1912–13," written after the death of his wife, Emma, from whom he had been emotionally estranged for many years. Among the most arresting of the numerous elegies that Hardy wrote later are "The Figure in the Scene," "He Prefers Her Earthly," "The Shadow on the Stone," and the self-elegy, "Afterwards," in *Moments of Vision* (1917). These poems include a resolute refusal to accept a deluded consolation, even though at times the speaker expresses the wish that the happiness of an earlier time could be recovered. Part of what prevents that recovery is the speaker's recognition, shared with us, that there has been a double loss. In effect, the person who died was already dead to the speaker in life because of an emotional estrangement. To return the person to life is not sufficient, because doing that does not overcome the distance that separated the speaker from her even during life. The impossibility of the double recovery prevents consolation.

The comparatively brief, deceptively simple "Rain on a Grave" from "Poems of 1912–13" provides a vivid example of Hardy's revision of the elegiac tradition. The poem has been read as the beginning of recovery and consolation for the speaker that is traditional in elegiac poetry.[5] In that reading, rain, as a sign of the tears that come with mourning, contributes to the vegetative cycle of growth and flowering that are frequent features of elegies. In fact, Hardy calls up those conventional elements, but he does so to transform and even transmogrify them by means of sexual implications. The rain appears to be not mournful but vengeful, in response to the dead woman's avoidance of water during life:

> Clouds spout upon her
> Their waters amain
> In ruthless disdain, –
> Her who but lately
> Had shivered with pain
> As at touch of dishonour
> If there had lit on her
> So coldly, so straightly
> Such arrows of rain.
> (*CPW*, II, p. 50)

Even without the context of Hardy's estranged relations with his dead wife, the erotic implications are evident. The diction suggests that the woman felt dishonor at being touched. This reading is especially likely because of the pun in "arrows of rain," which sounds like "eros" of rain and evokes the penetrating of her body. Poems of a traditionally elegiac sort do not mix sexual implications and a vengeful attitude in their evocation of loss and possible consolation.

The sexual implications continue when we learn in the closing stanza that "[g]reen blades" of grass will soon grow "from her mound," both her new grave and her *mons veneris* or female pubic mound, which becomes covered with hair during puberty. As did the arrows earlier, the blades indicate a violent aspect in nature rather than primarily a gentle, consoling one. The double meaning of "mound" suggests incongruously that in death the woman reaches sexual maturity. The stanza goes on to imply that through the body's decay, she will become part of the daisies on her grave and even "the sweet heart of them." She is their sweetheart, but, as decomposed matter, she also becomes their heart or central element physically. If we read "them" with emphasis, she has finally become a sweetheart, but to *them*, not to the speaker, her former sweetheart.

In the poem's middle, the speaker implies that during "the prime of the year" they strayed together as lovers on sunny days and clear evenings. But this was, by implication, during the "prime" of their lives, which is long past. The rain that now falls on her grave began not at her death but much earlier. The recovery of that sunny time, the reversal of the double loss that occurred first through disaffection and then through death, is more than the poem can accomplish. Even the assertion in the final line that "All her life's round" suggests a circularity in her existence and death that is less than consoling. She has become part of the natural round of vegetative death and growth, but she is no closer to an adult human love than she was in life.

Hardy's denial of deluded consolation to the speaker in his elegies often emerges in his use of negative language that appears at times as a kind of ghost or echo of what is ostensibly being said. This generating of overtones from negative statements, related to the multiple meanings in other poems mentioned earlier, is particularly clear in "After A Journey," one of the most ambitious and subtle of "Poems 1912–13," and in the slightly later "The Figure in the Scene." Both include an implied but emphatic denial that anything remains of the person that can be portrayed as positive or present. The negativity of these poems anticipates its prominent place in Hardy's late poetry. By means of negative language suggesting absence,

Hardy makes possible in surprising and vivid ways the recognition of a rich multiplicity of meanings while countering the speaker's delusions. The multiplicity, which can neither reverse the loss nor compensate for it, inhabits and expresses loss in an unusual poetic style that refuses the limits of conventional evocations of grief and relief.

"After a Journey" is a poem about repetitions with a difference, both repetitions that create something new and ones that cannot recapture a lost original. As we learn in the first line, the goal of the speaker's journey has been "to view a voiceless ghost" (*CPW*, II, p. 59). At the poem's end, the speaker asks to be brought "here again" in closing lines asserting that he is "just the same as when / Our days were a joy, and our paths through flowers." In light of the poem's directions and its recurring negatives, the assertion is more a protest at the inability to achieve an unvarying, changeless repetition than a convincing statement about a satisfying visit that can be repeated.

Although much of the poem is addressed to "you," it begins with a monologue that never turns convincingly into a dialogue with the "voiceless ghost." This ghost without a voice is the poet's dead lover, his muse, and a version of Echo, the mythological figure most closely associated with lyric poetry's repetitive language. Representations of echo occur throughout the poem by means of internal rhymes and end rhymes. The first instance of perfect rhyming in the end rhymes, "draw me" and "awe me" (lines 2, 4), provides the kind of echoing that the mythological figure of Echo practiced. That is, the later sounds are contained wholly within the former words, which have been foreshortened. In addition, every stanza includes lines in which exact or foreshortened repetitions constitute internal rhymes: "Whither, O whither" (line 2), "Through the ..., through the" (line 10), "At the then fair ... in the then fair" (line 20), and "bringing me here; nay, bring me here" (line 30).

The clearest evocation of echo occurs in the second half of the third stanza, when we learn that "you are leading me on" (line 17) to places known long ago, a waterfall and its cave, "with a voice still so hollow / That it seems to call out to me from forty years ago" (lines 21–22). The language suggests both that the cave, a place of echoes, still has a hollow voice and that the addressee, "you," has such a voice. But the voice, whether of the place or the "voiceless ghost," only "seems" to speak. The ghost's apparent speech in the second stanza is merely what the speaker thinks it might have found to say, embedded in questions about what it would say if it could: "Summer gave us sweets, but autumn wrought division? / Things were not lastly as firstly well / With us twain, you tell?" (lines 13–15). The illusion of the ghost's speaking occurs because the interrogative "you tell?" suggests that the speaker is responding to what the ghost has actually said.

The language's double effect resembles the dual character of an echo. An overtone gives the apparently literal language another meaning. This conceptual doubling, which occurs frequently in Hardy's poetry, also informs the phrase "leading me on." The ghost leads the speaker physically to spots they knew, but the act of this seeming voice amounts to leading him on in a figurative sense toward hopes that cannot be fulfilled. The speaker desires something that will be denied because the voice is not real.

The doubt, hesitation, and denial are evoked in the first internal repetitions, "Whither, O whither," in the final ones, "bringing me here; nay, bring me here," and between them. The "O" of apostrophe, which normally projects life, a voice, and a face onto something inanimate, is called up as an unactualized potential, since there is no direct address in the poem's opening. As part of a series of negatives that occur in every stanza, the "nay" (line 30) of the final stanza indicates that the speaker's wish will be denied. That denial has been predicted in the first stanza in the address to the "you" whose "coming and going" (line 8) is the fading in and out of an echo.

In that initial address, the speaker asserts that "Where you will next be there's no knowing" (line 5). Like "leading me on," this statement has overtones that enable us to recognize that the "voiceless ghost" speaks or is addressed in the context of qualifying negations and an emptying out of the illusory presence. With the phrase "no knowing," the first negation in the poem, the speaker indicates that he cannot predict where the ghost will be next. The same language, however, tells us what the place is. The place of "no knowing," where consciousness, our faculty for knowing, does not function, is death. Further, "no knowing" understood as echoic language tells us what the character of that place will be. It is a place, like the one figuratively created by the poem, in which a voiceless, echo-like sound occurs as the exact repetition of sound in "no knowing." The ghost will be "no-noing," that is, saying, in an echoic voice of denial, "no, no." Denial may also have been the ghost's habit during life. The poem both emerges from and tends toward this "no-noing," the undoing of apostrophe through a negation that turns "O" into the "no," "not," and "nay" of each stanza. The "O" that leads the speaker on in the third stanza, manifested by "mist-bow shone," "so hollow," "ago," "aglow," and "follow," in an insistent sequence of repetitions, leads in this poem's implications ultimately to the place of "no knowing," not to a place of consolation.

Hardy plays on "no" and "know" in an equally memorable but more condensed way in the final lines of "The Figure in the Scene," which exemplify his firm refusal of the consolations that elegies frequently offer:

Yet her rainy form is the Genius still of the spot,
    Immutable, yea,
Though the place now knows her no more, and has known her not
    Ever since that day.   (CPW, ii, p. 217)

The day in question is one in which the speaker sketched his female companion during rain that left "blots engrained" on the sketch. The poem's closing has sometimes been misread to mean, in a conventionally elegiac way, that the woman has become a *genius loci* or permanent, undying spirit of the place or spot.[6] But by "spot" Hardy means not only or primarily the place but the "blots" on the paper. By "still" he suggests not only or primarily her continuing presence but her stillness in death. By "Immutable" he indicates not that she is undying but that the spots of which she is the "Genius" or inspiration cannot be removed, any more than the effects of death can be reversed by elegiac poetry. What the place "knows" "more" "now" is her "no," the negation that she insistently represents. What it "has known" since the day she left is "her not." Hardy's refusal of elegy's potential delusions in "The Figure in the Scene" rejects resolutely and absolutely elements central to nineteenth-century conventions of elegiac poetry.

Late poems: the anti-self, negativity, and Beckettian language

The poems that Hardy published or prepared for publication during the last decade of his life are too numerous and heterogenous to enable comprehensive description. Many of them do, however, continue and elaborate elements we have already seen, including doubled perspectives and negative language. The doubling at times proliferates into multiple views and at times attains the status of an anti-self, while the negative language resists delusions and refuses conventional expectations.

The multiplying of views or selves is reminiscent of what D. H. Lawrence called the allotropic form of his fictional characters, their tendency to change state, as carbon does from coal to diamond. In "So Various," from his last volume, *Winter Words in Various Moods and Metres* (1928), Hardy presents in thirteen five-line stanzas thirteen versions of himself, twelve versions as apparently distinct individuals and a thirteenth that encompasses them all:

Now ... All these specimens of man,
    So various in their pith and plan,
        Curious to say
        Were *one* man. Yea,
    I was all they.   (CPW, iii, p. 208, lines 61–65)

As Yeats says, the artist "will play with all masks."[7] The multiple views of reality recall Wallace Stevens's "Thirteen Ways of Looking at a Blackbird," except that Hardy's subject and object are himself. The stanzaic form, with two longer lines that rhyme followed by three shorter lines that rhyme, suggests an internal division or a combination of opposites, in a way that resembles Hardy's formal reflection of doubling, or being twain, in earlier poems, including "The Convergence of the Twain."

The combination of opposites and multiplying of selves and voices occurs as well in "Voices from Things Growing in a Churchyard" (*CPW*, II, pp. 395–97), from *Late Lyrics and Earlier* (1922), but with an emphasis on echoic language and mortality that include the poetic speaker and the reader. In the final stanza, the dead who have spoken breathe as "maskers" (line 49) to those who linger, both the speaker and the reader. As "maskers," they are dancers in the dance of death, in which all participate, and they are personae, or masks, that a poetic speaker wears. Their "lively speech" (line 51), the language of the dead, is "murmurous" (line 53), or echoic, as in the rhymes of the refrain, "cheerily" and "eerily," which define the world's dual but conjoined character as night and day.

To learn from the dead and to take on their murmurous, echoic language as one's own refrain, as the speaker does in the final stanza of "Voices," is to become an anti-self, image, or mask in the sense that Yeats means those terms when he uses them in his autobiographical writings and elsewhere. For Yeats, to grasp one's anti-self is to achieve "the state of mind, which is of all states of mind not impossible, the most difficult to that man, race, or nation" (Yeats, *Autobiography*, p. 132). It is the moment at which the poet becomes "the opposite" of all that the poet is in "daily life" (p. 184). This moment, in which a form of freedom is attained, is part of poetic creation for Yeats, when he wears various masks, including that of "a mad old woman" on the Dublin quays (p. 359). Hardy evokes and achieves this state of being his own opposite in his late poetry when he adopts the voices of the dead.

Like Yeats, Hardy achieves the anti-self by taking on the voice of a woman who, as does Yeats's Crazy Jane, speaks independently of and against her male antagonists. In becoming the dead woman who speaks, Hardy anticipates poems by Seamus Heaney, including "Bog Queen" and "Punishment." In "'Not Only I,'" from *Human Shows: Far Phantasies: Songs, and Trifles* (1925), by taking on the mask of a dead woman Hardy's speaker expresses a multiple status in which the male poet becomes a she who is both "I" and "'Not only I.'" She says that "Not only I / Am doomed awhile to lie" (*CPW*, III, p. 101) in the grave because she has with her a multitude of attitudes, thoughts, and memories that are not quite "I" in any determinate sense. But her statement means as well that she is not the only one destined for the grave, since all of us die and "lie" in both senses of lying. She differs from those who remain behind, for her lying includes the poetic swerving from literal truth that makes the poem's words those of a woman who speaks from the grave. The poem achieves an ostensibly impossible feat, for the dead speaker expresses what those who have outlived her think: "'Here moulders till Doom's-dawn / A Woman's skeleton'" (lines 29–30). In defiance of this reductive view the poem's rhetoric asserts the persistence and the importance of all that is "[s]trange" and "unrecorded," "[l]ost" and "disregarded," by recording, preserving, regarding, and preferring its strangeness.

Equally strange are the poems in which the speaker's voice or one of the speaker's voices falls silent. This occurs in "Surview," the closing poem of *Late Lyrics and Earlier*, when the speaker recounts how his "own voice," whose language is printed in italics, talked to him in an accusatory way until "my voice ceased talking to me" (*CPW*, II, p. 485). The situation recalls both "Wessex Heights" and "'I Looked Up From My Writing.'" The poem that follows from and memorializes speech's cessation within the divided self evokes the uncanny, echoic effect of a falling silent resulting in a poetic speaking that continues the now silent voice by respeaking its words. This falling silent that we learn of through the strange continuation of its textual reflection and result anticipates the self-correcting, contradictory style and the tendencies toward silence in the much later work of Samuel Beckett.

Hardy achieves a culminating paradoxical effect in the closing poem of his *oeuvre*, "He Resolves To Say No More." Because of the formal resemblance of its five-line stanza to "So Various," this concluding poem extends the earlier one while also bringing it to closure. The poet who was so various now enjoins his soul in an apostrophe to be silent: "O my soul, keep the rest unknown!" (*CPW*, III, p. 274). He will not reveal the remainder, but he also refuses to know what rest is; his grave will be unquiet. By asserting that he chooses silence, the poet speaks as though he could control what he apparently could not earlier in "Surview," his voice's ceasing to speak to him, and what he absolutely cannot control as he faces death, the loss of speech. Hardy's use of apostrophe to enjoin silence boldly transforms a trope that traditionally implies the ability to speak. Hardy also links the affirmative "Yea" with "none" at the end of the first stanza, and thereafter negative statements reiterate that "What I have learnt no man shall know."

By shifting from "O" to "no" and to "know" Hardy achieves a final reversal of apostrophe's usual effects in a way that enables us to understand the poem's title, in the manner of Beckett's late style, as both so various and a falling silent. As Beckett writes in *Worstward Ho*, "Enough to know no knowing ... No saying. No saying what it all is they somehow say."[8] Hardy reaches the place of "no knowing" and no-noing from "After a Journey," where we know he always will next be. While he ostensibly chooses and accomplishes his fate, the silence of death, which he cannot avoid, he tells us in absolute terms that (like Joyce's Stephen Dedalus) he refuses to serve. Hardy resolves not only to say nothing but to say "no" more, to resist conforming even more frequently and more strenuously than before. He responds to pressures of society and mortality with a resisting, exclamatory statement, "no more," insisting that the pressures must stop. Through its multiple meanings, his style enjoins and enables us to *know more* when by attending to this poet's no-noing, in which he manages both to fall silent and continue, we become the strange continuators of his still but still stirring, echoing voice.

NOTES

1 The classic discussion of the difficulty in defining Romanticism is Arthur O. Lovejoy's "On the Discrimination of Romanticisms" (*PMLA*, 29 [1924], 229–53), rpt. in his *Essays in the History of Ideas* (Baltimore: Johns Hopkins Press, 1948), pp. 228–53.
2 A prominent instance of amphiboly in a modernist poem is Yeats's use of "from" in the final line of "Among School Children." In the second episode of *Ulysses*, Joyce uses subjective and objective genitive, and identifies it grammatically as such, in the phrase "*Amor matris*," meaning both the child's love for the mother and the mother's love for the child.
3 Harold Bloom, *A Map of Misreading* (New York: Oxford University Press, 1975), p. 21.
4 See the "Postscript" to Isobel Armstrong, *Victorian Poetry: Poetry, Poetics and Politics* (London and New York: Routledge, 1993), pp. 479–89.
5 See the interpretive headnote to "Rain on a Grave" by Tim Armstrong, ed., *Thomas Hardy: Selected Poems* (London and New York: Longman, 1993), p. 157.
6 This is the reading that Jahan Ramazani holds to in *Poetry of Mourning: The Modern Elegy from Hardy to Heaney* (Chicago and London: University of Chicago Press, 1994), pp. 62–63.
7 W. B. Yeats, *The Autobiography of William Butler Yeats* (New York: Collier, 1965), p. 318.
8 Samuel Beckett, *Worstward Ho* (London: John Calder, 1983), p. 30.

FURTHER READING

Bailey, J. O. *The Poetry of Thomas Hardy: A Handbook and Commentary.* Chapel Hill: University of North Carolina Press, 1970.
Bayley, John. *An Essay on Hardy.* London: Cambridge University Press, 1978.

Brodsky, Joseph. "Wooing the Inanimate: Four Poems by Thomas Hardy." *On Grief and Reason: Essays*. New York: Farrar, Straus, Giroux, 1995, pp. 312–75.

Buckler, W. E. *The Poetry of Thomas Hardy: A Study in Art and Ideas*. New York: New York University Press, 1983.

Christ, Carol T. *Victorian and Modern Poetics*. University of Chicago Press, 1984.

Clements, Patricia and Juliet Grindle, eds. *The Poetry of Thomas Hardy*. Totowa, N.J.: Barnes & Noble, 1980.

Davie, Donald. *Thomas Hardy and British Poetry*. New York: Oxford University Press, 1972.

Hynes, Samuel. *The Pattern of Hardy's Poetry*. Chapel Hill: University of North Carolina Press; London: Oxford University Press, 1961.

Larkin, Philip. *Required Writing: Miscellaneous Pieces, 1955–1982*. London and Boston: Faber & Faber, 1983.

Lucas, John. *Modern English Poetry from Hardy to Hughes: A Critical Survey*. Totowa, N.J.: Barnes & Noble, 1986.

Mahar, Margaret. "Hardy's Poetry of Renunciation." *ELH*, 45 (1978), 303–24.

Marsden, Kenneth. *The Poems of Thomas Hardy: A Critical Introduction*. New York: Oxford University Press, 1969.

Miller, J. Hillis. *The Linguistic Moment: From Wordsworth to Stevens*. Princeton University Press, 1985.

Tropes, Parables, Performatives: Essays on Twentieth-Century Literature. Durham, N.C.: Duke University Press, 1991.

Morgan, William W. "Form, Tradition, and Consolation in Hardy's 'Poems of 1912–13.'" *PMLA*, 89 (1974), 496–505.

Murfin, Ross. *Swinburne, Hardy, Lawrence, and the Burden of Belief*. Chicago and London: University of Chicago Press, 1978.

"Moments of Vision: Hardy's 'Poems of 1912–13.'" *Victorian Poetry*, 20 (1982), 73–84.

Orel, Harold, ed. *Critical Essays on Thomas Hardy's Poetry*. New York: G. K. Hall, 1995.

Paulin, Tom. *Thomas Hardy: The Poetry of Perception*. London and Basingstoke: Macmillan, 1975.

Pinion, F. B. *A Commentary on the Poems of Thomas Hardy*. London and Basingstoke: Macmillan, 1976.

Sacks, Peter. *The English Elegy: Studies in the Genre from Spenser to Yeats*. Baltimore and London: The Johns Hopkins University Press, 1985.

Taylor, Dennis. *Hardy's Poetry, 1860–1928*. New York: Columbia University Press; London and Basingstoke: Macmillan, 1981. 2nd edn., Macmillan, 1989.

Zeitlow, Paul. *Moments of Vision: The Poetry of Thomas Hardy*. Cambridge, Mass.: Harvard University Press, 1974.

INDEX